Thirty-three Years, Thirty-three Works

Celebrating the Contributions
of F. E. Abernethy, Texas Folklore
Society Secretary-Editor, 1971–2004

Thirty-three Years, Thirty-three Works

Celebrating the Contributions of F. E. Abernethy, Texas Folklore Society Secretary-Editor, 1971–2004

Edited by
Kenneth L. Untiedt
Kira E. Mort

Publications of the Texas Folklore Society LXXI

University of North Texas Press
Denton, Texas

10 9 8 7 6 5 4 3 2 1

Permissions:
University of North Texas Press
1155 Union Circle #311336
Denton, TX 76203-5017

The paper used in this book meets the minimum requirements of the American National
Standard for Permanence of Paper for Printed Library Materials, z39.48.1984.
Binding materials have been chosen for durability.

Library of Congress Cataloging-in-Publication Data

Abernethy, Francis Edward, author. | Untiedt, Kenneth L., 1966-
editor, writer of preface. | Mort. Kira E., editor, writer of preface. | Abernethy, Francis
Edward. Preface to Observations & reflections on Texan folklore.
Thirty-three years, thirty-three works : celebrating the contributions
of F. E. Abernethy, Texas Folklore Society secretary-editor, 1971–2004 /
edited by Kenneth L. Untiedt, Kira E. Mort.
Publications of the Texas Forklore Society ; no. 71. -- Denton, TX : University of North
Texas Press, [2016] | (Publications of the Texas Folklore Society ; LXXII)
This 71st publication of the PTFS series features a sampling of articles, presentations
and prefaces of previous books, all written by F.E. Abernethy. -- Preface | Includes
bibliographical references and index. | LCCN 2016037403I
ISBN 978-1-57441-655-8 (cloth : alk. paper) | ISBN 978-1-57441-663-3 (ebook)
1. LCSH : Folklore -- Texas. 2. Texas--Social life and customs.
I. Abernethy, Francis Edward
LCC GR110.T5 A35 2016
DDC 398.209764--dc23
LC record available at https://lccn.loc.gov/2016037403

*Thirty-three Years, Thirty-three Works: Celebrating the Contributions of F. E. Abernethy,
Texas Folklore Society Secretary-Editor, 1971–2004* is Number LXXI in the Publications
of the Texas Folklore Society Series

The electronic edition of this book was made possible by the support
of the Vick Family Foundation.

CONTENTS

I'll Sing You a Song

Reflections

PREFACE

I always tell my students that when it comes to writing, I can't teach them style. Style is something writers develop over time. It involves word choice, sentence structure and length, the use of figurative language, organization, and the skillful application of any other device writers possess in order to elicit a feeling from their readers. Some writers have very distinct styles, and some read like carbon copies of every other "house writer" responsible for formula novels that remain popular but don't show much quality.

Ab Abernethy had style. Read anything he wrote, and you'll hear him talking to you—casually, as if you were taking a leisurely walk together along the Lanana Creek Trail or sitting around a campfire at Sugar Creek after a day's hunt. Better yet, imagine you're sitting across from him in the TFS office on the SFA campus, trying to maintain your balance in a barely functional chair, swapping stories and talking out truths of the universe while shelling a bucketful of pecans he'd gathered on the walk to work. Yes, you can *hear* Ab in his writing, I think more than any other writer I've known. And his writing reads effortlessly. It was certainly not accidental, though. Everything from a preface to one of the annual publications, to an article on hunting or music or historical figures, to a presentation given at one of the meetings was unquestionably deliberate and, in its own way, sophisticated in structure.

This 71st publication of the PTFS series features a sampling of articles, presentations, and prefaces of previous books—all written by F. E. Abernethy. Ab served as Secretary-Editor of the Texas Folklore Society for longer than anyone else, and his three decades at the helm helped shape it into the prestigious yet familiar organization it is today. He was responsible for directing the move of the TFS headquarters to Stephen F. Austin State University in 1971, and for overseeing the daily operations of one of the state's oldest academic organizations through good times and bad—financially and academically. He regularly taught an introductory folklore course at SFA, and he encouraged many new members, guiding their research efforts and contributions to folklore scholarship through the annual TFS publications. To say the least, his editorial accomplishments were substantial; he edited two dozen volumes of the PTFS series, including the three-volume history of the Society (from 1909 up to the year 2000), which he wrote himself. Obviously, we're all indebted to Ab's dedication and contributions, for *everything* he did.

If you never met him, here's your chance. The works in this book represent his interests, his philosophies, his hobbies, his humor, his passions, and they are told in his very distinct voice. The chapters are arranged loosely, with four basic themes grouping the texts together. The first chapter features his thoughts on what connects us all through folklore. Another looks at many historical figures and events that shaped Texas and the Southwest, especially in our neck of the Pineywoods of East Texas. One chapter focuses on music, although you'll find song an integral part of several works in other chapters. The final chapter is reflective, and it includes pieces where he examined the events that shaped his life and his career.

Ab was, among many other things, a gifted photographer. Not too long ago, the chemicals he used for developing photographs he took were still sitting on the shelves in the small room in our office space where he had set up a dark room; the room now houses only our refrigerator and microwave, but the air filter remains on the door and the sink still works. Photos were important to Ab, and he made sure that TFS publications had plenty to add to the text of the articles. Rather than merely reproduce all the pictures that accompanied his works, I have chosen others that fit the articles featured herein—most were taken by Ab himself, and many of them he used in his self-published autobiography, which he had printed only for select individuals. Some you may have seen before, but most are very personal and come from his "archives." Where they seemed most appropriate, photos from the original publications have been reused, and I have included notations where Ab was responsible not only for the text, but also the photographs.

I have many people to thank for this book. As always, I appreciate the special relationship the TFS shares with Karen DeVinney, Ron Chrisman, and the staff at the UNT Press; without their help, our job of putting these books together each year would be much more difficult. In addition to the usual folks at Stephen F. Austin State University who continue to generously support the Society, including Mark Sanders, the Chair of the English Department, and Brian Murphy, the Dean of the College of Liberal and Applied Arts, I want to express special gratitude to a couple of other individuals. First, Kira Mort served as an intern during the Spring 2016 semester, and she worked on this manuscript from the beginning to (almost) the end. You can read more about her experience in the addition to this Preface. Also, I thank Megan Condis, the Director of Technical Writing at SFA, who helped coordinate Kira's internship.

Finally, I welcome Chalotte Blacksher to our team; she came in on the tail end of putting this publication together, but I thank her for her efforts to learn the mechanics of constructing a manuscript, and I look forward to working with her on future projects. Don't worry, Charlotte. There will be plenty for you to do on the next one.

I dedicate this book to Ab, on behalf of all the members of the Texas Folklore Society.

Kenneth L. Untiedt
Stephen F. Austin State University
Nacogdoches, Texas
May 22, 2016

To think I didn't know about the Texas Folklore Society until a few months ago! I'm very grateful to have had the opportunity to work on this collection. I guess it was my lucky stars that I crossed paths with Kenneth Untiedt in the first place. I came in as an intern, wet behind the ears, staring at the roadrunners on the walls and wondering what a "paisano" had to do with anything. At least I'm enlightened now, right?

That being said, this has been an incredible experience. I've always had a passion for legends and historical fiction, so once I became acquainted with the TFS—where has *this* been my whole life?—I realized I'd found a bigger treasure than the Spanish chest on the Camino Real. I may not have been born a Texan, but I certainly became one alongside Brer Rabbit, Old Rusty, Esteban, and the Lady in Blue. I was enchanted by each story as I read them for the first time—often taking longer than I probably should've with each! I laughed at Martha's "Adulteration of Old King David," cocked my head towards the Yellow Rose of Texas, hummed along with the songs of the Depression, and felt my inner adventurer stirring for all that treasure on the Camino Real. Soon enough, I was reading other stories that weren't even for the manuscript (always outside of the office, of course!).

It never ceases to amaze me how much you can learn about someone through the things they write. I never knew F. E. (Ab) Abernethy personally, but through his writing, I feel like I've better come to know him regardless. Puzzling over the ethological approach and the stimulus struggle, reaching down through the cracks of history to study these stories through my own unique lens. . . . Each story has taught me something about Dr. Abernethy, and at the same time, taught me something about myself. I've gained a real respect for the paisanos who've led this society throughout the decades, and I hope that a rookie paisano like me can do justice to at least one of them.

Working on this project had me sifting through countless files, pictures, stories, et cetera, all which taught me a great deal about Ab Abernethy, his life, and his interests. The more I learn about the man, the more I wish I'd had a chance to know him personally. I feel we would've been great friends. It's amazed me, how much we seem to have in common. With cute little critters like Twitchy running about, and the visible devotion Ab and Hazel had for each other, not to mention Ab's keen eye for photography—it's depressing to think I won't get to meet him in this life. At least I've better gotten to know him through this project, and I'm truly grateful for that.

Special thanks to Kenneth Untiedt, Secretary-Editor of the Society, for being generous enough to invite me to work on this project, and also to Dr. Megan Condis for introducing me to Ken. And may the Society live to carry on its fine work. Thank you all.

Kira E. Mort

Beginnings:
The Why and
the How

F. E. Abernethy as a young editor.

A PREFACE (In which the editor presents his credentials, among other things)

[from *Observations & Reflections on Texas Folklore*, PTFS XXXVII, 1972]

I know how you feel. I felt the same way when I first heard that the headquarters for the Texas Folklore Society was leaving Austin and The University of Texas campus. I could never imagine it anywhere else except at the place of the omphalos. Then the meeting was called to order, the motion was made, seconded, and passed, and the transfer was duly recorded in the minutes.

We moved during the burnt-out end of August, Wilson and I, in the midst of posting final grades, campus construction, and a quiet sadness. We sweated and cussed some as we packed the Society's materials in cardboard boxes and carried them out to the station wagon parked behind Parlin Hall. We took down the pictures of Lomax and Payne and Thompson and some Cisneros sketches that had been used in *The Healer of Los Olmos*. Frank Dobie's old felt hat with a turkey feather in the band was sitting on a filing cabinet, so we put it in. Very gently we loaded a box of Mody's paisanos, five or six of them. Wilson had deposited much of the early correspondence in the State Archives, but several boxes of old programs, advertisements, letters, and brochures remained as relics of our ancestors and of our beginnings. And there were the Society's publications, more than thirty of them that stretched back to Stith Thompson's Volume I in 1916. These make up our umbilicus, the visible chain of the Society's being, that makes us all a part of it from its inception in 1909.

The Texas Folklore Society is now headquartered on the Stephen F. Austin State University campus in Nacogdoches. I have hung the pictures, shelved our volumes, and filed the materials of our business. Our offices are in the basement of one of the campus'

original buildings. Our quarters aren't new and shiny, but then neither are we. The building, named after Thomas J. Rusk, is appro-
priately solid and comfortable, and the campus is located on the
old Rusk homestead. The pines reach tall to the sky here, and their
roots grow deep in the red dirt. This part of the country has been
Texas for a long time, and its history and traditions form a fitting
setting for the Society's headquarters.

The Texas Folklore Society Office, "Ab's office."

    As the new man on the job, I guess I ought to present some
credentials. Although I was born in Oklahoma, that area was Greer
County, Texas, when my grandparents settled there. Since those
first few months as an Okie I've lived in the Panhandle dust and
the Gulf Coastal swamps, five miles from the nearest mailbox and
in the middle of Big D. I began to consciously think Texas during
the centennial year of '36, and thereafter my education was liber-
ally seasoned with my own Texas Trinity—Dobie, Boatright, and
Bedichek.

Mody Boatright, TFS Secretary-Editor, c. 1960.

I shall do my best to keep the lid on my Texas chauvinism, but I am foolish about this state. It has blessed me bountifully in spirit and in store and I love it, head to toe, fingertip to fingertip. When you are in love with someone and you are really interested in her and not in your own reflection in her eyes, you are fascinated by every round inch of her, past and present. I feel that way about Texas and studying her folklore is getting to know her more delicately and more intimately.

This does not mean that I view folklore as an exercise in regionalism or provincialism. I do not. Nor do I view it as a snug nest to curl up in to retreat from the cold, sharp edges of the present. To me folklore is the ultimate, all-encompassing field of study. I see a decade, a millennium or an age go by, but the creature man remains the same, activated by the same urges, responding in the same way as did his ancient cave-dwelling ancestors. Only the symbols change. The gods shift their shape but continue to answer to the same needs, and folklore is the demonstration of this eternal kinship. A single seed contains the essence of all life, and the Texas and Southwestern folklore in this volume contains the essence of universal phenomena. The time and the place and the people happened in Texas, but the hunters and fighters and singers of songs are universals, representatives of the repetitions of history and the everlasting oneness of man.

A major concern of mine in Texas folklore has been stimulated by my association with the Institute of Texan Cultures. A tour of its quarters in San Antonio reminds us that we have the whole world in our borders, every ethnic distinction and every color, from blue-eyed Nordic to black-eyed Bantu. The phenomenon of folklore can be studied and enjoyed here in all its ramifications and derivations. I can envision a future TFS annual that is devoted to a survey and sampling of the folklore of the many different ethnic cultures in Texas, but we are going to have to fill some gaps. Our annuals are full of Mexican folklore, but there is remarkably little Negro folklore and even less Cajun lore. I had a student once who brought in Czech folklore, and another one from Brenham or thereabouts who talked a lot of German folklore but never got any down on paper. And as scarce as Indians are generally, there are still enough within our borders to talk to them about their own particular ways of life. We have an untapped treasure in the Southwest, but we are going to have to get to scratching if we ever hope to share it.

Editing this volume has been a pleasure. I have gotten together many of my favorites among Texas folklorists, and I have enjoyed visiting with them again. They are all my close friends and I hope you realize how much restraint was required on my part to keep from telling how great they all are as writers and as personalities. I am subjective about these people so if there is some article here that you don't like, don't tell me about it.

Hazel Abernethy.

I wish to thank Dr. Ralph W. Steen, the president of Stephen F. Austin State University, for his encouragement and assistance in getting the Society functioning on this campus; Dr. Roy E. Cain, the head of the English Department, for his generosity and support; and Mrs. Martha Dickson, the Society's secretary, for keeping our house—and this edition—in excellent and understandable order. And as always, I thank Hazel.

Observations and Reflections is dedicated to Wilson M. Hudson, Jr., former Secretary-Editor (1964–1971) and Fellow of the Texas Folklore Society. To him I owe the most.

Francis Edward Abernethy
Nacogdoches, Texas
April 18, 1971

Between the
CRACKS OF HISTORY

*Essays on
Teaching and
Illustrating Folklore*

Edited by Francis E. Abernethy

Publications of the Texas Folklore Society LV

Between the Cracks, the 1997 publication.

BETWEEN THE CRACKS OF HISTORY

[the *Preface to Between the Cracks of History: Essays on Teaching and Illustrating Folklore,* **PTFS LV, 1997**]

I wonder if folklorists follow historians like gleaners—or cotton strippers in west Texas—and collect the leavings from academic historians, all the tales and songs and traditions that the historians allow to fall between the cracks? Or that historians sweep under the rug? Or drop? Or choose to ignore?

Historians research, document, and file the facts of a happening. They are supposed to get the details right, but sometimes in following the letter of the investigation, they lose the spirit—which falls between the cracks of history where it is pounced on by the ever-lurking folklorist, who scarfs it up like a hog on a mushmelon.

Maybe its not just historians who let pouncable things fall between the cracks. Maybe folklorists follow doctors around for their droppin's and leavin's, and find out that urine relieves bull nettle burn and that tobacco eases the pain of a yellow-jacket sting and that chicken soup is as good for the flu as anything doctors prescribe. And maybe folklorists follow wildlife biologists and conclude that if they hear an owl hoot in the daytime, that owl is watching a buck walking. I hold firmly to that latter belief, by the way, and when the owl hoots I can see vividly in my mind's eye a big, old mossy-horned buck easing his way through a pine thicket.

On the other hand—

On the other hand, maybe historians followed folklorists at some dimly remembered past time to see what fell between the cracks as the folk passed along myths, legends, and folktales. Tell me, what history did not begin with the leavin's of folklore, the oral traditions that went back to the myths of the creation of the world and Eden, the legends of the great kings and warriors of Camelot, and the folktales that grew out of all these hand-me-downs and became the *Iliad*?

What science did *not* begin as folklore? Modern scientific mete-
orology was preceded by Zeuses and Thors and Jehovahs who
rumbled their presence with bolts of lightning and volcanic erup-
tions and with floods that drowned the world. The folk were using
levers, screws, and inclined planes as part of their inherited artifacts
before physics became an acknowledged science. A student could
easily learn his valence tables when chemistry was in one of its folkloric stages, when all matter was made of various combinations of
earth, air, fire, and water. In geology, that science and the whole
universe was simpler when folks thought that the earth was flat and
was twice as long as it was wide and that it was surrounded by the
great river Ocean and that it was created in 4004 B.C.—and that
it was created for man who was unique and its sole inheritor. And
the manipulation of holy numbers by the Mayans and Aztecs to
understand the peregrinations of the sun and the moon and the
seasons made mathematics a religious exercise long before it was an
academic discipline.

Singing and dancing, making music on drums and with flutes,
painting on walls and sculpting gods and gargoyles: all these
things began with the folk before the academic fine arts were ever
envisioned.

So, folklore might be that which falls between the cracks of
history (or biology or sociology, *ad infinitum*) but students and
teachers must not forget that long before these leavin's fell through
the cracks from the anointed hands of academia, folklore was the
beginning, the Alpha, and most probably will be the Omega.

All of which is a garrulous prelude to an introduction for this
volume's contents. *Between the Cracks of History* is partially peda-
gogical. The introductory essays, which were spawned at the Fort
Worth meeting in 1995, are concerned with defining, explaining,

and teaching folklore. Some of us have been immersed in folklore for so long that we assume that everybody defines and understands folklore the same way as we do. That is not necessarily the case, however, and it behooves the Society to pause periodically to examine basic premises.

The essays which follow illustrate the definitions and, with luck and latitude, illustrate the title of the book, *Between the Cracks of History.* Gideon Lincecum did not completely fall through the cracks of history, but when one encounters his name in Texas history books, he will not find much about Gideon as a fiddler. Chapters on west Texas history will discuss rodeos as one part of that area's social fabric but will probably neglect the machinations of the Bluebird Mare. East Texas histories will spend a long chapter on the East Texas oil boom of the 1930s but will leave out Mattie's Palm Isle and the other oilfield honkytonks of that exciting time. Burial rituals, oil camp customs, and railroad yarns—all are parts of the history of their times; but when historians tell us about handgun violence or an oilfield opening up or a train wreck, some of the personal remembrances, the folklore, falls between the cracks. Some of these leavin's lie around for years before a wandering folklorist picks them up, scratches through the grime on the surface and realizes he has found gold.

I tell my students, and anybody who will listen, that if they wish to study the world and mankind in all of their dimensions of time and space, then folklore is the teacher to whom they must turn.

For the sixteenth time, I thank this volume's contributors for the time and energy they spent writing and correcting and doing all the things one has to do to get a manuscript ready for publication. The Society has a strong and loyal and involved membership, if you haven't noticed.

Dan Angel (Stephen F. Austin State University President), Hazel and Ab Abernethy, and Senator Roy Blake.

The Texas Folklore Society thanks English Department head Patricia Russell and Liberal Arts Dean James Speer of Stephen F. Austin State University for their support. The Texas Folklore Society would not be here on the campus without the generous assistance provided by President Dan Angel and his administration. The Society has been on the SFA campus for twenty-six years, and several presidents have come and gone during that time. But all of this university's presidents have supported the Society generously and personally, and we hope that we have responded in kind. The Society cannot exist without the full commitment of its university host, which provides space, time, office expenses, and intangibles too numerous to mention. We appreciate the hospitality of our host.

And this editor and this Society thank Assistant Editor Carolyn Satterwhite for her work on this fifty-fifth volume of the Publications of the Texas Folklore Society—and for all her work as the Society's Secretary and Treasurer.

Francis Edward Abernethy
Stephen F. Austin State University
Nacogdoches, Texas
February 17, 1997

Carolyn Satterwhite, TFS Office Secretary.

Ab Abernethy, c. 1978.

THE ETHOLOGICAL APPROACH
TO FOLKLORE

Evolution, comparative anatomy, fetal development, and parallel physical reactions all indicate man's physical relationship with the rest of the animal kingdom. Ethology is the study of our behavioral relationship. That is, not only are all animals constructed on the same general pattern, but they also act alike and from the same motives. Everything for animals begins and ends with the food chain and with the problems of getting enough to eat. Animal behavior patterns are genetically selected to insure the group of fish, lizards, crows, monkeys, or men of having no more members than it can provide for over a long period of time and of maintaining these numbers in stable harmony. Folklore is one result of these genetically transmitted behavior patterns which man inherits from and holds in common with his animal ancestors. These behavior patterns—particularly sociality, territoriality, dominance, and sexuality—are modified by thought processes to fit the survival margin of his environment and are transmitted to the social group by symbolic language and example. The results are traditions and folklore which the society establishes in order to promote a stable social union.

SOCIALITY

Sociality, or the herding instinct, is man's most significant genetic drive. This instinctual grouping has multiplied his teeth and nails and has allowed a poorly armored and punily armed animal to survive. It is dependent upon the other drives for success. At least this is the pattern among the lower social animals, where social stability is dependent upon sufficient territory for the food supply and an established pecking order. This general social pattern is inherent in man as well as among the lower animals, but different human groups have modified this pattern in compromises with their environment. Many customs and traditions in folklore are the signs of adjustments and compromises a society makes with its animal drives, as well as being cultural sublimations of these drives. For example, a group recognizes the chaos inherent in an uncontrolled response to sexuality and evolves tales, rituals, moralities, and customs that regulate sexual practices in line with that which they consider necessary for the survival of the community.

Folklore has as its main purpose the solidifying of the group. It is social cement. The customs and the traditions of a group promote unity because they are familiar. Man, the animal, reacts negatively to the unfamiliar. He is either frightened by it and flees, or it activates his aggressive instincts. This is a survival quality. The animal that fails to react instinctively with fear or anger to the different and the unfamiliar will not live to pass his genes on to another generation. Therefore a community cherishes and cultivates its myths and traditions so that it can move and communicate within a pattern of the familiar. The people dress and talk alike, they all know the same songs and stories, and they all worship the same god in the same way. Those who know their lore and ways are insiders, are "the people," but those that don't are foreigners, and the group's ranks are drawn up tightly, like a ring of musk oxen, against the outsider who would destroy the unity and sociality of the group.

Karen, Acayla, Sierra, and Lee Haile.

Folk poetry, folk music, and folk dancing have as one of their original reasons for being the strengthening of the instinctual social bonds. Chanting, singing, and dancing satisfy an individual's psychological need for togetherness at the same time that they act as social synchronizers, causing a group of people to respond to the same stimulus on the same wave length. Singing and playing instruments harmonically gives the group a sense of personal blending with each other. The rhythmical chants and cheers at a ball game and the gospel singing at a revival meeting afford the audience with the same sense of social oneness and integration. And the swaying, jerking, rocking reactions to drum and song have the same purpose and effect in the Congo as they do in a university student center. The people become one in their common response to beat and sound. They are musically synchronized and the social bond is glued a little stronger and their chances for survival are a little greater.

Custom and ritual, and the proverbs, stories, religions, and songs that support them, were and still are means of social inclusion and exclusion, means of limiting population to the chosen. The religious group that selects those who can partake of its closed communion and the fraternities and sororities who control the gates into the college world of the Greeks are little different from the primitives whose rites of passage selected those they considered fit for survival in the group and eliminated the rest. Those who passed the test survived within the social strength of the group and were guided by leaders strong enough to protect the boundaries of their hunting grounds.

DOMINANCE

The sociality drive requires sacrifices on the part of the individual. Its commands come from the super-ego, that vehicle of traditions which is bent on maintaining a stable *status quo* in a tightly unified social group. The drives of dominance, territory, and sexuality are, on the other hand, selfish and id driven; and their satisfaction can, if not limited or sublimated, destroy the harmony of the social group.

Dominance is the strongest of the personal instinctual drives, and it is as necessary in its furnishing of group leadership and protection as it is destructive in the brutality that is sometimes its method. The individual desire for recognition and status produces the noblest as well as the most pathetic of results. This desire for rank and recognition is universal. No matter how low in the pecking order a man might be he must have something to satisfy his need for status or he will wilt in despair.

People have recognized that the struggle for dominance is a persistent pattern among all social groups except those that are on the fringes of survival. Under normal conditions there are surplus goods available and members of the group struggle to acquire these goods, whose ownership gives them prestige and elevates them in the pecking order of their group. Many of our traditional legends and folk tales are symbolic and figurative responses to this behavior pattern, especially those with the test motif, like the labors of Hercules. The legendary struggle for the room that is always supposed to be at the top is well illustrated by the stories of Theseus, Hercules, and Jason, among other legendary heroes, whose legends are stories of their trials in ascending the ladder to kingship and the top of the order.

On the other hand, many of the traditional folk tales are the lower classes' response to the pecking order that they have lost out in. Cinderella and youngest-best stories are the results of the wishful thought that patterns of social dominance can be broken and that youngest sons and the dispossessed without status can elevate themselves with the help of such supernatural agents as fairy godmothers and talking animals. Champions for the oppressed are the Robin Hoods and Jesse Jameses who rob from those who are high in the pecking order and give to those who are low. Religions, pandering to the hope that losers in the class-system pecking order will not always be losers, tell us that eventually the meek and lowly shall inherit the earth and be kings and wear crowns. These sorts of folk tales, like culture in general, are man's compromises with his behavioral instincts. They do not eliminate the social class system that is the result of this dominance drive; they merely turn it upside down. Man's attacks against the seeming injustice of established pecking orders are not attempts to destroy the concept of dominance, but to destroy the particular establishment in order to create another one that is more attentive to his particular interests.

Man might modify the dominance drive on earth and attempt to practice the most stringent type of equalitarianism, but his mythological world on his particular Olympus or in some other ethereal domain is one that has a distinct scale. Different gods, in most cases, serve different functions and rank differently on the scale of power. To counter this instinctual and continual struggle for dominance, which in a chaotic world increases the chaos, the Medieval Catholic Church and the folk evolved the mythological system which was to become known as the Great Chain of Being. The figurative became literal in the symbol of a golden chain which stretched from the foot of God's throne down to the lowest speck of dirt. From God, Christ, and Saint Peter, on down to the lowest seraphim through the pope, cardinals, and priests; from kings to commoners to serfs; through lions, eagles, whales; from the royal oak to the most servile weed; and from gold down to the most humble grain of sand; everything was in its proper rank in this most ordered of all disorderly worlds. Everybody was superior to some, inferior to others. The Chain hung straight down and no two links were ever side by side, so there was no need to struggle for dominance.

TERRITORIALITY

Territoriality as an inherited behavior drive is defined both individually and generally. Individual territory is that hypothetical space bubble which surrounds a person or animal and which is a sense of distance, both literal and figurative, that the animal wants to keep between himself and others. When too many are gathered together in too small a space, and this varies among both upper and lower animals, the individual goes into stress, and adrenalin is automatically released into the system to prepare the body for fight or flight. In folklore, social customs and manners evolve to regulate activities so that there will not be excessive invasions of this individual territorial bubble. In Japan the removal of shoes before entering a house, speaking softly, and "not hearing," are customs that have been selected because too many have been forced by high populations to live closely together in houses with paper and bamboo walls. Elaborate formalities and ceremonies are cultivated by the Japanese because they relieve some of the strain of continual close association. One does not have to wonder how to act in particular episodes of social contact if he has a prescribed set of rules. The higher the population density, the greater are the chances of personal territory violation, and the greater the need for established social manners.

Territoriality more generally defined is that sense of area that an animal has which gives him a feeling of belonging to a particular piece of land that will support him and his group. Male members of the cat and dog families mark the boundaries of their territory by urinating on their chosen markers. A grizzly bear marks his boundary with a scratch on a tree as high as he can reach. Bears that might wander into his territory can tell how big he is by the height of the scratch. A buck deer leaves his scrape and some well-hooked brush. Cities, states, and nations traditionally mark their boundaries with monuments and noticeable signs. At the present time the marking indicates lines of political separation, but among earlier peoples the line was religiously significant and was marked by consecrated stakes, totemic statues, gates, and bridges because territory itself had a religious significance. A group's territory was sacred to that specific group and received protection from the gods of the group, a concept that is much more significant territorially than the general animalistic concept of the sacredness of the Mother Earth. Rites of passage protected the individual when he crossed his boundary and left the protection of his gods and cleansed him when he returned. Present-day travelers still celebrate the crossing of boundary lines such as the equator and the 180th longitude, and children are very sensitive to the crossing of boundaries as they leave or return to their homes.

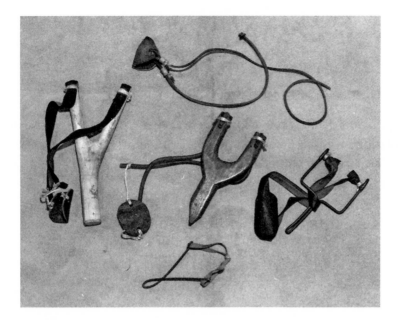

Some simple toys.

Many of our games, both for children and adults, reflect our concern with territoriality and the never ending struggle to gain and defend territory that exists for both man and the lower animals. King of the Mountain, Capture the Flag, and all the game and dance forms of musical chairs are sublimations of territorial competition. Games like Red Rover and London Bridge are similar in that foreigners are captured from another land and kept to serve in the new one. Such modern sports as football, hockey, soccer, and basketball are based on the idea of maintaining a defense of one's own territory while successfully invading the enemy's. Baseball is similar to Indian horse stealing. An individual, the batter, pits himself against the whole tribe (perhaps from Cleveland) and makes a raid on their

territory with the ultimate aim of getting home free. These perennial battles between towns and institutions, like chess and checkers,
take the place of earlier raiding parties and struggles for territorial extension. Theoretically these games are bloodless and follow
strict rules enforced by unbiased arbiters. They afford some males
the satisfaction of battle and the aggressive instincts while avoiding
the mayhem that accompanies it. Thus culture compromises with
instinct, and the result is a behavior pattern sublimated into folk
games, and the survival of the group is promoted.

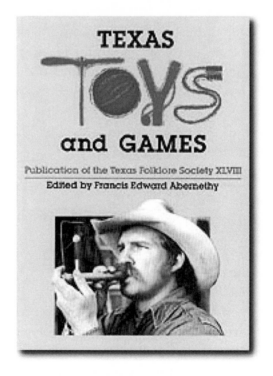

Texas Toys and Games, the 1989 publication.

The social picture is really a game with continual struggles for
dominance and territory and with the girls standing on the sidelines
cheering on the players. The first team contains the heroes. Others
sit on the bench as second stringers, and some aren't allowed to
play. There are definite rules and those who don't follow them are
thrown out of the game.

SEXUALITY

In the world of the lower animals, the male's energies are directed toward the acquiring of status and property and the maintenance of a social stability that will guarantee the continuation of both. The energies of the female are directed toward continuing the species by obtaining a male of the highest status and best territory possible. Dominant females get the dominant males and the species is guaranteed the continuation of the best of the genes.

That ultimate seedbed, the college campus, well illustrates the ethological principle and this particular behavior pattern. The queens of the campus migrate unerringly toward males of the highest social status, from the most powerful and affluent fraternities. Automobiles at one time constituted a male's territory and a strong sexual magnet, but at the present time off-campus apartments are the most attractive territories. Every campus has a student center that is divided into territories, and each of these areas belongs by common consent to the hippies, ag students, or frat lads whose numbers keep them occupied throughout the school day. And it is the males who secure the area, the table in the coffee shop or the group of easy chairs in the lounge, and it is the females who drift in as a result of their own choosing.

The female is not only the sexual chooser among the lower animals, she is the sexual aggressor. Our folklore has filled us with stories of the male animal's sweeping the female off her feet in an explosive passion of wooing, but among the lower animals the male does not react sexually until the female is physiologically ready and gives him the signal behaviorally. The world-wide acceptance of the double standard, therefore, is probably not so much a result of man's culture and conditioning as it is the result of some vague knowledge that the female really is responsible for all sexual consummation, excluding rape. This knowledge is a realization that universally aggravates the male ego, and man has compensated for what he knows as a fact by his fictions, especially his mythological fictions. Eve and Pandora are both good examples of the female-villain archetypes who have corrupted the world and have been the cause of all its ills. Perhaps this is so; the sexual drive is insistent and has been the downfall of more social units than King Arthur's Camelot. To the Hebrews and John Milton the temptation of Eve was more than man could resist, even knowing the commands of God. Like Eve, Pandora is another female who has been held accountable for the world's evils and Pandora's "box" is a fitting and universally understood symbol of the unstabilizing source of many of the male's problems. Lilith, Adam's first wife in Hebraic lore, took Adam's seed in his sleep and populated the world with demons. The Indians of Tierra del Fuego tell that in the beginning women ruled men, but finally the males banded together and with the help of supernatural power gained through secret ritual overthrew the women in a great battle. Our folklore indicates that the male is well aware of the sexual power of the female and is embarrassed by it.

Sexuality and the romantic foolishness that man's memory has invested it with has permeated every realm of folklore. It is the basic ingredient of all forms and degrees of folk literature, from epic to anecdote, and is the material backbone of most ballads and folk songs. Because of the intensity of the sexual drive and man's memory of it he has decided in his folk art that it comprises seventy-five percent (at least) of the contents of his waking moments and most of his dreams. This drive that the human male and female inherited from their animal ancestors is treated out of proportion to its intensity. Perhaps it illustrates the true power of the female in any social system, the power of an Eve or a Barbara Allen.

CONCLUSION

The ethologists are much maligned. To some of the stalwarts among the ranks of the illiberals, Konrad Lorenz, Robert Ardrey, Desmond Morris, Niko Tinbergen and company are apologists and rationalists for the most blatant forms of fascism, nationalism, racism, and male chauvinism. The proponents of ethology, however, like the followers of other sciences, have tried to arrive at their conclusions with scientific objectivity. Their purpose has been to gain insight into human behavior and to see it for what it really is, not for what man might romantically wish it to be. My conclusion, after using the ethological approach to folklore, is that behind every move that man makes is a wired-in behavior pattern which man holds in common with many of his animal kinsmen. This means that man has little control over what he does, only in how he does it. The "how" is his folklore, his culture, his way of life.

BIBLIOGRAPHY

Andrew, Richard J. "Evolution of Facial Expression," *Science,* Vol. 142, No. 3595 (November 22, 1963), 1034–1041.

—. "The Origins of Facial Expressions," *Scientifc American,* Vol. 213, No. 4 (October 1965), 88–94.

Ardrey, Robert. *African Genesis.* New York: Dell Publishing Co., Inc., 1970.

—. *The Social Contract.* New York: Atheneum, 1966.

—. *The Territorial Imperative.* New York: Atheneum, 1966.

Calhoun, John B. "Population Density and Social Pathology," *Scientific American,* Vol. 206, No. 2 (February 1962), 139–148.

Esch, Harald. "The Evolution of Bee Language," *Scientifc American,* Vol. 216, No. 4 (April 1967), 96–104.

Gerard, Ralph W. "What Is Memory?" *Scientific American,* Vol. 189, No. 3 (September 1953), 118–126.

Gray, James. "The Language of Animals," *The Languages of Science.* Greenwich, Conn.: Fawcett Publications, Inc., 1963, pp. 96–109.

The Human Species (special edition), *Scientifc American,* Vol. 203, No. 3 (September 1960).

Langer, Susanne K. "The Lord of Creation," *Fortune,* Vol. 29, No. 1 (January 1944), 12–128; 139–154.

Lorenz, Konrad Z. "The Evolution of Behaviour," *Scientific American,* Vol. 199, No. 6 (December 1958), 67–78.

—. *On Aggression.* New York: Harcourt, Brace & World, Inc., 1966.

Morris, Desmond. *The Human Zoo.* New York: Dell Publishing Co., Inc., 1969.

—, and Ramona Morris. *Men and Apes.* New York: Bantam Books, Inc., 1968.

—. *The Naked Ape.* New York: Dell Publishing Co., Inc., 1969.

Primate Ethology. Desmond Morris, ed. Garden City, New York: Anchor Books, 1969.

Rule, Colter. "A Theory of Human Behavior Based on Studies of Nonhuman Primates," *The Graduate Journal,* Vol. 8, No. 1 (1968), [A publication of The University of Texas], 23–59.

Tiger, Lionel. *Men in Groups.* New York: Vintage Books, 1970.

Tinbergen, Nikolaas. *Social Behaviour in Animals.* London: Associated Book Publishers Ltd., 1966.

Wynne-Edwards, V. C. *Animal Dispersion in Relation to Social Behaviour.* New York: Hafner Publishing Co., 1967.

—. "Population Control in Animals," *Scientific American,* Vol. 211, No. 2 (August 1964), 68–74.

Ab asserting his territoriality

The Crew of *The Pride*, a young Ab Abernethy on the right.

WHEN YOU CALL ME THAT, SMILE! OR FOLKLORE, ETHOLOGY, AND COMMUNICATION

It was now the Virginian's turn to bet or throw in his cards, and he did not speak at once.

Therefore Trampas spoke. "Your bet, you son of a _____!"

The Virginian's pistol came out, and his hand lay on the table, holding it unaimed. And with a voice as gentle as ever, the voice that sounded almost like a caress, but drawling a very little more than usual, so that there was almost a space between each word, he issued his orders to the man Trampas: "When you call me that, *smile*!"

The Virginian by Owen Wister

The basic premise for this paper is that much of folklore is a cultural response to genetically implanted behavior patterns which man holds in common with all his animal kinsmen, and that communication is one form of this folklore.

THE ETHOLOGICAL APPROACH

Our physiological kinship with the rest of the animal kingdom is amply supported by a study of evolution and comparative anatomy. Our behavioral relationship, the study of which is ethology, is equally supported by an observation of the basic drives or instincts that most animals hold in common—those of sociality, dominance, territoriality, and sexuality. Man's folklore is his cultural response to these drives. For example, the customs and traditions and religious beliefs which a group holds in common enforce the sociality drive, or herding instinct, and bind them together in a strong, survivable unit. The dominance drive for the establishment of a pecking order is illustrated in all folk contests and in folk tales of Hercules and

Jason and their ilk who must overcome obstacles to take their places at the top. Territoriality, so necessary for an animal's procreation and survival, is illustrated by games, both intellectual and physical, by chess and football, in which teams struggle to penetrate and gain new territory while protecting their own. And sexuality, which the females of the various species control for the continuation of the species, is a basic ingredient of all kinds of folk song and literature and of folklore itself because the folk have always known that without continuing fertility and the sexuality that operates it all other factors of life are meaningless.

This brings us to communication, which is one kind of folklore, and which will be discussed from the viewpoint of the ethologist, that is, as one aspect of inherited behavior patterns that all animals hold in common. The bases for all human communication are behavior traits that man shares with other animals, and these traits have been genetically transmitted throughout the human race. Man has, however, gone beyond the lower animals, primarily because he has a better memory and therefore a higher ability to reason, to choose among courses of action. He has chosen instinctive communication signals—such as touching, waving, or crying—he has modified them to suit his culture, and he has passed these new distinctive hand shakes, peace signs, and love songs along through later times and other spaces. This is his folklore, most of which is putting his genetic drives into symbolized forms.

COMMUNICATION BY SIGNS AND SYMBOLS

Communication is the voluntary and involuntary transmission of information (includes feelings, attitudes, states of mind, reactions) from one animal to another. The four ways animals communicate are by smell, touch, sight, and sound.

Communication is achieved by means of signs (or signaling) and symbols. Theoretically the lower animals communicate by signs only. Their signs—their cries, gestures, and scents—are the results of genetic reactions and conditioned responses to internal feelings or external situations. Other animals hear them, see them, feel them, or smell them and react or respond to their signals. One dog enters another's territory, smells the signs the home dog has left on the fireplugs and utility poles, and loses some of his confidence. Mourning doves in the springtime romantically lean against one another and bill and coo. Bees return from a scouting expedition and do a dance indicating the direction and distance from the hive of a new pollen source. And whales moving in groups keep continual "songs" going that keep the group in contact with each other.

People communicate by signs also. They emit odors that communicate to those nearby that they have been under nervous or sexual tension. They touch, slap, grab, and shove each other to attract attention or to announce their moods. They smile, frown, blush; their bodies are continually moving in response to their own feelings and external conditions. And they laugh, cry, moan, and sigh according to their moods. These genetic responses and conditioned reflexes are signs and signals man holds in common with other animals and with other people, whether they are members of his culture or not.

One of man's distinguishing characteristics is that in addition to being a sign user he is a user of symbols in his communication. A symbol is dictionarily defined as something that is used in place of, stands for, or represents something else. The "something else" can be abstract (feeling, state of mind) or concrete (a person, place, or thing). Communication within a human group is accomplished mainly by means of cultural symbols which are meaningful only within the particular group. To English speaking people the word *table* represents a piece of furniture with a flat top and enough legs to keep it up and stable. To the Spanish, *mesa* stands for the same thing. The Eskimos communicate tactilly by rubbing noses; Americans touch lips. The association of the idea with the symbolic response is conditioned by the culture which uses it. These symbols are his culture's folklore, traditionally circulated and continually changing.

Man and the lower animals share four different methods of communication. They are olfactory (smell), tactile (touch), visual (sight), and acoustical (sound).

OLFACTORY COMMUNICATION

Olfactory communication is the transmission of information by use of scents. In the evolution of communication among animals it is the simplest and most primitive form, first used by the female of the species to announce sexual readiness.

The one-celled paramecium usually reproduces by cell division but it may also reproduce sexually by conjugation. At the time of sexual readiness it emits a chemical attractant which will call in a mate and at the same time repel those that it cannot mate with. On a much higher evolutionary plane, among mammals the female in a state of estrus sends forth a chemical or olfactory signal when she is ready to copulate. Females among humans at the time of physiological readiness also broadcast an estral odor, but man's olfactory sense is too undeveloped and blunted to perceive it, except vaguely.

The estral odor, along with other odor stimuli secreted by the apocrine glands during sexual arousal, are signals in the olfactory communication system. They are genetic and/or conditioned responses to situations. Olfactory symbols are scents that he has created to stand for certain desirable olfactory signs, usually sexual signs. Perfumes with a musk base are used by females as aphrodisiacs (consider My Sin, Aphrodesia, Intimate, Tabu, Wild Desire, Soul Kiss); that is, the female removes her natural odor by washing and substitutes a manufactured scent that is recognized as titillating in her culture. This substitute scent is an olfactory symbol.

Although the sexual musk base is the dominant odor, there are many variations of the blended secondary odors of spices and flowers, and various groups express their own folk preferences. Mediterranean peoples lean to heavy, oil-based odors, while Asiatics traditionally prefer flower scents, and the Nordics use the lightest scents of all. The Atakapan Indians of the Texas Gulf Coast boiled the oil from alligator tails, allowed it to get rancid, then coated their bodies with it. The resultant bouquet was their socially distinguishing smell and also kept off mosquitoes.

Olfactory communication in folklore has purposes that are other than sexual. It is one way of communicating with the gods in some cultures. The burning of incense and aromatic woods during worship services is to attract the gods' attention. This holds true with the Greeks' sacrifice of hecatombs as well as with other burnt offerings, especially among the early Hebrews. Noah, when he finally came to land "took of every clean beast, and of every clean fowl, and offered burnt offerings on the altar. And the Lord smelled a sweet savor" and leaned out and looked down upon him and blessed him.

TACTILE COMMUNICATION

Tactile communication is the transmission of information through touch. The primates, especially the large social primates, such as the chimpanzees and baboons, are continual social touchers who spend much of their time leaning against one another and grooming one another. The initial result is comfort and cleanliness; the principal result is the strengthening of the social bond. Another tactile signal among primates is mounting, which communicates dominance. In a contest for territory or sexual favors, the weaker male, in order to appease the dominant male, will present himself as if for copulation. The dominant male will mount him not for direct sexual purposes but to demonstrate his dominance. This is ancestral to hugging or the formal abrazo. The hugger is dominant; the huggee is sub-dominant.

Man communicates tactilly through both signals and in symbolic communication. Tactile signals include any type of touching that has as its purpose the gaining of attention or the expression of a mood. One person taps another on the shoulder so that the tappee will look in the tapper's direction. Or one leans against another person for comfort or touches him or straightens his tie to demonstrate affection. This is grooming similar to cats licking one another. The folklore that evolves from this need to communicate by touch includes the formal handshake and abrazo and all the modern ways of swapping skin. Rubbing noses, western kissing, and the religious practice of the laying on of hands are also tactile symbols; that is, each kind of physical contact represents more than merely the touching of skin, and each is a formalized representation of something else, usually an emotion.

Ab Abernethy and Jack Duncan, 2009.

VISUAL COMMUNICATION

Visual communication is the transmission of information through movements, postures, and other externals which can be seen. Visual communication among most mammals, especially the primates, occurs in three ways—by gross movements, or the stance of the entire body or its parts; by raising of the hair over the whole body, down the back, or on the head and face; and by facial expression. These are genetically implanted signals which man holds in common with his animal kinsmen. We bow up or cower, smile, frown and pout, back our ears and flare our nostrils; and even though we don't erect our hair as well as our furrier friends do, we still have the physiological mechanism to do it; and sometimes the hair does stand up on the backs of our necks or we get goose bumps that raise what little hair we have. Man's visual signs include blushing, smiling, frowning, and all sorts of gestures and body postures which are informal, non-traditional, and are the immediate results of a situation or state of mind. This is body language, and is a holdover from our evolutionary past. For example, the smile is the relique of the baring of the teeth in a defensive posture.

Visual symbols are those gestures which a culture has formalized into traditional and recognizable patterns. This is our folklore. Included in it are all sorts of sign language, including the peace sign and the black power sign as well as the insulting signs such as the stuck-out tongue and the extended middle finger. (The flashed middle finger as well as the Italian thrusted forearm are both sexual symbols asserting male dominance in the same way as in the primates' mounting signal, and these gestures are technically improper when used by females.) Also included is the dress style that cultures and subcultures affect to announce their membership in classes, clubs, groups, and lodges.

ACOUSTICAL COMMUNICATION

Acoustical communication is the transmission of information through sounds. Among humans this includes telegraphy, hand clapping, and whistling, along with communication by voice or any instrument that is an extension of the voice (a saxophone as well as a telephone).

Most of the mammals communicate vocally, and this vocalizing functions as a result of the sociality drive, holding the herd of cattle or whales together; of the dominance drive in voicing aggressive intentions; of the territorial drive, as the herd bull paces his territory bellowing both an invitation to females and a warning to other males; and of the sexuality drive, as the birds and mammals whistle and howl their readiness. As the most complex of communication methods vocalization is highly elaborated in some animals, even to including learned dialectal differences that exist among certain species of birds and seals, to mention two.

A couple of fine birds.

Vocal communication is man's most highly developed skill. Vocal signals are those cries, sighs, laughs, and moans which a person emits under internal or external stimulation. All humans cry and laugh, and they yell when they are hurt and growl when they are angry. Each culture, however, selects about thirty phonemes from the 10,000 sounds the human animal can make and with these phonemes creates words, or sounds which stand for something in particular. These words are vocal symbols, because they are substitutes for the thing itself. The word *cat* is a traditional way of arranging sounds in order that one in our culture might transmit the idea of a cat. The word is a substitute, a vocal symbol, and it is our folklore, being continually shaped and reshaped, corrupted and refined as we use it and pass it on to our progeny.

CONCLUSION

Communication among humans consists of folklore, conditioned reflexes, and inherited behavior patterns. And probably folklore is the least of these. Spinning off the studies of Albert Mehrabian and using his figures, the Total Impact of Communication is 7% verbal (the word itself) + 38% acoustical (the sound of the word) + 55% visual (the gestures which go with the word). The verbal part, the words we use, mean very little by themselves, but the sound of the words said and the stance of the sayer—all these together communicate. There are many ways to say "What a lovely dress" or "I hate you." Both can be spoken in a way to mean the opposite of the explicit meaning of the words. Hamlet asks Ophelia, "Are you honest?", meaning "Are you chaste?" She answers, "My lord?" with two, simple, one-syllable words whose meaning—anger, embarrassment, amusement?—depends entirely on tone of voice and whatever visual signals she might send. And it was all right for Trampas to impeach the Virginian's maternity as long as he smiled when he said it.

The folklore is the word said, the figure of speech, the language and dialect, and whatever traditional gesture, smell, and touch that accompanies the word. These are the symbols that one generation of a culture passes on to the next, and this symbolic communication is consciously performed. But underlying and amplifying this level of communication are all his years of being conditioned in his culture and all the blood, bones, and nerves that are a part of his genetic makeup. And here is where most of the sound of his words comes from and the look on his face and the movements of his body as he speaks. And it is on this level that he meets his past and all those animals he came down the evolutionary road with. On this level, he howls and snarls and stomps his feet in threat or cringes in submission, tail between his legs. And on this level he becomes *almost* as honest about what he really means as his animal kinfolks.

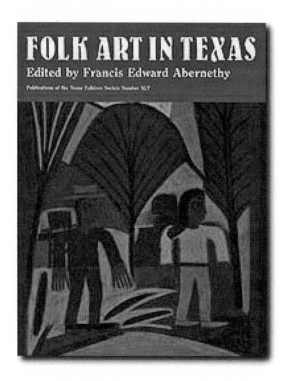

Folk Art in Texas, the 1985 publication.

FOLK ART IN GENERAL, YARD ART IN PARTICULAR

[Originally, text and photographs by Francis Edward Abernethy]

This folk art project began on a flight from DFW to Austin. I was with a jazzman friend, and we got into a two-hundred-mile discussion of art. He had ordered a cord of wood, and the black man who delivered and stacked the wood arranged it in obviously contrived designs. My friend catalytically remarked that he hated to break down the cord of firewood because he was destroying a work of art.

We contemplated the impulse that would give rise to such an ephemeral art form and began to consider other common but either unnoticed or taken-for-granted manifestations. I had recently purchased a new Stetson and had had it steamed and shaped according to my inclination and one of the latest styles. We agreed that shaping hats was an art in addition to being a craft. The knowledge of the craft was necessary to know *how* to do it. The feeling for the added dimension of art—for the flow of the curve of the brim, and the balance and symmetry of the crown—was necessary to know *what* to do. The art of the hat had gone beyond the utility of it.

As we surveyed our fellow passengers we found a Pentecostal lady with no makeup but with a very elaborate hairdo. Seated close by was a young black girl whose crowning glory was both braided and cornrowed. Our conclusion, which was certainly nothing new, was that all people have an artistic impulse, a desire to elaborate, ornament, decorate, and personalize the utilitarian objects that are parts of their lives. In a mass-produced world of clothes and houses and people there was this urge to tie on ribbons, to gild lilies, to add a dimension to things in order to distinguish them from others of the same species and to give them personalities to share with their owners.

So that's what this book is about—the art that all people are involved in, the decoration and ornamentation that man puts on himself and on his properties, the unnecessary that he adds to the useful to make the article more pleasing to his eye.

The main purpose of all art—of all things that man puts his hand to—is to bring order out of chaos. If man has a lifelong devotion to any one goal—and it is a goal admirably searched for but seldom reached—it is to get some order in his life and in the little world he moves in, to get stability in his days and his years, in his own and his world's past. So he arranges the hours of his day and the boundaries of his territories, and he stacks Troy and All Gaul and Waterloo and the Fourth of July in a neat historical pile. Then he writes his poetry in ordered iambic pentameters and sings his songs in regular ballad stanzas and draws the Creation nicely framed on the ceiling of one grand room as if it were happening every time someone looked at it. And the artist who draws the Creator becomes the Creator himself, making new worlds, controlling new visions, separating light from darkness, dry land from the ocean's water. The Artist—like Jehovah of Old or a child with his toys—makes worlds that are his. They are ordered, disciplined worlds that he can sit back and enjoy and observe.

Another purpose of art is communication. The soul sits in silence, brooding, imagining, fantasizing forms that symbolize its being's being. Out of the depths with sound sepulchral, it tolls, "Know me! I am! I have heard and seen and been!" And like Lazarus come back to tell you all, it strains to tell you all. The ordinary says only words with futile gestures to tell the world who he is. The artist sings forth his soul's release for a little while or with flexing spatula spreads his fragile spirit on a canvas. Art is one answer to the sociality drive; the artist yearns to communicate with his herd and be responded to.

The practice of art is also like the playing of games. It is the result of the stimulus struggle, man's desire for the optimum amount of intellectual stimulation—not the most, but the best. The nonspecializing, hyperactive, extremely curious upright biped called man that nature selected for survival is physiologically and neurologically equipped to lead a continually questing life. When life's pace slows he becomes bored; when life becomes too fast and too frantic, he panics. He therefore seeks this optimum, the mean between boredom and panic, and his art as one form of his recreation reflects this. Music played too softly loses its impact; music played too loudly causes pain. Continual pastels produce aesthetic lassitude; the lavishness of rococo eventually offends the eye. "The optimum" never means "the most." Peter DeVries said, "Nothing is so boring as unrelieved novelty." But unrelieved order also becomes boring, so a straight line or a musical note is waved or curved or shaped into the form of a buffalo or a ballad, and variations on the norm become elaborations and ornamentations—they become art. The optimum, the art that satisfies the eye or ear, is neither totally predictable nor totally unpredictable, and art is the search for the desirable mean.

One slogs through a mire when he attempts to explain either who "the folk" are or what art is, and he wades even deeper when he deals with those terms in tandem. We are dealing with visual art, which can be defined as color and form arranged to satisfy aesthetic expectations. Lines are drawn, paint is applied to a canvas, clay is molded: these are common media for art. But artists frequently go beyond these forms and create with fabrics and metals, wood and stone—anything on which a line can be drawn, anything that can be shaped or arranged.

Much art that is produced is not art for the sake of art, but is art that is produced as an aesthetic embellishment of a person or place or thing, each of which can exist and function independently of its ornamentation. For instance, man unadorned is beautiful enough to satisfy his Creator, but the traditions of cultures require that hair be styled, faces be painted, and bodies be jeweled and attired in ways that please the eyes of the general. Pots are thrown that are sufficient to carry water from here to there, but sometimes color is kneaded into the clay and lines are drawn on the surface, and later artists write odes to Grecian urns on which the art has become more important than the craft and its use.

The folk—the common denominators among the carriers of a culture's customs—are artists, ever pleasing their own and others' eyes with colors and forms which they create or apply to themselves and the things around them. Some create folk art in the most acceptable academic sense of the term; that is, they follow the use of color and form in the long-standing traditions of their culture. They learn a craft and the art that embellishes it from their elders, who learned it from the ancients. The traditional forms and colors are passed to them by word of mouth or demonstration. These folk artists create variations on the traditional formulas, but they stay within the well-understood conventions of their group. They craft a warm and durable quilt in a double-wedding-ring design. They sculpt headstones out of limestone with lambs and angels and shrouded urns adorning the memento mori. They hammer tin or cut metal to create crowing cocks and running horses as weather vanes. These are not the fashionable art forms of high culture; they are the products of artisans, and they grow out of craft traditions— and they represent the traditions and tastes of a homogenous group of people.

The term *folk art* was once applied to the paintings and sculptings of primitive artists, the untrained who paint and sculpt for their own pleasure, little caring for conventional standards or academic criteria. This type of artist is now referred to as a "naive artist" to separate him from the implications of the word *folk* with its emphasis on tradition. This Grandma Moses type of folk art at its worst is no better than what a third grader brings home. At its best it has a simplicity and honesty that is singularly refreshing and delightful. Cecilia Steinfeldt's *Texas Folk Art* is this state's study of its best-known naive artists.

Sometimes folk art is the expression of the folk individually, and what these individuals do to create an artistic milieu is not necessarily in their culture's traditions. These persons are untrained, perhaps unskilled, and as creators they do not think of themselves as artists, perhaps as decorators. This type of art does not usually grow out of a craft, nor is it created for sale. It is a personal response to the dynamic inner urge to personalize one's territory and possessions, to communicate identity, to assert identity. The best illustration of this is in yard art, that species of space art that one regularly views as he drives down streets, roads, and highways—past houses with petunia-filled washpots, with bottle trees and wheel-lined driveways, with a front yard museum of ornamental hedges and rock gardens and farm machinery. No two yards are alike, and the objects are usually resurrected discards, what to other people would be junk. But the creator has arranged color and form to satisfy his aesthetic expectations, and this arrangement of color and form is as much art as a mobile I once saw in a London art museum that consisted of license plates and hub caps.

Beauty is in the eye of the beholder.

Yard art is a response to the dominance and territorial imperatives. The artist is displaying his personality (his ego, his dominance) in his own territory, like a buck deer hooking brush and clearing scrapes. He establishes personality by using artifacts that he feels represent him, things to which he is sentimentally and emotionally attached. The artistic decoration of one's yard is no more than an extension of making up one's face and selecting clothes and decorating the rooms in one's house. An occupant paints walls, hangs pictures, sets pot plants and books and *objets d'art* on shelves, and he makes his interior territory his own. Some do the same to their yards.

I stopped by a house in Johnson City during the daytime, when *As the World Turns* was on the television. John Dixon, the soap's consummate villain, was temporarily blind, so the lady of the house didn't have much time for me at first. She gave me the run of the place, however, and said that I could photograph anything I wanted to—the wheels, the painted gourds, the row of dressed Mrs. Butterworth syrup bottles, and the centerpiece—a magnificent bottle tree with all blue bottles on a large white cedar-tree trunk. When her soap was over she came out, and we both speculated on and looked forward to the episode when that rascal John would get his just deserts.

When we got around to discussing other things, I asked her why she had decorated her yard thus, and she said because she had wanted to. I asked her why she had created the bottle tree, and she said because she liked bottle trees; she thought they were pretty. I have since decided that those are the ultimate motives for the creation of most folk art: because the artists want to and because they like it. These arrangers of form and color want to decorate, and they do, without much consideration of motive. It is the same with the forms they choose; they collect what pleases their personal eyes and innards and seldom ask why.

The lady from Johnson City was proud of her bottle tree and had gone to considerable trouble to collect and attach the dark blue bottles. To her and to other yard artists along the highways, the trees were pure decoration, to serve no purpose except to please the eye. The bottle tree, however, had its beginning in a reason. It was a product of the Afro-American tradition, and its purpose was to protect its house from evil spirits. The belief was that lurking spirits would be attracted to the array of sparkling colored glass and that they would be lured into the bottles and would be unable to escape. The bottle-tree people I talked to were white, and none of them recognized the mystical, utilitarian purpose of their creations. They just liked bottle trees and thought they were pretty.

I visited with a man who lived on the edge of Madisonville. He had a mailbox mounted on an old water pump. Arranged in the front yard were a riding cultivator, a turning plow, and the inevitable black washpot filled with petunias. He was a retired farmer, and these were some of the implements left over when he came into town. He had brought a part of his life and personality with him and established them in his yard as his totems.

Farm tools and machinery are popular forms of yard art. They represent a simple and romantic rural past. Their users nostalgically love the forms for what they represent personally and historically. Iron stirrups, hames, and singletrees hang on garage walls or as mobiles to decorate carports. Cultivators, walking drills, go-devils, and Georgia stocks are arranged as artifacts in the yard museums of their interests. Wagons of all sizes are used, and I'm sure that in a front yard somewhere one could locate an old binder or combine. But maybe the combine is too modern. Yard art machinery is usually antique, relics of the horse-drawn era.

A man somewhere east of Waco had a yard that was completely enclosed with a fence made out of cultivator wheels welded together. The gates and swing arbors were made of cultivator wheels, all cleanly silver painted and in good repair. The whole of it startled the eye, but it was certainly ordered and symmetrical. The constructor was a retired welder who had access to a wonderful lot of cultivator wheels. Rather than let them rust back into the soil he applied his talents to circumscribing his territory with them.

Welders as a class seem to be creative. A knowledge of the craft gives the welder a power over iron that requires artistic expression, and they are the ones who make the artistic chain and iron supported mailboxes and wheel-gates. Welding projects in high school ag shops frequently wind up in parents' front yards.

Much of the yard art I encountered had been arranged by retired people who had previously lived active lives. When they had fixed everything around the house, planted and maintained gardens, chicken yards, and fruit trees, manicured and landscaped their yards, they had an energy that still had to be burned in doing. So they welded elaborate gates, or built little windmills and well sheds, or tightened their fleeting holds on their territories with personalized fences.

On one long, lonesome road in the Blacklands I visited an old widower who lived in a well-kept shotgun shack with a white-whiskered rat terrier and a back yard full of birdhouses and whirligigs. He welcomed my company, talked about a past that was vivid and active, and said that he decorated his back yard with whirligigs because they brought some movement and activity, a sense of life, to his yard. He fed birds and built birdhouses because he needed something to putter around with and because their life and movement were a precious seasoning to this final inactive time of his life. The artifacts also added an artistic dimension to an otherwise drab landscape.

I discussed the ubiquitous black washpot planter with numerous ladies along the way, and nearly all of them remarked on the unsuitability of the washpot as a planter. The pot was pure decoration, usually purchased at a flea market—as were many of the yard art items. The pot was not good as a planter, I was told, because it wouldn't drain. I was counseled to put a lot of gravel in the bottom should I decide on one for my own yard. Twice I was told of disasters to washpots when hardheaded husbands insisted they could knock a small drainhole in the bottom, ultimately creating several pieces of concave cast iron. Washpots pressed into service as flower pots are artistic, not utilitarian.

Bathroom fixtures in the yard reflect a certain whimsy on the part of the user-artist. Usually they are used as planters, with a white enamel bathtub containing a full fern garden. One sink I encountered was wired to a pine tree and held a lush cascading ivy. A commode with chrysanthemums made a lovely display of gleaming white and green and gold. This bathroom-variety humor in yard art depends on a surprising incongruity. These creators are responding to that sense, straining or shocking in order to attract the eye of the passerby.

Rocks of all varieties abound, some serving territorially to hem in flower gardens, some standing monolithically for the sake of their own solid selves. All kinds of rocks are used, but the yard artist's greatest affinity is for petrified "rocks," as they are sometimes described. Most decorators express a sense of pleased wonder at the antiquity of the petrifactions as well as awe at the process in which wood could be turned into stone, almost like water into wine. Their difference constituted a natural beauty.

Bleached skulls—horned cow skulls in particular—receive considerable attention from yard artists. Some of the art reflects a conscious concern with the Texas mystique as symbolized by the longhorn cow, and the skull is a reflection of the romantic interest in the rural and the antique. I think that many people like cow and horse skulls because they like cows and horses, and here's the elemental structure that doesn't require care and feeding. One humorous horse skull sported a straw hat; the gaudiest one was painted red, blue, and black.

The most striking yard adornment I encountered was an elliptical arrangement of twenty-five bicycles in a front yard near Tyler.

A red-white-and-blue turning plow, a wagon, singletree mobiles, painted milk cans, and earthenware jugs completed the decor. I shall not attempt to interpret the bicycles.

The principal motif in yard art is the circle, in the form of wheels and tires. They are everywhere—adorning gates and fences, supporting swings and washpots, circumscribing flower beds, standing as guardians along driveways. Wheels within wheels—"The little wheel turns by faith; the big wheel turns by the Grace of God!"—exist in every sort of plane. It is a natural choice. According to Gestalt psychology—with which every yard artist is intimately acquainted—the circle has a perceptual "goodness" (*Pragnanz*) to which all persons are innately sensitive. In a descending scale of goodness, to clarify this abstract notion, are the square, triangle, and the star. Only the wheel can be rotated through 360 degrees and maintain the same form. It can also be moved through all its planes and always be symmetrical. One can complete its form accurately by seeing only a small arc of its circumference. The circle is the form most satisfying to man's innate desire for order and predictability.

The circle represents perfection. When the Pope asked Da Vinci if he could draw, the artist took a piece of charcoal from the fireplace and drew a perfect circle on the papal wall. When Dante described God, he pictured Him as three concentric circles. The medieval universe consisted of concentric circles with the earth as the center. Fortune, to Boethius and other medievals, was a great wheel immutably turning. Ezekiel's great vision of the ultimate truth was a wheel within a wheel up in the middle of the air. And what was good enough for Dante, Boethius, and Ezekiel in their magnificent contemplations of the universe is certainly good enough for your casual folk artist who merely wishes to personalize his yard, mark his territory, and get some attention from neighbors and passing motorists.

Yard art does not qualify as folk art with some critics because in its hodge-podge individuality it is not in the respected parade of tradition (like quilting patterns or painted Pennsylvania hex signs). But if we accept the definition of the folk as the common denominator of a culture and of art as the aesthetic arrangement of color and form, we have in yard art the two side by side, even if they are not wedded. These artists are as much folk decorating their yards as they are when they're stitching the Lone Star on a quilt cover. And they are arranging their culture's colors and all sorts of traditional forms to satisfy an aesthetic expectation. So, stretched though the definition might be, these are the type of folk who put a red-and-green turning plow on a stump in the middle of the front yard and are mightily pleased by the looks of it—that is, until someone decides the whole yardscape would look better if the plow were flanked and balanced by two silver cultivator wheels.

A true herpetologist.

SNAKELORE

[Paper presented at the Eighty-Second Annual
Meeting of the Texas Folklore Society, Sherman, Texas,
April 10, 1998]

And the serpent said unto the woman, "Ye shall surely not die [from eating of the tree of knowledge]; for God doth know that in the day ye eat thereof, then your eyes shall be opened, and ye shall be as gods, knowing good and evil."

Soon thereafter, however, God discovers their transgression and asks the man, "Who told thee that thou was naked?"

And *shamelessly* the man said, "The woman whom thou gavest to be with me, she gave me of the tree, and I did eat."

And the woman blamed it on the serpent: "The serpent beguiled me and I did eat."

And God put a mighty curse on the serpent: "Because thou hast done this, thou art cursed above all cattle, and above every beast of the field; upon thy belly shalt thou go, and dust shalt thou eat all the days of thy life. And I will put enmity between thee and the woman, and between thy seed and her seed, and they shall bruise thy head and thou shalt bruise their heel."

And those reared in Old Testament tradition have grown up killing snakes.

When I was growing up on the Washita ranch, I am sad to say that we killed snakes. Grandad, sitting on a walking horse, shot the head off of a crawling rattlesnake with his pistol, or at least that's how he told it. I watched in fascination as Ring, one of the ranch's greyhounds, would swoop up a snake, give it a great shake, and then fling it in the air—in uncontrolled and sometimes danger-ous directions—to land limp and lifeless on the prairie. We took any dead snake and hung it belly up over a fence to make it rain. On later inspection, I would always find that it had twisted, dead though it was, back to a stomach-down position—for which reason it did not rain during the Thirties in the Panhandle of Texas.

Of course, the snake had no problem shifting its position on the fence, because folk wisdom reminds us that a snake will squirm and will not die until the sun sets.

I learned very young the good snakes from the bad and caught coachwhips, puff adders, king snakes, and bull snakes when they crossed my path. The ranch hands regularly warned me that if I aggravated a coachwhip (*Masticophis flagellum*) sufficiently, it would chase me down, wrap me up in its coils, and proceed to whip me till the skin fell from my bones. As if that were not enough, under extreme provocation it would run its twin tongues up my nostrils and suck out what little brains I had.

I periodically brought serpents to the house, where (I am ashamed to say) I showed them to my invalid aunt who entertained me by going berserk at the sight of anything reptilian. This was not as bad as my son-in-law's uncle and aunt, who when they were around six and seven respectively caught rattlesnakes, broke off their rattles, and then turned them loose to prowl the prairies in silence. The children were not found out until their mother confronted them with a Folger's coffee can filled with rattles.

Deedy Abernethy with a snake.

So I present my credentials as a herpetologist from my youth, point out that at one time I regularly led college biologists on snake hunts in the Big Thicket and on the Pecos, and in 1959 I was one of two herpetologists on a pioneering biological expedition into the barrancas del Cobre, Tarahumara, and Urique. In addition to which I have a bumper sticker on my pickup that reads, "This truck brakes for snakes."

I was prompted to writing this paper by being snakily misquoted at last year's meeting. I forgot exactly what the misquotation was, but it had to do with differences between water moccasins and natrixes, or common water snakes. To clear up which, let me say that "water moccasin," "cotton mouth," and "stump tail" are common names for the *Agkistrodon piscivorus*, a venomous, surly-spirited pit viper equipped with fangs that can inject serious doses of hemotoxic poison. Natrixes are large, dark, and lance-headed like the moccasin. And natrixes have nasty, aggressive dispositions. But they are long-bodied and nonpoisonous. If, however, you come across a stocky, two-to-three foot, lance-headed, slate-colored snake which is about as wide as your foot and *which looks like it is smiling*, it is a moccasin. If it pulls back into a coil and opens its mouth and the mouth is white, it is a cotton-mouth moccasin. And if your eyesight is any good at all, you should be able to see that it has an elliptical, cat-eyed pupil that makes it look mean and adds evidence of its being a water moccasin. The common water snakes are round eyed. Really, this difference is not hard to recognize, even at a distance.

The simplest way to catch a snake is to put something flat across its neck where it joins the head, then put the index finger on the head while clamping down on the neck with the thumb and middle finger. With large snakes, a full-hand grip behind the head is recommended. Another method, particularly useful with water snakes, is to grab the complete head in the hand and hold it firmly, even while the remainder of the snake is coiling about your arm. Raymond Ditmars suggests grabbing the snake by the tail, swinging it back between your legs, and then clamping down. Thus, one pulls the snake back outward between his legs until he comes to the head.

What the head might be doing to one's backsides during this operation is a matter Ditmars fails to address.

Then, after you catch the snake, you must know how to handle it without disrupting its delicate skeletal structure—or getting bit. Sometimes the results are unpredictable. Doug Davis, a student of mine at Lamar, had reached the climax of his tour, guiding Career Day students through the biology department. He had showed them skeletons and various pickled fetuses. In conclusion he wrapped Chloe, the department's huge chicken snake about his neck and was explaining to his completely impressed and fully attentive students the art of snake handling. Some lad asked, "Mr. Davis, how do you know he won't bite you." Doug could not help but smile. He said, "You must never squeeze a snake." But being suggestible, he squoze, and Chloe automatically struck his nose like the blow of a fist. And instead of snakelike, slashing and recoiling, it hung there. Losing all composure, Doug screamed, "Git him off," in a muffled nasal tone. But by this time his charges were at the far back of the room or hanging from the fans. Doug, looking like Pinocchio, had to prize Chloe off with his fingers. By the time Doug got to my class, he was darkening around the eyes, his nose noticeably chewed. The next day his eyes were black and his lip was poked out and his nose looking like ground meat left out in the sun.

Let us return to the Hebrews, whose god put a cultural curse on snakes generally. (We have no idea on what *kind* of snake that primal one was in The Garden—poisonous? Nonpoisonous?) Sir James G. Frazer in his *Folklore of the Old Testament* presents the Biblical Paradise Lost tale along with a dozen or more Middle Eastern variants and arrives at an epitype, or original, of what he calls "the perverted message" tale type. This *original* Paradise Lost story was more logical and provided us with a more compassionate god and with smarter primal parents than *Genesis* did. In Frazer's epitype story, God creates a world and puts a man and a woman in it. In the Garden he puts a Tree of Life and Tree of Death. He then calls *his messenger, the snake,* to him and tells him to tell the folks in paradise not to eat of the Tree of Death for in that day they will become mortal and die, but to eat of the Tree of Life and live forever. There is no confusion here between the Tree of Death and the Tree of Knowledge. The snake takes the road to Eden, but on the way he develops a jealousy and thinks, "This is really unfair, that they should have immortality while I have it not!" So the snake does the old tree switch, and the man and woman *mistakenly and misguidedly* eat of the Tree of Death and become mortal, and the serpent eats of the Tree of Life and becomes immortal. And it has been that way ever since, with man doing his three score and ten and then departing, while the snake sheds his skin every spring and is reborn and immortal.

The equating of the Tree of Death and the Tree of Knowledge of Good and Evil is found in the Hebraic version only, and gives us some idea of an early Hebraic intellectual ambivalence. And of course, a snake does shed his skin soon after it emerges from hibernation, but it might shed its skin two or three times annually, depending on its growth rate.

As in Frazer's and other Middle Eastern myths, the snake has been universally considered the messenger of the gods. The Greeks and Romans had in-house messenger snakes which they honored with plates of milk. The Japanese considered that the albino black-rat snake was a fitting messenger to the gods and kept it comfortable and well fed. Malaysians send their prayers to the gods through lethargic native adders that they drape around in their temples. The Hopi and Zuni dance with snake messengers annually, sprinkling them with water and corn meal, then sending them to the four points of the compass to address the gods on their behalf.

In addition to being a messenger for the gods, the snake, which is universally represented as both a symbol of immortality *and* as a phallic symbol, has attained godhead itself in many cultures. In west Africa, the Dahomean god Damballah is a great snake who is worshipped as the intercessor between man and the creator. In India the god Shiva is a snake in one manifestation, and his adherents subject themselves to awful rituals in which they pull snakes through holes cut in their tongues. The Indian Naga (cobra) gods were once worshipped with human sacrifices. A cobra goddess ruled Lower Egypt. In China the serpent was a phallic-fertility god, and in Japan the

God of Thunder was a snake. The Mayans worshipped the winged serpent Kukulcan, and the Aztecs worshipped the same winged serpent Quetzalcoatl, a combination of a quetzal and a rattlesnake.

And one of the American Revolutionary flags featured a coiled rattlesnake under the warning, "Don't Tread On Me!"

The list of reptilian deities could go on and on, demonstrating without doubt mankind's interest in and dependence upon the good will of snakes from the time of creation.

Texas snakelore contains the folk beliefs found over most of the US. Texas is blessed with the milk snake (*Lampropeltis triangulum*), a banded snake that follows cattle, latches on to teats, and sucks them dry. And reportedly, there are those who have seen an old jersey cow waddling into the lot with the snakes hanging from all four teats. The colorfully banded milk snake is frequently mistaken for the banded coral snake (*Micrurus fulvius*)—a neurotoxically poisonous snake, kin to cobras. The folk mnemonic guide, "Red and yellow killafella; Red and black venom lack" is to be applied at this point.

Let us not forget the hoop snake, or stinging snake (*Farancia abacura*, or mud snake), which has a tail sharpened into a stinger. This is the serpent that seizes its tail in its mouth and rolls after its victim like a living bicycle tire. When it catches up with a small boy, it uncoils and spears him in the calf of the leg with its tail-stinger, and the boy falls over immediately to suffer an agonizing death. In reality, the mud snake is most gentle. It uses its sharp tail to anchor in mud as it searches for amphiuma eels. The mud snake does have the disconcerting habit of tapping your arm with the tip of its tail, its stinger, when you first pick it up.

Rattlesnakes (the Crotalidae) do not swallow their young to protect them. A snake's stomach enzymes are very powerful and would turn a snakelet to mush in a trice. Also, rattlers add more than one rattle a year, every time they shed, and cannot be aged by the number of rattles. And they do not necessarily rattle before they strike. When they are hunting, they *never* rattle before they strike. Rattlesnakes can go just about anywhere, and putting a grass or hair rope around a sleeping bag won't keep one out—and I question the prickly pear corral story that is the subject of José Cisneros' classic print.

On a Texas State Herpetological meeting held on the King Ranch, we came upon a vaquero who had killed a large rattler, and had built a small fire, and was burning the snake to keep its mate from following him and taking vengeance.

The frightening puff adder or spreading adder (*Heterodon contortrix*) is really a smooth-mouthed, toad-eating, hog-nosed snake, which goes into a death feign as soon as it is seriously challenged. A large hognose can rear and spread like a cobra and is most intimidating. Some affirm that the puff of an adder contains a killing poison. When spreading and puffing fail to work, the hognose rolls over on its back, hangs out its tongue, and feigns death. You can roll it over on its stomach and it will immediately roll on its back again, a dead giveaway. A test of one's nervous system is to let a spreading adder strike at his hand without moving it. This snake cannot bite seriously, having only rear-placed teeth which it uses to pierce puffed-up toads before swallowing them.

And let us not leave out the glass snake, which is really a legless lizard (*Ophisaurus ventralis*) that looks like a fat garter snake with longitudinal green and white stripes. When it is struck or grasped, it writhes frantically to escape and breaks into two or more parts. What is happening is that the tail joints are separating from the short, main body. The tail parts twist and turn, while the body part lies still. Most self-respecting predators will be attracted to the lively tail parts while the body quietly slips off into the grasses to grow another tail. Folklore opines that the body will come back, find its broken parts, and rejoin itself. The glass snake does not have to do that; it quickly grows another tail. For the snake watcher, again the eyes are the clue. Look this reptile in the eye. If it blinks, it is a lizard posing as a snake, not a real snake. The folk belief in glass snakes inspired the 1754 flag of the Albany Plan, that pictured a snake cut in several parts under the motto, "Join or Die."

Although snake meat is low on the customary folk-food chain for most Americans, fried rattlesnake is considered a delicacy by some, and canned snake meat can now be purchased in specialty food stores. The Asiatics, whose cuisine has wider variety than ours and who do not have our anti-serpent propensities, eat snake regularly, being partial to the large pythons. The Hong Kong Chinese have a fall banquet of snake meat, which is supposed to prepare them for the rigors of the coming winter. During my snaking years at Lamar, when we finished the autopsy and posting of a large rattlesnake, we cut the body into two-inch sections and took the pieces to the student center, where they were dipped in batter and fried and we ate them for supper.

The snake is reputed to have all sorts of curative powers, again based on the folk belief in its immortality and its phallic form and reproductivity. Partaking of the dried internal organs of a snake promotes virility, according to some Orientals. The Greek Pliny recommended applying snake blood to the face to eliminate zits. Most of us know that a dried snakeskin tied about the head cures a headache and is equally efficacious strapped against other parts of the ailing body. A rattle stuck in a hatband is also a headache cure. Snake oil is used to cure rheumatism and all sorts of eye, ear, and nose problems, and snake oil salesmen were common on the American frontier. I visited an apothecary shop in Juarez that had hundreds of dried rattlesnakes hung and boxed that were sold to be boiled in a soup to cure internal problems, including cancer.

Snakes can sneak up on us anywhere.

Jehovah should be satisfied with the state of snakehood at this end of the 20th century. We have about run out of snakes. They have become endangered species. I spend considerable time on the Angelina and Neches rivers and in the woods and creeks of East Texas, and I can tell you that snakes are a lot harder to come by now than they were a generation ago. During these first warm days of spring one should find water snakes draped over all the button bushes that line the river banks. He should find moccasins reclining on wet logs and rattlers sunning on flat rocks and king snakes wrapped about each other in their annual procreations. But it is not so. The snake population is dangerously low, and no one knows exactly what has caused it. Probably DDT had something to do with depopulation directly or it affected the food chain, particularly among the amphibians. I used to catch bullfrogs (*Rana catesbeiana*) regularly and easily, but I have not *even heard* a bullfrog chorus for over twenty years.

In 1962 the Texas Herpetological Society had its annual hunt on the King Ranch. We drove the roads at night and sacked dozens of snakes as they crossed or warmed themselves on the pavement. When the TFS met at Kingsville in 1990, Hazel and I drove the back roads from there to Corpus and never saw snake-one. Thirty years ago, one could not drive far without at least seeing a *dead* snake on the highway. Now, how many snakes do you see compared to the number of possums, coons, skunks, and deer that are DOR, Dead on Road. We are woefully scarce of reptiles and amphibians. The circle of life has been broken. So I ask all members to go forth, tie yourself to a large serpent, and cry, "Hebrews, spare this snake!"

A harmless chicken snake.

A beautiful Flower Mountain doe.

THE EAST TEXAS COMMUNAL HUNT

Twenty-five million years ago—or thereabouts—a marked climatic change took place in the earth's history. The great forests began to diminish in size, and broad grasslands took their place. In the shrinking forests a struggle for dominance was taking place between two groups of tree-dwelling primates, the ancestral great apes and ancestral man. The apes turned out to be the fitter of the two species in this battle, and they forced their weaker kin first to the fringes of the forests and then out on the broad savannahs. Those early men who could not adapt to the new environment perished. The smartest and the strongest survived, occupied a new biological niche, and began their evolutionary journey to what we call the modern man.

What nature selected to survive was an upright biped with high forward eyes, arms freed from the work of locomotion, an opposable thumb, and a highly developed brain. Because he did not have the speed of a deer, the armor of a turtle, the spines of a porcupine, or the fecundity of a rabbit, he could not afford to be as stupid as any of them. What he did have and that which kept him alive was a combination of qualities that put together made him a match for the other animals. He had brought from his life in the forests a sense of color and depth perception. He could run, swim, and climb as well as most animals, and he could think and throw things better than them all. And somewhere along the evolutionary way he had picked up a gene that had given him a hunter instinct that was as strong as a cat's. He was a hunter of meat, strong red meat that gave him enough nourishment at one feeding to allow him to sit around and enjoy the fruits of thought and nourish the arts of his culture.

This instinctive hunter was also a social creature, and he had sense enough to know that if he wanted a woolly mammoth for supper he had better take some tribesmen with him on the hunt.

Or maybe a signal was genetically transmitted to these very early men that caused them instinctively to mob their quarry, to hunt communally. Many animals are genetically triggered to hunt in this way. Sharks will mob a whale, crows will mob an owl, and wolves work in mobs and packs to pull down their game. Are the acts of these animals rationally planned, are they the result of social conditioning, or is mobbing an instinct that is genetically transmitted from one generation to another? Does man react to this same pack instinct when he succumbs to mob hysteria? It is my belief that he does. But whatever causes this patterned reaction, either genetics or challenge and response, the communal hunt is one of the oldest social activities in the history of man, and its customs and traditions are hallowed by antiquity.

The communal hunt, although it is not called that, is still a tradition in some of the heavily wooded areas of East Texas. The deer hunters there call it "making a drive" or "having a race." There are places in the Big Thicket and in the baygalls of Tyler and Polk counties and in the forks of the Angelina and Attoyac rivers where the brush is so thick that still-hunting or trying to walk up a deer is futile because the game is walled off by myrtle and yaupon and choked-up second growth. The only way a man can put any venison on the table is to get his friends together and shovel in a bunch of hounds in hopes that they can push a buck through a clearing where someone can get a shot. This is a communal hunt and it is practiced today in East Texas and in other parts of the South much as it was ten thousand years ago throughout the world.

There are a lot of traditions, rituals, and beliefs that go with the communal hunt. East Texans accept and practice them because this is the way the old-timers trained them to hunt, and because these customs maintain a stability and sense of order in what could be a very chaotic situation. The customs are practiced now for the same reason they were practiced in the remote past; they promote the survival of the group.

Before the Bushmen of the African Kalihari Desert make a big drive, the hunters ritually separate themselves from the rest of the tribe. Sex is considered weakening and is taboo, as is everything else not directly connected with the hunt. The hunters sing and dance their past hunts and act out their hopes for a successful drive. They prepare their hunting arms and pray over them to get them the power necessary to strike down strong, fast game.

The gathering of East Texans before a hunt is in much the same spirit. The group becomes a male club with a strong sense of community and kinship. The world of women, business, and the city is cut out of both thought and conversation. There might not be a formal blessing of arms and ammunition, but there is much cleaning and handling of guns and sharpening of knives and serious consideration of their individual attributes. A gun that has served its master faithfully over a large bundle of years has lots of soul and frequently a name, always female. "You start that old buck in my direction," a hunter will say, "and I'll have Bess invite him to dinner." A knife that has held a good edge for a generation receives the same kind of personal attention and respect. The ceremony of the pre-hunt gathering is blessed and concluded with the passing of the bottle—once around just to cut the phlegm.

A cool morning at deer camp.

The driver is the chief of the hunt in every sense. He is the acknowledged best hunter and woodsman in his group, and he knows the hunting grounds down to the last fat-pine stump. In many cases the hunting ground is land that his ancestors have hunted generations before him. The driver sets the rules for the hunt: whether or not to catch the dogs if they are running a doe, how close the hunters must stay to their stands, and what kind of deer to shoot for camp meat. No one questions his authority in the placing of standers or the location for the casting of the dogs. When all of the hunters are on their stands, he casts the dogs and makes the drive. He stays behind the dogs, and if he sees that a buck has been started, he fires a shot to let the standers know that one is moving.

The signals that the driver uses with his standers and his dogs are at least as old as the medieval ballad of the first meeting of Robin Hood and Friar Tuck. In that old song-story Friar Tuck calls his dogs with one long blast on his horn, and Robin Hood calls his men to him with three. Long, single blasts are still used to call in the hounds at the end of the race, and three short blasts mean for the standers to come in. Two short blasts mean for the stander to holler where he is. East Texas hunters use the same kind of horn that Robin Hood and his predecessors used, a cow horn with a small bell, about a foot long and scraped down to resonating thinness.

The driver is the dispenser of justice. In the thick woods during a hot race it is necessary to know exactly where everybody is. A hunter who leaves his stand could miss the deer or in his wandering about turn the deer away from another hunter or head it out of the hunting grounds. Or he might wander into an area covered by another stander and get caught in the large amount of buckshot that is slung when a buck comes flagging through these thick woods. There is also a chance that a hunter might go to sleep when the sun starts thawing him out about ten o'clock in the morning, or he might get caught looking in one direction while the deer is sneaking out in another. And hunters have been known to get buck fever and miss a real meat shot. In such cases the driver exacts the penalty for conduct unbefitting a good hunter: he cuts off the offender's shirt tail. The amount of shirt tail varies with the sin. If a man misses a fairly difficult shot, he might lose only an inch or two. If he is caught asleep on his stand after a buck has walked right through him, the driver will cut his shirt tail off right up between his shoulder blades. All of this is done in the spirit of fun, but the message is unmistakable.

There is no telling where or when shirt-tail cutting originated, but my theory is that it is either a circumcision or castration substitute, probably the latter. If it is a circumcision substitute, the ritual implies the ignorance and inexperience of the hunter by forcing him to repeat a ritual associated with the early puberty rite of passage into manhood.

More probably, shirt-tail cutting is a castration substitute that the southern American hunter derived from the Indians. Castration was a common punishment among Indians, as it was among most early societies. Aeschylus in *The Eumenides* refers to castration as a punishment among the early Greeks. During historical times the Pueblo Indians castrated certain males and made them *mujerados* to be used for ritual pederasty, and as late as the eighteenth century the Karankawas of the Texas Gulf Coast used castration as a tribal punishment.

In any hunting society the worst crime would be to foul up a hunt in such a way that game, vital to the tribe's survival, would be lost. A man who proved himself to be useless or detrimental to the hunting group might be castrated and forced to do squaw labor. Castrated males, referred to as *berdaches,* were sometimes forced to wear the dress of a squaw also. The close association of the frontier American and the Indian brought about the borrowing of many skills and customs. What probably is a shadow of this primitive form of punishment is meted out to any hunter who shows that he is not up to the group's standards.

Another function of the driver is to conduct the rite of passage when a young hunter makes his first kill. The ritual among primitives usually takes the form of applying the animal's blood between the youth's eyes for good vision, on his legs and arms for strong running and good aim, and above the breast bone for strong lungs. In East Texas the blood is applied to the initiate's face only. Behind this ritual is the belief that a boy becomes a man and qualified to take a wife when he is able to put meat on the table.

Inherent in the contagious magic of this blood rite is the belief in the power of the blood itself. To the primitive mind blood was more than a physical ingredient necessary to life; it was life itself. The Bible says in the book of Leviticus (17:11), "For the life of the flesh is in the blood." A cup of blood was a cup of life, and the blood of a strong animal was the essence of strong life. When a young hunter is daubed with the blood of the first deer he has slain, he is invested with the vitality and strength necessary to aid the survival of his hunting group.

Another office of the driver is to see to the awarding of trophies and the division of the meat. The one who kills the deer gets the head, the hide, and the feet, as did Atalanta when she slew the Calydonian boar in the Greek Golden Age. On some drives the killer and the driver get a ham apiece, and the rest is divided among the standers. Sometimes the killer, to gain status, will renounce his lot or just put in for a little stew meat. The spirit of the interdependence of the group is strong, though, and traditionally the meat is divided among the heads of the families present. Lots are drawn for the portions, and the killer and the driver draw with the other standers. The driver, in addition to his lot, receives the liver. This custom is a relic of the belief that the liver is the seat of strength and courage. It is awarded to the chief because of the group's dependence on him.

Keeping the head of a slain animal, especially a large animal that the tribe depended on, was a regular practice among primitive hunting societies. Sometimes they hung the head or the skull on the wall and laid gifts before it and made speeches to it to propitiate the soul of the dead animal. Otherwise, some feared, the spirit of the animal might return to plague its killers, or it might go out and warn others of its kind away from the hunting grounds.

The head was considered by some primitives to be the repository of the animal's spirit. The brain was the stuff of the spirit and was either offered directly to the gods or the shaman ate it for the gods. The skull, as the home of the spirit, was saved and honored because the hunter believed that the spirit went forth and animated another of its kind, if it were properly treated.

Some groups saved head trophies as a mark of their love and respect for the animal. The Indians of the Great Plains and the Ainu of Japan believed that the buffalo and the bear, respectively, were their staffs of life and that these animals loved them and offered themselves to be slain that the tribes might live. Just as it is the hunter's part to kill, it is the bear and buffalo's part in the natural scheme of things to be killed.

Coat racks made out of deer feet reflect the ancient belief that the animal's speed and endurance lay in the marrow of the leg bones, and the bones themselves were often saved and enshrined with the head.

From the first hunters to the latest the post-hunt conversations have been about the same thing: what happened on the hunt. In talk the drives are made again, and everybody gets to tell what happened during the chase in his part of the woods. Part of this talk is for the pleasure of telling. Practically, this is a study period, and the comparing of notes is a lesson on how deer move through the woods and how to hunt. This communion around a pine-knot fire or in a camp house and the talk about the race and the virtues and vices of the various dogs affords about as much pleasure as the hunt itself.

After a meatless hunt, when nobody has popped a cap or cut a hair, when the only thing that came over a stander was an old hammerhead with a faun hanging from each teat, there is usually some speculation about the forces beyond their control that hindered the hunt. There is general agreement about these forces among East Texas hunters. A wind out of the northeast will bed deer down so tight that you couldn't pry them up with a crowbar. Sometimes it causes them to ball up in a baygall like a gob of worms in a Prince Albert can. The moon can also be a disturbing force. The deer walk when the moon can be seen in the sky, so the full moon that shows only during the night when it is illegal to hunt is not the hunter's friend. An owl can be a help, because when he hoots during the daytime a buck is walking. A man might blame a missed shot on the last deer he skinned, because when he broke the tail while he was skinning it, he automatically was fated to miss his next shot. Some hunters have personal fetishes that are as potent to them as the old

Zuñi hunting charms, and if they go hunting without their good luck pieces or fail to wear a particular hat or well-blooded pair of hunting pants, they are figuratively snake bit before they ever get started.

Why does a man hunt? A large part of it is the desire to escape from the responsibilities and complexities of urban living to a fairly simple world with uncomplicated rules and values. For some, hunting is a good excuse to spend time in the woods watching birds and squirrels and armadillos, or maybe it is one of their few chances for long periods of uninterrupted thought. For most, the hunt represents the primeval challenge that is also an invitation. There lies in most men the belief that the Earth Mother will provide for her children, if the children are fit to survive. This is the basic drive for gardeners, fishermen, and hunters, for all those who are continually checking to see if they can live off the land. The meat that a hunter puts on his own table, like the vegetables he raises, is sweeter than that which he buys at the supermarket.

These are secondary reasons, however. The main reason that man hunts, and gathers naturally on a communal hunt, is that hunting is part of his genetic make-up. Man is genetically and biologically a hunter, an omnivorous predator. He is a hunter of animals, a predator after his own kind, and a prowler in search of knowledge. He is always hot on the trail of something. Doctors hunt for new cures; lawyers hunt for clients; and professors hunt new meaning to *Finnegan's Wake*. The word *hunt* is much used in man's vocabulary. His literature is filled with stories of the hunt; and readers, watchers, and listeners are in full vicarious cry with the rest of the pack as the hero harries the villain—as Orestes trees Aegisthus, and Hamlet finally bays Claudius, and Matt Dillon cuts down the unshaven bad men who trouble the ringing plains of windy Dodge. Man is always ready to gang up and make a hunt and it doesn't make much difference whether he is part of a posse or a mob. Self-consciously, though, he is equally quick to hide this hunting instinct, or at least to sublimate it, so that this drive will be acceptable in a society that has its oxen pole-axed and its chickens plucked and its hogs scalded and scraped far from its sensitive sight.

But for some there comes the time in the fall when the wild call comes, when the air is amber and rich with autumn, and great antlered bucks rattle their racks on pine saplings. Then the Earth Mother calls her children to the harvest—the fox squirrel to the mast of the white oak tree, the boar coon to the last late berries, and the buck hunter to the chase. The time of the hunt is the Earth's last soft gladness before the old cold sorrow of winter, and to him who loves her she opens her greatest treasure. "Come live awhile with me," She says, "and it will be as it used to be, when man and the land were clean and green together in their youth."

First big buck.

Bill Clark, Pat Barton, and Ab outside Pat's cabin.

RUNNING THE FOX

An East Texas fox hunt is more than a hunt. It is a convocation that binds its following together with closer than Masonic ties. The wine is drunk and the bread is broken, but no blood is spilled. The race is the thing, and it is the running of it that is the measure of its significance, not the reward in the end. And the pursued is as important as the pursuers.

Two pickups with pens in the beds pull over to the side of a two-rut, red-dirt road and cut their lights. Men get out and talk and argue for a while, then open the gates to the pens and the hounds spill out—red bones, blue ticks, black and tans, lemon spotted. They scatter in the darkness, each yelping his own personal cry. Then the men wait until pretty soon an old bitch hits a hot trail and in singles and in groups the pack hearkens to her until all are pounding through the woods, pursuing the same quarry. The men get back to their trucks and drive the country roads, stopping silently to listen every few minutes, hunting the best seat in the house to hear the music of the pack. When they find that particular hilltop, they stop, build a fire to cut the chill, and listen and speculate and talk. This continues till the fox trees or goes in the ground. By that time it is usually around sun-up, and they start rounding up the dogs, driving, stopping, and blowing long, clear blasts on their horns. They don't miss work the next day, but a hunter can usually be distinguished by his sleepy look.

There are a lot of stories about the dogs and the men and the foxes that get together on these cold East Texas nights, and there is probably an element of truth to some of them.

A bunch of high school boys from Kirbyville were running lines on an old slough off the Sabine, and they were all bedded down around about midnight. They heard a rustling noise and some light feet running, and some of them looked up just in time to see this little gray fox trotting and picking his way right through the center of the camp.

That was something to talk about, and they did while they listened to a pack of hounds sounding and heading in their direction. The yelping got closer and closer, and all the boys were standing up when the pack went right through the middle of camp, muddying up blankets, scattering the food, and knocking pots and pans all over the place.

The boys cussed, straightened up some, and crawled back between their blankets. Just as they were dozing off, the fox loped through again, this time sort of grinning and looking them over. One of the boys missed him about a yard with a stick of firewood, and they all settled down to some serious listening to the pack, which sure enough was headed their way. They were about half ready when the dogs came pouring through the camp again, baying and squawling on a hot trail. This time they flung every pine knot and mud clod they could get their hands on, and the dogs ran on through with a yelp and a holler here and there.

That was all the sleep for the night, so three of the boys went off to run the lines and the rest put on the pot and went to straightening up the camp again. An hour later, after the talk had shifted from the fox to fishing, it happened again. At the time the hounds were out of hearing and nothing seemed to be stirring outside the ring of fire. Then the little gray came through like a hummingbird, ran just outside the circle of light, and was gone before you could say, "There's that damn fox!" Then the pack topped a rise about two hills away, and you could tell by the sound that they were running the same old trail. When they hit the camp, the camp hit them—skillets, firewood, clods, everything that could be thrown or swung—and that was the end of the race for that night.

Going home the next day, the boys stopped at a snuff-and-soda-pop country store, and the first thing they were asked was had they heard the race the night before. They allowed they had and

the old man told them about Little Gray, the smartest fox in Newton County. Usually Little Gray led a long race over the ridges and
treed when he got tired of the fun. Last night, though, he must've
been in a bad mood. He took the pack through every baygall and
briar patch in the county, seesawed through half a hundred bob-
wire fences, and then must've led them over Baird's Bluff. Damn
near killed every dog in the bunch!

There's another smart fox up in Sabine County. This one's
named Rusty and he's old enough to be gray-headed. Everybody
chased Rusty and they had a lot of respect for him. They'd even set
up some ground rules for chasing him. They'd never run him more
than once a week and usually kept him for the Friday night race,
and they never ran him with more than twenty dogs in the pack.
The fox hunters broke in the young packs on Rusty because they
always knew where to cast so they could pick up a trail in a hurry.
Rusty had his stomping ground and everybody knew what it was,
and they put out dead chickens for him regularly just to keep him
happy. They loved old Rusty and looked out for him; you might
tell a Sabine County fox hunter that his favorite hound was a cold
trailer, but just don't say anything about Rusty.

Well, Old Man Jim Hughes' boys came home a few days for
their daddy's birthday a couple of springs ago, and as usual they
spent every night out on a red-dirt hill listening to a race. The last
day they were home they decided to run old Rusty, so Mr. Jim
checked around and nobody'd run him that week, so that night
they cast the dogs near Rusty's stomping ground and sat down to
wait developments. Somewhere out in the dark old Rusty unlim-
bered and started circling, running figure eight's, and just generally
cutting up. There were twenty dogs running true, not a babbler in
the bunch, and Mr. Jim and his boys sat on a ridge around a fire and
listened just like the king and his court at a concert.

There was just one outsider in this group. He was a young fellow from Beaumont who'd come up with Alec, Mr. Jim's youngest
boy. This fellow had been hearing dog talk for three days straight

and almost considered himself a fox hunter. He was dressed for what he thought a fox hunter ought to look like, and later on that night when he heard the dogs barking treed and everybody started off through the woods in that direction, he felt that now was his time to shine. He trotted off ahead of the family, who weren't running, just long striding, and chorused the dogs till pretty soon he found them, yelling and squalling and bawling and running as high up the side of an old bent magnolia as they could. And there sitting about twenty feet out on an old crotch limb was Rusty, completely unconcerned about all the noise going on below. He'd made a good race, had helped the dogs put on a good show, and was waiting for what he figured would happen next. The men would tie off the dogs, and he'd hop down and run back to his ground where he'd find a dead chicken hung up in a tree. That was the way things went.

But he or nobody else had figured on this young fellow from Beaumont, who as soon as he saw him, pulled out a .22 pistol and began firing wildly in Rusty's direction. Well, old Rusty took one surprised look and fell limp across the limb he was sitting on. The dogs hushed and stood still, some of them slinking off through the woods with their tails between their legs. And Old Man Jim Hughes, who'd just come up flanked by his boys, said, "Well I'll be damned!"

And that was about it. Luke Hughes tied the young fellow's hands with a lead rope, and Old Man Jim made a noose with another one. They'd already got the hanging rope over a limb, and I guess that would have been the end of the fellow if Rusty hadn't got to laughing so hard that he fell out of the tree.

There never were two old men who liked to fox hunt as much as Dad Wilson and Bert Tunstall from up at Woodville. They were both older than the courthouse and so deaf they couldn't hear it thunder. Every day you could find them on the square talking at the tops of their voices to each other and the other old-timers, and any time there was a big fox hunt on, Dad and Old Bert would be there talking dogs and trying to hear who was running. They judged most of the bench shows in Tyler County and kept a pretty good bunch of blue-tick hounds to run whenever they could get somebody to go along and help them around.

Dad's grandson Charlie took them out east of Hillister one cold spring night, and they cast the dogs about nine o'clock. The pack struck a trail right off, so they drove to the top of a sand hill near the railroad right-of-way and fired up some pine knots and settled down to enjoy the race. Their conversation was always sort of short during the running and generally was about which dog was leading or which one was just babbling or running the trail the wrong way. And this was a cold, still night and you could hear the pack nearly all the time, especially when they topped a hill, even though they were taking the fox away.

"There's old Jug leading the race again," said Dad.

"Too coarse-mouthed for Jug," replied Bert. "Sounds like Sadie to me."

"Sadie ain't that fast."

"Jug never led anything but his tail."

And this went on till the pack had run out of hearing, and they were getting ready to get in the pickup to find a better stand. About that time, though, the T. & N.O. freight out of Shreveport topped a rise and blew for a crossing about a mile off.

"I-God," Dad said, "don't tell me that ain't Jug."

"You better gitcha a hearing aid," Old Bert told him back.

And that T. & N.O. kept coming up one hill and going down another, blowing at ever logging road on the line.

Bert said, "Damn, they shore are coming, ain't they?"

And the old man said, "They *shore* are."

By that time the freight had hit the hilltop and was blowing the long whistle for the Hillister crossing, and the ground was trembling and the trees were shaking, and the two old men just stared into the fire. It had passed in a couple of minutes, and you could barely hear the sound of the engine as the tracks took the train through Big Turkey Creek bottom.

Old Man Tunstall shook his head and spit into the fire. "Well, sir, I don't know whether that was Jug or Sadie leading, but, by God, *that* was a race!"

And Dad said, "I-God, it *shore* was!"

The immediate sources for the above stories were David Shepherd of Port Arthur and Mrs. Ruth Garrison Scurlock and Charles Merrill of Beaumont.

The hunter.

J. Frank Dobie, TFS Secretary-Editor.

DOBIE'S ONLY CHILD: THE TFS IN 1926

[Paper presented at the Seventy-Fifth Annual Meeting of the Texas Folklore Society, San Marcos, Texas, March 30, 1991]

—◆—◆—

Calculating Calvin Coolidge was the president in 1926. Dan Moody had defeated Ma Ferguson in the Texas governor's race that year, and both candidates had taken strong steps to curb the political power of the Ku Klux Klan. Patriotism, prosperity, and prohibition were the three planks that Texas politicians stood most firmly on. And everybody felt prosperous except the farmer, who was raising more and getting less.

By 1926 the Twenties were in full roar, and the culture shock suffered by that decade's elders must have been massive. Few times standing so close together have such a sharp line of distinction as that which existed between pre- and post-WWI. The world before WWI had been Jeffersonianly rural with all the conservative moral values of that way of life. The post-war Twenties were urban and in direct reaction against all reliques of Victorian morality.

The Twenties had begun and had continued with a material prosperity such as ordinary Americans had not known before. With jobs to be had and good wages the American people were able to buy cars, radios, phonographs, and a host of labor saving electrical appliances. They paid to see professional sports. They went to college and Europe. They borrowed money and bought things on credit. They lived better than any American pre-WWI society, and they tried to be everything their parents were not.

Female style in 1926 had achieved the asexual flat look, bustless and buttless, that announced that recreation, not procreation, was the purpose of sex. Ironically, the young Flappers who had earlier divested themselves of their corsets to free their bodies for the Shimmy and the Charleston, by 1926 were wearing tube-like foundation garments to flatten out their curves. We must remember that this was the world of our now-sainted mothers and grandmothers.

While the Twenties jazzed around in its worldly ways, J. Frank Dobie was strong in his guidance of the Texas Folklore Society.

Dobie concluded a letter to Byron Shipp (April 27, 1929), the Society's Treasurer in 1929, by saying, "If I can be of any assistance at any time, night or day, call on me. The Texas Folk-Lore Society is the only child I have." It truly was Dobie's "only child," and he gave it his undivided attention in the late Twenties and early Thirties. Dobie poured every bit of energy he had into recruiting members and contributors and into collecting folklore—and into editing and publishing and distributing the Society's publications. This massive charge of vitality, like B12 shots and vitamin pills, was what it took to get the Society strong enough to take care of itself.

The Society gathered for its twelfth annual meeting at the Y.M.C.A. Auditorium at the University of Texas on Friday evening and Saturday afternoon and evening, April 23–24, 1926. The Texas State Historical Association met on Friday also and Dobie participated in both meetings. The two societies scheduled their meetings together in 1925 and 1926 so that members could attend both meetings. John Lee Brooks discussed Paul Bunyan stories, which journalists jumped on and made into hot items in subsequent newspaper stories. The meeting had some interesting papers, some of which were seminal for Dobie's later work, such as papers on lost mines and white mustangs. The members closed the meeting Saturday night with a demonstration of square dancing "to the squeaking music of country fiddlers from Bandera county," according to Marvin Hunter of *Frontier Times* (June, 1926), who was responsible for their appearance.

One significant result of that 1926 meeting was Dobie's resolution to save the longhorn. Dobie loved longhorns, both for themselves and as a symbol. The longhorn for Dobie "suited the wide, untamed land and the men that ranged it" (*Longhorns,* 42) and represented all the survival qualities that Texans and Dobie romantically believed in. Dobie had also been talking with Will C. Barnes, who was to be the one who would re-establish the breed with a herd at the Wichita Mountains Wildlife Refuge near Lawton, Oklahoma.

According to the *Dallas Journal* (April 27, 1926) Dobie might have been stirred to action also by a statewide news story about a longhorn being offered to the San Antonio zoo and being considered a rarity. The upshot of Dobie's dwelling on the literal extinction of the longhorn from the world's stage was his writing an article for *The Cattleman* in April—"The Texas Longhorn's Dying Bellow."

Dobie with longhorns in his office.

Perhaps more importantly, Dobie put through a save-the-longhorn resolution at the TFS meeting that same month to be sent to the state legislature. Fannie Ratchford, then the recording secretary but later the stern guardian of the Wrenn collection at U.T., wrote the resolution in the minutes as follows:

"The following resolution presented by J. Frank Dobie, Secretary of the Society, was adopted:

"Whereas, the old-time Texas longhorn was, with cotton, the basis of the commercial prosperity of the State;

"Whereas, in song, romance, and sentiment the old Texas longhorn is forever linked with the human and soil background of the State; and

"Whereas, the Texas longhorn is now bellowing his last bellow and is nearer extinction than the American buffalo ever was,

"Therefore, we of the Texas Folk-Lore Society recommend that the Legislature of the State of Texas appropriate sufficient funds and provide adequate means for preserving in its original purity the long-horn breed—the most history-making breed of cattle the world has ever known" (VI, 240).

I am sure that legislators read the resolution. It appeared in papers all over Texas. But it never made the congressional minutes. Nevertheless, history has generously but mistakenly given Dobie and the Society the public credit for saving the longhorns from extinction. I have even been told that even by members of the Longhorn Breeders Association, and the matter was something I always took for granted. Dobie certainly did arouse public opinion, but Will Barnes was ultimately responsible for establishing the first herd. Barnes got three thousand dollars from the federal government; he painstakingly gathered a small herd of typical longhorns; and he put them on the Wichita Reserve. Their progeny are still there. Dobie and the Texas Folklore Society did *not* go out personally and round up the herd, but they both played a large role in the salvation of the Texas longhorn, for which Texans and mankind generally should be eternally grateful.

Five years later, in 1931, Dobie and his friend Graves Peeler did establish a small longhorn herd near Mathis in the Brasada (Worcester, 80–82). Dobie's herd was moved to Fort Griffin near Albany in 1948, where it is today. Clifton Caldwell of Albany told me that the University's Bevos were taken from this herd.

Another matter of historical interest that cropped up in 1926 is perhaps the reason for Dobie's relationship with and hostility to the

American Folklore Society and its academic approach to folklore. He did not begin this way. When he took over the Society in 1922 he accepted the level of membership that included membership in the AFS and subscription to the *Journal of American Folk-Lore*. He kept this level when he reissued the pamphlet in 1924, although he did delete Leonidas Payne's 1910 statement, "The official organ of this society will be the 'Journal of American Folk-Lore.'" For Dobie the official organ of the Society would be the Publications of the Texas Folklore Society.

Early in his professional life Dobie was a member of the AFS and attended the December 28, 1922, meeting at M.I.T. in Cambridge, Massachusetts. He gave his "Weather Lore of the Texas Mexican Border" at that meeting and was elected to a three-year term as Councilor (JAF XXXVI [1923], 198). The following year, while he was at Stillwater, he attended the AFS meeting in New York, was re-elected as Councilor, and presented a paper entitled "Some Representative Legends of Texas and the Southwest Current among Anglo-Saxon Americans." One can use such an academically cumbrous title as that only within closed scholarly circles, and he was obviously playing the AFS academic game full out. During that year also he had two articles accepted for publication in the JAF, "Texas-Mexican Border Broadsides" and "La Canción del Rancho de los Olmos" (JAF XXXVI [1923], 185–195).

That same year, 1926, *The Journal of the American Folk-Lore Society* carried the review of his darlingest child and his most important work to date, *Legends of Texas*. The review was not what he would have wished. In a section of long, fulsome, signed reviews it was tossed in at the last, in a brief, unsigned review, alongside a book the AFS panned—and it was damned with exceedingly faint praise:

"Professor Dobie has compiled a large collection of tales and legends which are of unusual local interest. They include Legends of Buried Treasure and Lost Mines influenced greatly by Spanish intrusions; Legends of the Supernatural; Legend of Lovers; Legendary Origins of Texas Flowers, Names and Streams; and Miscellaneous Legends. Most of the legends show very little Indian influence but are more typical of the tales white men tell which are locally attributed to the Indian. The collection is of more interest to the local historian than to the student of folklore in general. The Editor is to be congratulated on the hearty support which the many contributors bring to the work" (JAF XXXIX [1926], 91).

I do not doubt but that the review disappointed, pained, and angered him. I know that circa 1925–1926 is the cutoff date of his association with the AFS, and the review is coincidental with that date. The Society will have no further affiliation with the AFS, and Dobie's hostility will be increasingly evident. He does not merely express his independence from this "parent" society; he is openly antagonistic in his regular attacks on the scientific method of folk-lore investigation, to Dobie a mark of the AFS. The AFS at the time was around four hundred strong, not a lot larger than the TFS, and from reading the programs, not a lot more interesting. It was, how-ever, peopled by the great names in folklore, mostly names from the eastern academic establishment, and names of people whose recognition Dobie wanted.

Another point of interest in the 1926 TFS proceedings is four articles on Negro folklore in that year's annual, PTFS V, rechristened *Rainbow in the Morning* by Wilson Hudson in the 1965 reprint. These articles are noteworthy because they illustrate four attitudes toward blacks held by Texas, Southern intellectuals of that time. And they are significant because historically—and in a way ironically—they were instrumental in preparing the way for racial desegregation.

Before we look at the four articles, let us look at the Negro in American culture in 1926.

The Twentieth Century before World War II was a time of dis-covery of black culture, of blacks themselves. Blacks, who had been slaves-chattel-aliens for many years, were just a few years beyond Emancipation, and they were now only barely beginning to take shape as a part of American culture. The study and appreciation of their folklore—their culture and traditions and beliefs, their songs and stories—were the first steps toward racial understanding and eventual integration.

On the national scene, Negro art forms were becoming accepted fare in all levels of society. Joel Chandler Harris with his

Uncle Remus tales might have done more than anyone to bring the richness of black life and culture into white consciousness. He was widely known, read, and loved throughout the United States. Roark Bradford's *Ol' Man Adam and His Chillun,* from which Martha Emmons got her "Adulteration of Old King David" and Marc Connelly got his Pulitzer Prize winning *Green Pastures,* was written in the same spirit. The Fisk Jubilee Singers were international performers of Negro spirituals and impressed people with the beauty and the seriousness and depth of feeling of a race who had long been singularly out of the framework of consideration.

In spite of modern protestations by the NAACP and some black activists, Amos and Andy, Molasses and January, Hambone, and Rochester—all of whom were much loved by white audiences— were in the vanguard of the integration movement, whether they meant to be or not. Even minstrelsy, with its stereotypes and "darky" songs, played a part in integrating black culture into the dominant white society.

The Texas Folklore Society from its beginning to World War II was involved in the exploration and discovery of black culture. Its first publication, in 1912, was Will H. Thomas's monograph, "Some Current Folk-Songs of the Negro." Dorothy Scarborough presented Negro folk music studies at meetings and published in *Coffee in the Gourd* (PFTS II, 1923) her important study of Negro blues as folk songs. This was before John Lomax began his serious work with black folk music. Spiritual singers regularly were featured performers at TFS meetings. And when Kittredge made his first visit to the TFS in 1913 Lomax took him to hear Negro preaching and singing at an Austin church. (PTFS XXXIII, 6). Among later contributors, the best known collectors and tellers of Negro tales in the Society were Martha Emmons, A. W. Eddins, and J. Mason Brewer. John Henry Faulk studied and wrote about Negro church and religious life. Hardly a meeting went by before WWII without some presentation in the field of Negro folklore, and the Society regularly carried Negro folklore in its publications. Because Negroes' position in society was in a state of flux at the time, the attitudes of the presenters were similarly various.

Dobie recognized this variety of attitudes toward blacks in his preface to *Rainbow in the Morning* and said, "The editor disclaims any responsibility for the opinions and information set forth by the varying contributors on the subject of negro folk-songs printed in this publication. If one wants to spell negro with a capital N and another with a little n, the editor has nothing to say; if one considers the negro as a shining apostle of sweetness and light, another as a gentle old darkey, and still another as 'phallic kinky,' it is none of the editor's business" (PTFS V, 4). This is the same Dobie who in the Forties in the midst of his involvement in the Raney affair, fell into disrepute among some Texans because of his liberalism, particularly because he espoused voting and education rights for Negroes.

Editorial distancing such as Dobie's, especially in an academic journal, would be unacceptable in our present ethnically enlightened times, as would most of the attitudes toward blacks found in the Society's first fifteen years of presentations. But we must not forget that we are talking about a different historical time, and social historians must never forget that they cannot judge past moralities by present-day standards. This is called generational chauvinism, the belief that only the values of one's own generation are valid. Dobie and the TFS writers were the most educated and sophisticated people of their time and culture, but they were products of their times. Scotus and Aquinas believed in a geocentric universe, Thomas Jefferson had slaves, and respectable western folk of the nineteenth century believed that society would collapse if women got the right to vote. Abraham Lincoln did not believe that Negroes should be given citizenship and denied the doctrine of social equality for blacks (Randall, 118). And many educated antebellum Southerners had no more guilty consciences about the presence of slavery than did our own parents and grandparents of the Twenties and Thirties have about the presence of Jim Crow laws. It was status quo, a fact of life.

Thus, when one reads the 1926 articles by John Strecker, Natalie Carlisle, Gates Thomas, and Richard Harrison one must remember that he walks through a world that is now three generations old.

John K. Strecker was a scientist with an interest in Negro folk beliefs. Strecker published three PTFS articles on herpetological folklore, one in 1925 and two in 1926. He was Texas' leading herpetologist at the time and was librarian and curator of the Baylor University's natural history museum, now called the Strecker Museum. Most of Strecker's folklore of reptiles and amphibians was folk beliefs that he had heard from blacks and which he wrote down in his version of a Negro dialect. John Strecker reported Negro folklore with a gentle but patronizing amusement at the beguiling simplicity and bizarre superstitions of the black folk. Strecker was interested in more than relating humorous anecdotes about Negro superstitions, however. His main interest was in their primitive state, and he refers to the best of his folkloric sources as "blackfolk, descendants of African tribesmen, untainted by alien blood" (V, 56). Strecker bemoans the fact that more folklore was not collected from antebellum blacks close to their old world (V, 71) because his main interest was in the evolution of the tale, song, or belief from its African source to its 1926 modern version. This is certainly in line with modern folkloristic pursuits.

Natalie Taylor Carlisle was a prominent Houstonian and a member of the Southern plantation aristocracy, which was a main ingredient in her depiction of black folklore. Her "Old Time Darky Plantation Melodies" from Washington County begins with a current romantic attitude toward old-time blacks that she remembered from times past: "As many Southerners have observed, the old time darky's trusting religious faith, his loyalty to his daily tasks, his love for 'old marse' and 'ole mist'ess' and his richly flavored sayings make a very attractive memory" (V, 137). Mrs. Carlisle was writing from the same framework as many movies made in the Twenties and Thirties, where happy Negroes sang as they worked in the cotton fields or gathered near the front porch at sundown and sang and danced for "old marster" and his family.

Gates Thomas, brother of Will Thomas, was a plantation-reared, English department head at Southwest Texas State College. Thomas's study, "South Texas Negro Work Songs," was of secular songs that he had collected in the Colorado River bottoms in Fayette County. His paper is fairly academic with an introductory discussion of the other literature in the field. He writes, however,

with an unromantic view and precedes his discussion with the following introduction: "The work-song I have in mind is a product
of economic and labor conditions and, so far as I can observe, is
found in its most authentic state among the 'lusty, phallic, Adamic'
Negroes of South Texas, shiftless and shifting day laborers and small
croppers who follow Lady Luck, Aphrodite, and John Barleycorn.
From just these unidealized Negroes have been gathered the work-
songs that I wish to present. . ." (V, 154).

Richard Clarence Harrison, who was TFS president in 1925–26
and was head of the English department at Texas Tech, was far
ahead of his time in the movement toward racial understanding and
equality. In his "The Negro as Interpreter of His Own Folk-Songs,"
Harrison discusses the literary and artistic progress of the Negro
that was taking place around 1926. In his introduction he recognizes his time's problems: "The greatest impediment to advance-
ment has come from the two hundred and fifty years of political
bondage that weighed upon the Negro up to the close of the Civil
War. The second greatest hindering force has been racial preju-
dice, which was intensified, if not engendered, by the conclusion
of the Civil War, and which has been directed towards the Negro
ever since. A third impediment has been the tardiness with which
the country, especially the white and black races of the South, has
responded to the need of educating the liberated Negro" (V, 144).
This was a very liberal statement for the 1920s—perhaps for the
Thirties, Forties, and Fifties too—and stands alone among decades
of articles about blacks and their folklore.

These were the liberals of their time, not our time. And liberalism is relative, with all types and degrees, then as now. TFS interest
in blacks and black culture was one force that paved the way for the
interest in the 1950s that marked the beginning of desegregation.
The stories presented blacks humorously and patronizingly, *but
sympathetically*, and in a way that was acceptable and readable by
contemporary audiences and in a way that bridged the gap between
two cultures that in 1926 were miles apart.

The year 1926 was not a climactic year for the Texas Folklore
Society. Interesting things happened that year. But then interesting

things happened every year. Every meeting time put some program arranger to the test of interest and entertainment and the problem of putting on a show that would be remembered. Every publication was preceded by editorial crises of major or minor proportions, depending on how close one was to the book. Interesting things happened every year because interesting people have always been a part of the Texas Folklore Society. The time of '26 was chosen because it was far enough away to be history but close enough to be a part of our lives in the Society.

Perhaps not as sociologically significant but equally interesting in the nation's tabloids of 1926 is the story of the adventure of Aimee Semple McPherson. Aimee is an established figure with the Society because Hermes Nye and Lu Mitchell sang her song at Society meetings so long that it became a tradition. Aimee was an evangelist of sweetness and light (as opposed to her contemporary Billy Sunday, whose evangelical ploy was to scare hell out of his audiences) whose Angelus Temple in Los Angeles was topped by a rotating, illuminated cross that could be seen for fifty miles. She packed audiences in, and she put on a show with music, lights, and drama. Then one day in May after she had gone bathing in the ocean, she disappeared. Half of southern California turned out to search for her, most thinking that she had swum out to sea and drowned. Howsoever, a month later she turned up on the Mexican border, reporting that she had been kidnapped by three men but had escaped from her captors and had walked miles and hours through the burning desert sands. Miraculously, her shoes were unscuffed and she had not broken a sweat. She was greeted in L.A. with a hallelujah chorus that began to go off key as investigators traced her adventure to a cottage by the sea and a month-long tryst with her radio director. As Lu Mitchell sings it in her version of "Aimee Semple McPherson":

> They found a bungalow with a breakfast nook,
> A folding bed with a worn-out look.
> The slats were busted and the springs were loose,
> And the dents in the mattress fitted Aimee's caboose.

The Way Things Were

An East Texas sawmill.

THE GOLDEN LOG: AN EAST TEXAS PARADISE LOST

I first heard the following East Texas story, with its Paradise Lost theme (A1331), ten years ago from a student of mine at Woodville, Texas, High School. She told it with only the scantiest of detail, and I do not remember whether she accepted it as fact or as fantasy. More recently Walter Lavine of Ruliff, Texas, told me a variant of the story; this time the setting was across the river in Louisiana. I have been passing this tale on for several years, every time I discussed the sources of *Paradise Lost*. In comparison with the first version I heard, current versions have grown; but this has been a growth in detail, not a change in essence.

> There used to be a place where the sawmill and the commissary were on one side of a big, deep creek and the settlement on the other. But the people never had any trouble getting across because there was a big golden log spanning the creek and it was easy to walk across.
>
> Since this was the only crossing for many miles either way, the mill boss and everybody really kept an eye on this golden log to keep anything from happening to it, and there was a general understanding that the log was to walk on and nothing else. But the women got to chipping off a little every once in a while and trading it in to the commissary agent for new clothes and bedspreads and things like that. Everybody in the settlement was doing real well and they didn't need the money, but that's the way they were.

93

Well, they chipped and whittled on the sly and the log got smaller and smaller, but they cut it down so slowly that nobody ever noticed it. There were a few more people than usual falling in the creek, but still nobody thought much about it—except the women, of course; they knew.

Finally one day a new bride came across, going over to get some flour and a new enamel water dipper. She got to the middle of the log, looked all around, but didn't see anybody, so she bent over and chinked herself out a piece of gold and said to herself, "I believe I'll get me a new dress to look pretty in for the dance next Saturday night." She walked a little farther and said to herself, "It won't hurt to have some new shoes to go with it"; and she looked all around and then cut another little chunk out. She got across the log, stopped, and thought, "Takes a new hat to really get started in." One more look and she stepped back to the log, leaned out a little, and sliced a long sliver right off the top.

That last sliver was all it took. The log cracked and popped real loud and sank right to the bottom of the deepest hole in the creek. The mill boss heard the noise and came running down from the office. He caught her standing there and she had to tell what she had done, so he told her and her husband to pack up and leave the settlement. He took the commissary agent to the county seat and had him thrown in jail.

After that nothing seemed to go right at the mill. Every time the creek rose nobody came to work. They tried to build a bridge but it washed out every time there was a heavy dew. Finally it got so bad that the mill had to shut down and everybody left.

Nobody can tell you where that place is now. Some say it's in the Thicket; others say it's in Louisiana. But they all agree that a man could sit in a rocking chair on his front porch and shoot a deer any afternoon and that they baited their trotlines with five-pound bass. It must have been some place!

This story is fairly typical of tales which an older generation romantically spins about the good old days when the forests were filled with game, the rivers were teeming with fish, and living was easier, happier, and less complicated. It was thus in Eden when Adam and Eve, the sun grown round that very day, had dominion over the fish and fowl and every living thing that moved upon the earth. The setting is an East Texas paradise which furnishes all things that are necessary for life; it is an idealization of a secure rural existence.

Hazel and Ab Abernethy, newlyweds.

The new bride and her husband are our Adam and Eve. This time, Adam is entirely out of the action of the story and is mentioned only as he leaves. As in the biblical tale, the woman becomes the culprit and is guilty of the crime that brings about their expulsion. Unlike the story as told in Genesis, here the man has no hand in the immediate business; but we can safely assume that he is guilty through knowledge of the deed and by association, as was Adam. Both Eve and her East Texas counterpart were unable to withstand a temptation to advance themselves. Eve succumbed to a desire for knowledge and equality with the gods, while our bride lusted after material riches and a desire to elevate herself sartorially to the level of the bosses' wives. In both cases, ambition and a thirst after worldliness lost the world for all concerned in the story. Sir James Frazer in *Folk-Lore in the Old Testament* discusses the fall of man in the various mythologies, but does not consider any, except the Hebraic, which emphasize the wickedness of the human being as we see it in Eve and the young bride.

The commissary agent plays the devil in our story. In most mythologies man loses his paradise and finds death because he is misled by a messenger from God or is duped by an evil one who has intercepted a message from God. In Genesis, Satan as the serpent leads Eve to the luxury of the tree of knowledge instead of the necessity of the tree of life; in our story the crooked commissary agent offers material luxuries instead of the simple necessities of life. The main difference between the two tempters is motivation. Biblically the tempter is personified Evil, whose motivation, very vaguely presented, seems to be a mischievous desire to cause trouble. We know even less about the commissary agent than we do about the biblical serpent. Our only conclusion is that he was ambitious for wealth. There is no evidence that he was trying to cause dissension among the mill hands or that he was antagonistic toward the mill boss, as Milton's Satan was toward God.

The mill boss can easily be equated with God. This is not difficult when one recognizes the mill boss's authority in a sawmill community. He hires and fires; pays off, gives credit, and collects; arbitrates disputes; and is the supreme power from whom all blessings flow. In this case he settles the problem with speed and decisiveness, and poetic justice is rendered to all major participants. The same swift and immediate justice is found in the biblical version: "Therefore the Lord God sent him forth from the Garden of Eden, to till the ground from whence he was taken."

The central symbol in the community is the log, considered in the telling as a part of a tree. The tree is used universally as a symbol of life and fertility, and here the log—golden, to emphasize its intrinsic value to the community, and typical in its central position of sacred trees in Germanic and Celtic folklore—insures the prosperity and the continuing livelihood of the community. Frazer, in *The Golden Bough,* points out that the tree-of-life concept is made more specific among certain primitives, the Maoris for instance, when they fabricate tales in which trees become the umbilical cords of mythical ancestors, connecting the present generation to their parent stock and to an other-worldly Paradise. The East Texas golden log is also a silver cord, an *umbilicus* which links the children of the settlement to their material sustenance, the sawmill and the commissary. When the log is finally cut in two, the people are separated from their sustenance, maternal in its way, life in paradise is lost, and they are forced to leave their idyll to make their livings elsewhere—and their sorrow is greatly multiplied. As Roark Bradford concludes his tale, "Eve and That Snake": "So de Lawd bailed ol Adam's trover and leveled on his crop and mule, and put Adam and Eve off'n de place. And de next news any yared of old Adam, he was down on de levee tryin' to git a job at six bits a day."

A Legend of the Trail.

LEGENDS OF THE TRAIL

[A legend is a traditional prose narrative that has a historical setting and real people as characters. It deals with extraordinary happenings, even supernatural events, in a realistic way. Legends are folk history which document heroic or dramatic events of a culture's life.—*Abernethy*]

The following happened in August of 1886 on the Camino Real de los Tejas, where the Trail crosses Onion Creek southwest of Austin.

1886 was the drouthiest year in over a generation, and the wells had dried up, and the black land on Tobe Pickett's farm had cracks in it wide enough to swallow a jackrabbit. María, who with her husband Pablo were Tobe's hired help, walked alongside a great wide crack on her way to cut prickly pear for the hogs. As she looked into the depths of the crack, thinking to see a trapped jackrabbit, her eyes caught the gleam of old metal. A closer look revealed a crack's-width view of a large chest with an iron chain around it.

María had found the chest of gold the Spaniards had buried on the Camino Real when they were attacked by bandits a hundred years earlier—before Spaniards became Mexicans. María marked the spot and told her husband, and they waited and planned how they would get the chest out when nobody could see them.

They waited three days for Tobe to go into Austin and give them some privacy—and the night before the day that Tobe was supposed to go to town, leaving them time and space to dig up the chest and become richer than the governor of Texas—they heard a rumble of thunder in the northwest. It began to rain. It rained for a day and a night. And the creeks flooded and the wells filled and the black land became a gumbo that could bog a burro. And everybody rejoiced. Everybody, that is, except Pablo and María, who searched for days for evidence of their crack and the hidden treasure the Spaniards had buried along the Camino Real de los Tejas. But the land had swelled with the moisture and the crack had closed.

Finally they searched no more. "Sea por Dios," said Pablo, in resignation. "The gold is not meant for us."

"You are right," said María. "We will live the lives we have."

And that great chest of gold with a chain wrapped around it is still buried alongside the Camino Real de los Tejas. We have had a drouth this year; perhaps the earth is cracked once more down to the old Spanish treasure chest. Es la voluntad de Dios that some traveler—some day—on the King's Highway will find it. Let it be one of us.[1]

Now, I do not absolutely vouch for the veracity of that tale. I tell it as it was told to me. I can also tell you about several pack loads of Spanish church crosses and chalices and plates of gold and silver that to prevent their theft were dumped into the Attoyac River at the Camino Real crossing in San Augustine County.[2] And there are six jack loads of unimaginable wealth secreted at the bottom of a pond that lies close by the Camino el Caballo, the Smuggler's Road that left the Camino Real and looped around Spanish customs in Nacogdoches.[3]

The Camino Real is a corridor of myths and legends as ancient as the tracks of the first people that walked it. The Caddo Indians, who traveled the Trail and lived alongside it over a thousand years ago, have a tale which says that they came to East Texas out of a land of darkness. They brought corn with them and seeds for squash and pumpkins, and they journeyed from their dark, unknown past in the east to a new world of light on the Angelina and the Neches where the Trail crosses those rivers. And they met travelers with their greeting of "*Tejas*"—meaning "friend"—and gave Texas its name.[4]

The first Europeans to travel the Camino Real came as the result of the tales of great wealth hoarded among the Indians of the Southeast. Hernando de Soto and seven hundred men set out from St. Petersburg, Florida, in 1539 to find this wealth. Three years later the De Soto remnants were down to three hundred men and *up* to seven hundred hogs, but no treasure. Now under the command of Luis de Moscoso, they reached East Texas, tattered and torn and much poorer than the Caddo Indians they found at Guasco. These Caddos lived near the Old Spanish Trail where it crosses the Neches

River in Cherokee County. Desperately searching for a route back to Mexico, Moscoso sent ten mounted scouts down an Indian trail that would become El Camino Real. They reached the Guadalupe River near present-day New Braunfels, but finding the natives to be as destitute as they were, they turned back up the Trail to Guasco. Moscoso and his men did get back to Mexico, but by boat, unfortunately not by the Camino Real.[5]

In 1690, 150 years later, when the Spanish came again to the Camino Real—this time to the land of the Hasinai Caddo, whom they called the Tejas—they followed the legend of The Lady in Blue. The Spanish began, however, in 1685 following *not* the legend but the reports of the landing of the Frenchman LaSalle on Spanish soil near Matagorda Bay. The Spanish were on him like a hound on a rabbit the moment he landed, and in 1689 Alonso de Leon found his pitiful French remnants at Fort St. Louis.

Franciscan Father Damian Massanet accompanied Alonso de Leon on the 1689 search for LaSalle. Father Damian came to New Spain following the legends of the miracles of Mother María de Jesus of Agreda, Spain. She was The Lady in Blue, who—according to stories she had told sixty years earlier in 1631—had by the miracle of bilocation (an enviable miracle of being in two places at one time) visited the land of the Tejas without leaving her convent in Spain. She said that while she was in the New World she had instructed the Tejas in the mysteries of Catholicism and had saved many souls for Christ. Father Damian encountered a group of these Tejas Indians in the vicinity of La Salle's Fort St. Louis.

The wily Tejas, as eager after gifts as my six-year-old grandson, with utmost sincerity told Father Massanet that they were familiar with the stories of God, his Son, and the Holy Mother—and of course, The Lady in Blue. They begged that Father Damian send missionaries among them to teach them Christianity—and don't forget the presents!—even as a Lady in Blue had taught them years before when she had come down from the East Texas hills to their villages. Father Damian, ecstatic and convinced that this was the miracle of the Mother María, promised that he would return with Catholicism—and gifts—the following year when the corn was ripe.

In the spring of 1690, an entrada under Alonso de Leon and Father Damian Massanet came to "Cenis," a large Hasinai Caddo settlement near the Neches River (in the same general area as the village of Guasco that Moscoso had visited), and established a Franciscan mission. The Spanish dedicated Mission San Francisco de los Tejas on June 1, 1690. This tribute to The Lady was the first permanent European establishment in Texas on the Camino Real.[6]

Now that the Spanish had this Imaginary Kingdom at the far end of what was to be the Camino Real they decided to equip it with a governor. Consequently, in 1691 the viceroy appointed Don Domingo Terán de los Rios as the first governor of this newly created province among the Tejas. Terán planted the royal standard at every campsite on his gubernatorial entrada, claiming the land for Spain. His standard was *not* the flag of Spain, however, but was a banner that had the Crucified Christ on one side and the Virgin of Guadalupe on the other. Then he gave the land of the Tejas the unhappy title, "Nueva Reyna de Montaña de Santander y Santillana." Imagine, if you will, singing "The Eyes of Nueva Reyna de Montaña de Santander y Santillana are upon you"!

Governor Terán's bitterly cold tenure in Texas was not a happy one. His explorations in the winter of 1691 were expeditions out of hell, if there is an icy hell, and he reported to the viceroy that "the difficulty was so great that I [can] not find words to describe it." Our first Governor of Texas concluded his report with words to the effect that if he owned hell and Texas, he'd rent out Texas and live in hell. This catchy insult was later copied by other intruders into the Lone Star State.[7]

According to popular legend, Louis Juchereau de St. Denis is the trailblazer of the Camino Real. He was not, of course. The many trails from East Texas to the southwest had been traveled for centuries, but St. Denis, with his Frenchman's élan and panache, became the most famous. In 1714, St. Denis and a small band of Frenchmen and Caddo Indians rode the Camino Real corridors from Natchitoches through the camps of the Nacogdoches, then through the southern route to Paso de Francia and Mission San Juan Bautista on the Rio Grande.

Louis de St. Denis.

The St. Denis story is hard to believe, even now. Can you imagine Diego Ramon's surprise when this *Frenchman* showed up on his doorstep at San Juan Bautista? Now look who's coming to dinner! And then St. Denis spent two years successfully playing bureaucratic politics with the Spanish, marrying Diego Ramon's granddaughter, and finally being hired (Can you believe it?) in 1716 to guide the Domingo Ramon expedition up the Camino Real, this time all the way to the founding of six missions and a frontier outpost at Los Adaes, the end of the Trail for the Spanish. I think St. Denis fully qualifies as a semi-legendary figure on the Camino Real.[8]

I would like to cite the St. Denis-Domingo Ramon entrada of 1716, as the coolest, most casual and laid-back expedition that ever went up the Camino Real. It has to be legendary in some sense. The troops were supposed to march twelve to fifteen miles per day, but they were continually stopping to chase deserters or find lost horses, or children. They spent all day March 17 fishing, and the churchmen claim that they caught 300 fish. Several other days were spent hunting and fishing—or when somebody got sick. March 26–29: "These four days," Ramon says, "I remained in this place because a soldier's wife gave birth to a child." Ramon camped on the Conchas River five days "so that all of the people would have plenty of time to confess their sins and pass Holy Week." They also went wild horse hunting on this stop. May 5 was a wedding day: "a soldier was to be married to Anna Guerra, an occasion that was celebrated with a feast prepared by his companions." June 2: "This day I remained here, because it was such a fine day." Eight days later: "This day I remained here, because it was a good camping place and because we wished to celebrate the Feast of Corpus Christi." Captain Ramon almost did not finish his diary because on the fourth of May he ran a horse race with a Frenchman that included snatching his hat from the ground while riding at full speed, and Ramon fell off his mount.[9]

The Domingo Ramon travelers were welcomed to East Texas—when they finally got there—by an Indian woman speaking Spanish. This was Angelina, an enduring legend of the Camino Real. Friar Isidro Espinosa tells in his trip's diary about "a learned Indian woman of this tribe (Hainai Caddo), reared in Coahuila," who met the Domingo Ramon entrada and thereafter acted as an aide and interpreter between the Spanish and the Indians.[10]

Angelina assisted the Spanish and the French during the period of exploration and settlement between 1712 and 1721 and was described by contemporaries as being "learned," "sagacious," and "famous." She was obviously greatly valued by the Spanish who named the Angelina River after her, and she would have shaken her head in wonderment had she known that she achieved such legendary stature that a county, a college, a river, and whole page in a Lufkin telephone book would carry her name—and that nationally famous artist Ancel Nunn would draw a picture of her that made her look like a movie star. I think I see Linda Darnell in that role.[11]

If the Camino Real ever decides it needs its own saint or the blessing of one who definitely has the ear of God, it should appoint Father Antonio Margil de Jesus as its guardian angel. Father Margil walked the length of the Texas Trail twice—barefooted! sixty years old! and with a double hernia!—and this was after he had walked all the way from Costa Rica, with side trips through the Yucatan. Father Margil carried no food, only a staff, a cross, and a breviary. He ate one meal a day consisting of a broth of herbs and greens.

He slept only three hours a night, the remaining time being spent on his knees in prayer with arms outstretched in remembrance of Christ's suffering on the Cross. Father Margil's religious zeal was already legendary before he traveled the Camino Real to East Texas, and stories about his walking on water and turning water to wine had sprung up wherever he had preached.

Margil's Nacogdoches legend grew out of the terrible drouth of 1717–18, when the Indians' crops failed and La Nana and Banita creeks dried up and the Spanish were surviving on crow meat. According to legend, Father Margil spent a night in prayerful supplication and received a vision. On the next morning he proceeded to a high bank of La Nana Creek, about a hundred yards upstream from the Camino Real crossing. Here he struck his staff against the rock bank and two springs began to flow. The people were saved, and the springs were known thereafter as Los Ojos de Padre Margil, the Springs (or Eyes) of Father Margil. The City of Nacogdoches has purchased the traditional site of the Holy Springs, and it has now been cleaned and protected. The holy waters still flow (or trickle or seep), and I regularly bottle some for my friends who need its curative and procreational powers.

Pointing out the seeping spring, The Eyes of Father Margil, on the Lanana Creek Trail in Nacogdoches.

Another legend of Father Margil of the Camino Real was the tale of his encounter with the panther. The padre was traveling the Trail from Nacogdoches to Bexar when during the night a panther (*sic* "tiger") killed his baggage mule. When Father Margil awoke to the deed the next morning, he indignantly summoned the panther in from the woods, ordered him to kneel, and then loaded him with the dead mule's baggage. That panther had to carry the gear all the way to San Antone, where he was finally unloaded, pardoned, and allowed to return to his hunting ground. He was also sternly lectured about molesting mules that belonged to Roman Catholics.[12]

Legends on the Camino Real stuck to Father Margil like ticks on a bird dog. He is credited with starting the flow of the San Antonio River[13] and with conferring the name on the Brazos River.[14] I would strongly recommend that the name of Father Antonio Margil de Jesus be invoked at all deliberations involving El Camino Real.

Margil Park, in Nacogdoches, Texas.

And in the dramatic history of the Old Spanish Trail, who can forget that bloody conflict, The Chicken War. Two mighty nations,

Spain and France, faced each other in an uneasy truce across a gulley called the Arroyo Hondo, the eastern boundary of the Province of Texas. In Europe, this fragile truce broke into warfare, and the French in Natchitoches happily heard about it before the Spanish got their news. Thus, on the morning of June 19, 1719, French Lieutenant Philippe Blondel mounted a sneak attack on the mission at Los Adaes on the Spanish frontier. His army of seven soldiers surrounded the mission and captured all the occupants, which consisted of a lay brother and a soldier. The battle fought and won, the dastardly Frenchmen raided the mission's henhouse and captured all of the chickens. Unfortunately, when the lieutenant tied his squawking brace of hens across his saddle, they made such a racket that it spooked his horse, which plunged bucking through the pines and dashed the Frenchman to the ground. In the confusion that followed, the lay brother escaped and spread the word through San Augustine, Nacogdoches, and finally to Domingo Ramon's fort on the Angelina. Panic ensued and the Spanish fled down the Camino Real to Bexar. East Texas was once more devoid of Spaniards, which vacuum gave the bellicose French second thoughts: they had *won* the war but they had *lost* their best and only market.[15]

Antonio Gil Y'Barbo was the founder of Nacogdoches, a mercantile village begun in 1779 at the crossroads of the Camino Real and Trammel's Trace. The enduring and much circulating legend of the Y'Barbos—and all of the old Spanish families of East Texas—was that they were pure Andalusian Spanish, who had come straight to East Texas from Seville, through French New Orleans, if you can imagine! This put them a cut above the more recent Mexican imports.

As it turned out, the Aguayo entrada of 1721, which was the time of the arrival of the First Families, brought a very mixed package of beggars, debtors, and jailbirds—much like colonials elsewhere. Of the 110 men recruited, 107 were taken from the jail at Celaya and one was sent by his father. As to the legend of ethnic purity: forty-four of the settlers were indeed classified as Spanish. The rest were classified as such ethnic mixtures as *mestizos, coyotes, mulattoes, lobos,* one free Negro, and one Indian from Sapotlan. These settlers reproduced and married among the French in Natchitoches and the Indians all around them. They soon created a Spanish-Creole colonial culture that grew along the Camino Real from Los Adaes back toward the missions around Nacogdoches.[16]

In East Texas, "A True-Born Spaniard is a Contradiction."

These "Spanish" settlers were brought up the Camino Real by the legendary Marques de San Miguel de Aguayo, who (as one story goes) excused himself from a card game in Mazapil, rode fifty miles back to his hacienda near Saltillo on the Camino Real, slew his wife and her lover, rode back to Mazapil and finished the card game. He rode ten horses to death and silenced five mozos in the process, and his card playing friends never knew he had left the building.[17]

All the tales of the Camino Real have not been told. Spanish treasures still lie hidden along the Trail—and The Lady still walks. The Lady in Blue appeared at Sabine Town, at the Camino Real crossing of the Sabine River, two hundred years after she had first appeared to the Caddos of East Texas. She came this time in 1844 to nurse and care for the victims of the black-tongue plague. And when the sickness was over, she disappeared again.[18]

Seventy years later, in 1916, Uncle Matt Pantalion of Nacogdoches saw The Lady on the Camino del Caballo on the dusk of Christmas day. She was dressed in a flowing white and blue robe, and she was standing by a large white-oak tree on the side of the road. She looked at young Matt, sighed sad and lonely, and then ghostily faded away into the darkness of the forest background. You very well might question some of the tales I have told, but I *know* that this legend of the Camino Real is true because I took a picture of Uncle Matt standing by that very white-oak tree.

ENDNOTES

1. J. Frank Dobie. "In a Drouth Crack." *I'll Tell You a Tale.* Boston: Little, Brown and Company, 1931. 282–290.
2. J. E. Mayfield in Blake Papers, Vol. 45, p. 287, Special Collections, Steen Library, SFASU.
3. Uncle Matt Pantalion. Letter to author, in March 1972.

4. F. Todd Smith. *The Caddo Indians: Tribes at the Convergence of Empires, 1542–1854.* College Station: Texas A&M Press, 1995.
5. James E. Bruseth and Nancy A. Kenmotsu. "Soldiers of Misfortune: The de Soto Expedition Through Texas." *Heritage* (Vol. 9, No.4, Fall 1991): 12–17.
6. William C. Foster. *Spanish Expeditions into Texas, 1689–1768.* Austin: University of Texas Press, 1995. Chapters II & III.
7. Ibid. Chapter IV.
8. Donald E. Chipman and Harriet Denise Joseph. "Louis Juchereau de St. Denis: Canadian Cavalier." *Notable Men and Women of Spanish Texas.* Austin: University of Texas Press, 1999.
9. Domingo Ramon. "Diary of his Expedition into Texas in 1716." *Preliminary Studies of the Texas Catholic Historical Society* (Vol. II, No.5, April 1933).
10. Espinosa. "Diary." 16.
11. Diane H. Corbin. "Angelina." *Legendary Ladies of Texas.* 15–19.
12. Stephen F. Austin. "The Prison Journal of S. F. Austin." *The Quarterly of the Texas State Historical Association* (Vol. II, No.3, Jan. 1899): 185.
13. J. Frank Dobie. "Stories in Texas Place Names," *Straight Texas* (PTFS 13, 1937). Hatboro, PA: Folklore Associates, Inc., 1937. 69–70.
14. J. Frank Dobie. "How the Brazos River Got Its Name," *Legends of Texas* (PTFS 3, 1924). Hatboro, PA: Folklore Associates, Inc., 1964. 211.
15. "Chicken War." *Handbook of Texas.*
16. Eleanor Claire Buckley. "The Aguayo Expedition into Texas and Louisiana, 1719–1722." *The Quarterly of the Texas State Historical Association* ([Vol. 15, No.1, July 1911): 25–28.
17. J. Frank Dobie. "The Marques de Aguayo's Vengeance." *I'll Tell You a Tale.* 117–123.
18. Joseph F. Combs. "The Legend of the Lady in Blue." *Legends of the Pineys.* San Antonio: The Naylor Company, 1965.

The Lady in Blue.

MARÍA DE AGREDA: THE LADY IN BLUE

There were women of legend in the Americas long before the Europeans arrived, even though we don't know who they were. But we do know that all cultures, the American Indian included, recognized the great ones among themselves by elevating their status into the realm of legend or myth. The legendary ones always have some touch with reality and real time and space and history. The creatures of myth are from the early dawn of time or from other worlds.

The first woman of Texas legend after the coming of Church and chains and armored horse and rider was a fair and loving figure somewhere between the world of legend and myth. She was The Lady in Blue and her story in the earliest history of Texas is as that of the bringer of a soft and generous Christianity to the tribes of the Southwest and East Texas.

The story of The Lady in Blue probably started with the Franciscan Friar Juan de Salas who ministered to the Indians of south and west Texas in the 1620s. Father de Salas was a strong and loving man who had traveled widely and earned the affection of those Indians among whom he moved. Particularly did the Jumanos admire him, and they begged that he come to visit them on their ground on the Río Concho, near present-day San Angelo. In 1629 Father de Salas was able to go.

In 1629 the Custodian of the New Mexican area, Father Alonzo de Benavides, received from Spain thirty Franciscan friars to send out from San Antonio de Ysleta (near El Paso) to minister to the Indians. He sent Father Juan de Salas and Father Diego López to the Jumanos of the Río Concho, who had long been requesting missionaries. Father Benavides questioned the Indians who came to guide the padres. This is his account in his *Memorials* published in 1630: "Before they went, we asked the Indians to tell us the reasons why they were with so much concern petitioning us for baptism, and for Religious to go to indoctrinate them. They replied that a woman like that one whom we had there painted—which was a picture of the Mother Luisa de Carrion—used to preach to each one of them in their own tongue, telling them that they should come to summon the Fathers to instruct and baptize them, and that they should not be slothful about it. And that the woman who preached to them was dressed precisely like her who was painted there; but that the face was not like that one, but that she, their visitant, was young and beautiful. And always whenever Indians came newly from those nations, looking upon the picture and comparing it among themselves, they said that the clothing was the same but the face was not, because the face of the woman who preached to them was that of a young and beautiful girl." In describing the clothing the Indians pointed out the regular nun's habit but emphasized the cloak of blue which the saintly visitant wore. She came to be referred to by the fathers and the Indians as The Lady in Blue.

The friars de Salas and López who went to the Jumanos found much to their surprise that the Indians were already well instructed in the doctrines of the Church. They attributed this to the visitations of The Lady in Blue, so without further teaching they baptized the chief and the entire tribe of ten thousand people. Before they left the encampment, according to Benavides' later report, the sick came by to be healed by the power of their new religion. The healing lasted from three o'clock one afternoon until ten o'clock the next morning: and "instantly they rose up well of all their infirmities, the blind, lame, dropsied, and of all their pains."[1]

Father Benavides soon returned to Mexico City, where he received orders to return to Spain and report the progress of the Church in the New World to his superiors. His *Memorials* of 1630 is the result and the report of his work, and it was received with high favor among his superiors. Of course, the report of the miraculous conversion of the Jumanos was a part of this report and was the occasion of much comment. The result was that he was sent on April 29, 1631, to the town of Agreda, on the border of Aragon and Castille, where Mother María de Jesús had earlier declared that by the miracle of bilocation, being in two places at one time, she had been visiting the Indians of the New World over the past ten years.

Father Benavides arrived in Agreda on the last day of April in 1631 and said in a report, "Mother María de Jesús, Abbess now of the Convent of the Immaculate Conception, is about twenty-nine years of age, not quite that, handsome of face, very fair in color, with a rosy tinge and large black eyes. The style of her habit, as well as that of all the nuns of that convent, who are twenty-nine in all, is the same as ours; that is, it is of brown (pardo) sackcloth, very coarse, worn next to the body without a tunic, undershirt, or skirt. Over this brown habit is worn a white one of coarse sackcloth with a scapulary of the same material and the cord of our Father Saint Francis. Over the scapulary they carry the rosary. They wear no shoes or sandals other than boards tied to the feet. The cloak is of blue cloth, coarse, with a black veil."[2]

María Fernández Coronel, or Mother María de Jesús de Agreda, was born into a very devout Catholic family in Agreda in Castille in 1602. She took the vow of chastity when she was eight, and when she was sixteen she persuaded her parents to convert their house into a convent and take the vows themselves. As a nun in this convent María wore no shoes but sandals made of wood or straw. She wore a cassock of coarse brown sackcloth next to the skin, covered by a white habit tied by the knotted cord of St. Francis, and over all this she wore a mantle of blue for the Virgin Mary.

María was deeply and mystically contemplative from her youth, and in 1621 when she was eighteen her contemplations became miracles. She began going into trances, and in this state she was transported to the New World in a wild and primitive country and moved among savages, who, when she spoke, understood her even though she spoke in Spanish. And when they spoke she understood them even though they spoke in their own language. She visited different tribes during the period between 1620 and 1631, making around five hundred trips, sometimes completing as many as four visitations a day, and she told them about Christ and the Mother and God's wounds and Mary's tears for the suffering of mankind. She was martyred on one visit, receiving many wounds and a crown from God for her suffering. This visitation occurred, she said, in the Indian kingdom of the Ticlas, or Theas, or Techas (manuscript spelling was confused), in the northeastern part of New Spain, in the part of the New World that they would call Tejas.[3]

Benavides had written the report of his visit to the Jumanos in 1630. Although Mother María did not have any more trances in which she was transported to the New World after 1631 and we have no reports of a Lady in Blue appearing among the Indians, the story continued in its circulation both in the Old and New Worlds.

In Spain the story was familiar to Father Damien Massanet, one of Mother María's adherents who went to the New World to pursue this inspiration along with his professional pursuit of souls for the Mother Church. Father Damien in his studies of the legend concluded that the Theas, Ticlas, or Techas Indians of which Maria spoke were the Tejas Indians, the name then popularly attributed to the Hasinai Caddoes of East Texas. In order to continue this line of investigation he obtained a station at Mission Caldera in Coahuila. His chance to meet the Tejas came in 1689, when he accompanied Alonzo de Leon on an expedition to search out and destroy all Frenchmen in New Spain. They found the burnt remains of La Salle's fort, and they made their first contact with the Tejas. De Leon wrote the following account of the latter episode in a letter of May, 1689: "They [the Tejas] are very familiar with the fact that there is only one true God, that he is in Heaven, and that he was born of the Holy Virgin. They perform many Christian rites, and the Indian Governor asked me for missionaries to instruct them, saying that many years ago a woman went inland to instruct them, but that she has not been there for a long time; and certainly it is a pity that people so rational, who plant crops and know there is a God, should have no one to teach them the Gospel, especially when the province of Texas is so large and so fertile and has so fine a climate."[4]

In another note de Leon says of these Indians, referring to María: "They are very fond of blue because of the mantle of the venerable mother."[5]

The woman who came to the Tejas was certainly no one sent by the Church, so this was accepted as further indication of María's supernatural presence. The result of Damien Massanet's meeting with the Tejas in 1689 was that he promised them that he would come to them in the following year "when the corn was ripe." He went to East Texas in 1690, founding the missions San Francisco de los Tejas and Santísimo Nombre de María before returning to New Spain (probably either Monclova or his College at Querétero) and writing an account of his journey. He concludes this account with what he calls "the most noteworthy thing of all, namely this: While we were at the Tejas Hasinai village, after we had distributed clothing to the Indians and to the governor of the Tejas, that governor asked me for a piece of blue baize in which to bury his mother when she died; I told him that cloth would be more suitable, and he answered that he did not want any other color than blue. I then asked him what mysterious reason he had for preferring the blue color, and in reply he said they were very fond of that color, particularly for burial clothes, because in times past they had been visited frequently by a beautiful woman, who used to come down from the hills, dressed in blue garments, and that they wished to do as that woman had done. On my asking whether that had been long since, the governor said that it had been before his time, but his mother, who was aged, had seen that woman, as had also other old people. From this it is easily to be seen that they referred to the Madre María de Jesús de Agreda, who was frequently in those regions, as she herself acknowledged to the Father Custodian of New Mexico, her last visit being in 1631, the last fact being evident from her own statement, made to the Father Custodian of New Mexico."[6]

Legendary Ladies of Texas, the 1981 publication.

The end of this part of the legend occurred with the abandonment of the East Texas missions in 1693. Father Damien, on his return to East Texas in 1691, found that although the memory of The Lady in Blue remained in Indian stories, her precepts were poorly attended. The Indians became openly hostile toward the Spanish and indifferent to Catholic teaching. Completely disillusioned, Father Damien and the friars left the Tejas in 1693, and San Francisco moldered back into the red dirt on which it was built.

The Lady in Blue legend continued to circulate among the Indians and Spanish of East Texas, and in later years, according to later stories, she returned to bring comfort to other East Texas settlers. In the early 1840s, during the late winter and early spring, the Sabine overflowed and isolated many of the river-bottom settlers. The black-tongue plague, or malaria, struck, and whole families sickened and many died. In the midst of the plague a mysterious lady in blue appeared to look after the sick. She stayed and cheered and healed the sick until the plague abated; then she disappeared as mysteriously as she came.[7]

According to other stories the ghost nun still wanders the Camino del Caballo, the old Smugglers Road that skirted the customs and outposts at Nacogdoches. She cries sadly from time to time, perhaps in mourning for the vanished Tejas whom she came to save.[8]

So what happened? Were The Lady in Blue's appearances examples of mass hysteria among Indians, psycho-phenomena similar to our flying-saucer sightings? Or was it the ultimate con game played by the Indians on the Spanish in order to get the gifts the priests handed out along with their more abstract blessings? *Or,* are there stranger things in heaven and earth than we and Horatio ever dreamed of in our philosophies—and is this a prime example of the miracle of bilocation? If it is a miracle, as her adherents believed, was she transported in body or in spirit, a point of contention among Agredistas of that time? She said that in some of her transportations she took crosses with her which she evidently left with Indians, because she could never find them thereafter, which would seem to indicate corporeal bilocation. Those who faltered on the threshold of belief in corporeal bilocation were reminded of the power of God in the manipulation of miracles and told of the numberless angels who could dance on the head of a pin.

Interestingly, in *The Catholic Encyclopedia* and in *The New Catholic Encyclopedia,* to mention only two standard reference works on Catholic faith and practices, nothing is said about María's miraculous trips to the New World. She is discussed as the friend and advisor of Philip IV, and she is much discussed as the author of the very controversial *The Mystical City of God and the Divine History of the Virgin Mother of God* (3 vols. Madrid 1670), which was periodically on and off the Inquisitional Index. María claimed that she was transported in 1627, this time to the Celestial City, where God commanded her to write the definitive biography of the Virgin. Not to be unreasonable, he gave her eight angels as assistants and then showed her all the stages of the Virgin's life. Very disturbing to some of her readers—especially French readers who, her supporters said, read Spanish poorly—was the description of the Virgin's nine months in her mother's womb. More interesting but equally disturbing was the chapter on the Immaculate Conception, which *The New Catholic Encyclopedia* evaluates as "though perhaps crude, was not, as was alleged, immoral."

Mother María and Father Margil and the marvelous Texas legends that went with them were the last flickerings of the Medieval Age of Faith and were, in a sense, anachronisms. Erasmus from his lofty Renaissance perch had already surveyed the superstitions of the Church and the folly of its people and its pieties—and he had laughed to scorn that part of the institution that proliferated Franciscan anti-intellectualism and he had stood agape at the outrageously miraculous saints legends. Erasmus spoke for most men of enlightment of the Renaissance.

But who can tell what dreams there are that men must have, what miracles and madnesses, what inspirations and insanities that they *must* have to guide their ways into strange new worlds. The Lord provided the Jews a pillar of cloud by day and a pillar of fire by night. He just might have given the Spanish The Lady in Blue.

NOTES

1. The episode with the Jumanos is a paraphrase of *The Memorial of Fray Alonso de Benavides,* 1630, Mrs. Edward E. Ayer, trans. (Albuquerque: Horn and Wallace, Publ., 1965), pp. 57–63.
2. Carlos Castañeda, "The Mission Era: The Finding of Texas, 1519–1693," *Our Catholic Heritage in Texas, 1519–1936* (Austin: Von Boeckmann-Jones, 1936), I, 197.
3. José Antonio Pichardo, *Limits of Louisiana and Texas* (c. 1810), Charles Hackett, trans. (Austin: University of Texas Press, 1934), II, 480 ff.
4. Charles Heimsath, "The Mysterious Woman in Blue," *Legends of Texas,* PTFS III, J. Frank Dobie, ed. (Hatboro, Pa.: Folklore Associates, Inc., 1964/1924 c.), 134.
5. Pichardo, II, 144.

6. "Letter of Fray Damien Massanet to Don Carlos de Siguenza, 1690," in *Spanish Exploration in the Southwest, 1542–1706,* Herbert E. Bolton, ed. (New York: Barnes and Noble, Inc., 1967/1908 c.), p. 387.

7. Joe F. Combs, *Legends of the Pineys* (San Antonio: The Naylor Co., 1965), pp. 76–89.

8. Harry G. Pettey, "Names and Creeks Along Historic Road Are Stories in Themselves," *The Daily Sentinel,* Nacogdoches, Texas, July 9, 1963, II, 1.

Charreada: Mexican Rodeo in Texas, the 2002 publication.

CHARRERÍA: FROM SPAIN TO TEXAS

The self sufficient Spanish conquistador-rancher-hacendado who brought the wild new land of America under his control, who branded the cattle and horses and made them his, who (far separated from Madrid and Ciudad Mexico) made his own laws and enforced them—this man became the Mexican who loved the land and its soil and he loved the spirit that he had made. This close Mexican identity with the land and love of the land was the spirit that made *charrería* and its celebration in the *charreada*.

Charrería is the traditions and the skills of the *charro*, the ideal Mexican on horseback and his spectacular use of the lariat in roping and handling stock. The *charreada* is the gathering of teams of charros and charras to perform a series of formalized exhibitions of roping and riding.

The charro, who is the center of charrería tradition, goes back in history to Spain, where the term at first had a negative connotation and implied rusticity and crudeness. But language grows, and the term *charro* soon became respectfully applied to skilled horsemen, in the same way as did *caballero*. A recognized pride and machismo was part of being a charro, and his pride in himself was announced by his beautiful charro regalia and the splendid trappings for his horse.

The story of the charro is woven into the history of Mexico.

The Spanish began bringing horses and cattle into the New World in 1519. By 1537—less than twenty years later!—there were so many cattle and horses in Mexico that ranchers were required by the Spanish authorities to have an annual roundup to brand and castrate stock and to see that all the stock was with its rightful owners. This New Spain became a land of ranches and the land of the daring and skillful men on horseback who managed them.

This annual roundup of range cattle, or *rodeo del ganado*, is the sixteenth century beginning of the charreada, the Mexican rodeo and the ancestor of Texas rodeos.

Ranch headquarters were far apart in colonial New Spain and after 1821, in the Mexican Republic. The ranchers and their vaqueros had little time or opportunity to meet and socialize. The annual rodeo became that time. Families of the ranchers involved in the roundup gathered at the roundup grounds, near one central hacienda. Then after the work of the roundup was finished, the hacienda that sponsored the roundup gave a celebration for the hacendados and vaqueros of all the ranches that had participated in the roundup. They had a barbecue and bands played and people danced, and this celebration became meeting and mating time for the rancher-frontiersmen of Spanish Colonial and Mexican times.

Natural exhibitionists as all males are, the vaqueros and the young sons of the hacienda showed off their skills and their bravery to win the hearts of the women present and to arouse the envy of their peers. The man-on-a-horse became the unit that was the center of the whole stock raising world of Spanish and Mexican ranching, and the purpose of the exhibition was to demonstrate the expertise of the man on horseback who was responsible for the success of that ranching world.

By the twentieth century the charro, the man of horseback, became the symbol and the representative of the spirit and the pride of heritage of the Mexican people. He became to Mexicans what the cowboy is to Texans, only more so. The charro was not simply a vaquero, a working cowhand. He was more likely to be the landed gentry, or the son and heir of a hacienda. Nowadays, he is usually a city dweller. The charro was the best of men on horseback, riding with style and ease, recalling the heroic charros who fought against the Spanish in 1821, against the French and Maximilian in 1865, and against governmental corruption in the Revolution of 1910. In his dress and in his machismo the charro represents the heroic and dramatic in Mexican history and tradition. Every Mexican is a charro or charra at heart.

The charreada, the exhibition of the equestrian skills of the charro, is the national sport of Mexico and is its celebration of that country's spirit and its love of the dramatic. The charreada, unlike the Texas rodeo, is practiced for style, not speed, and it is competition among teams, rather than among individuals. It is entered into for applause and admiration and for the patriotic celebration of Mexican tradition, never for money. No one pays an entrance fee.

Unlike the Texas long-oval rodeo arena, the charreada takes place in an exhibition area that looks something like a frying pan. The pan part is the *rueda* or *plaza*, a circular arena forty meters in diameter. Most of the events, or *suertes*, take place in the arena. The audience's stand is at the end of this arena. The pan handle is called the *lienzo*, or alley. The lienzo, in addition to being one special competition area, is the alleyway through which all the teams come into the arena.

The charreada, as it evolved from the Spanish roundup celebrations three hundred years ago, is begun with prayers in the chapel to Our Lady of Guadalupe. The opening performance is the *desfile*, the parade of the teams of charros and charras, accompanied by the association's officers and local dignitaries, with the Mexican flag and the flags of Texas and the United States. A mariachi band brings the teams into the arena with the playing of the "Zacatecas March" and the national anthems. Religion and patriotism are ever present, as is mariachi music and the baile that often follows the charreada.

The charreada is highly structured and is divided into *suertes*, or competitions among teams of charros. (*Suerte* really means "luck," but in this case a suerte is a competition.) The suertes begin with *La Cala de Caballo*, the presentation and the examination of the qualities of the horse and its rider. After this introductory demonstration, the main competitions begin. The first two suertes, team roping of running mares and tailing the bull, take place in the alley. The rest of the events take place in the arena. Sometimes the ladies, the charras, perform their team demonstrations, the *Escaramuza*, or skirmish, at the end of the competitions in the lienzo and before the suertes in the arena. The charras are all beautifully costumed and perform intricate team maneuvers riding side saddle. The competitions in the arena include wild mare and bull riding and amazing displays of ropesmanship as they lasso mares and bulls from afoot and on horseback. The final event is the *Paso de la Muerte*, which consists of the charro's leaping from his running horse to the back of an unsaddled and unbridled wild mare and then riding the wild mare to a halt with only the mane to cling to. One can see why the Paso de la Muerte is the final act of the charreada competition and why it is called the Pass of Death.

All of these events are performed with the most scrupulous attention to the welfare of the bull or wild mare. The mistreatment of an animal brings the judges' and the audience's censure.

As in the early colonial days, after the demonstrations of horsemanship the charros and the audience visit, have a barbecue, listen to mariachis, and have a baile. The charreada is an important cultural and social occasion and the Mexican people's reminder of the drama and the romance of their rich history and heritage.

The importance of the charro, the *caballero*, and the *vaquero* in Mexico goes back to their colonial beginnings and their history in a nation and a people whose lives were built on the ranching tradition. The skills of the man on horseback, in peace or in war, were the exercises of survival. And these men on horseback became— and remain!—their culture's heroes. During the late nineteenth and early twentieth centuries, the popularity and the skills of the charro were displayed in all sorts of exhibitions all over the world. In 1894, charros were a celebrated attraction in Buffalo Bill's Wild West Show, and their showmanship was displayed in South America and in Europe and Britain.

These performances were equally admired among their own Mexican people and gradually all of the displays of riding and roping came together in a structured form, called the charreada.

After the Revolution of 1910–20, in 1921 the National Association of Charros was founded in Mexico City. This was a movement of mainly urban charros who were athletes who trained to become skilled in the arts of the lariat and horsemanship. Their purpose was to maintain and promote Mexican nationalism and the spirit and identity of Mexico through its charro symbol. In 1933 the National Federation of Charros was created. It has become the parent organization of charro and charreada associations in Mexico and the United States. The San Antonio Charro Association, chartered in 1947, was the first accredited charro association north of the Rio Grande.

Texas can boast of seventeen chartered charro associations, in addition to dozens of hometown and horse-pasture charreada arenas. San Antonio alone has four associations. Bruce Shackelford, in his "Twenty-First Century Charrería," says that there are fifty-seven registered associations in the United States, the greatest number—thirty-nine—being in California. And there are four in Illinois!

The popularity of charreada competitions in Texas has increased with the continual arrival of immigrants from south of the border. In an alien land, the charreada reminds them of home and is a symbol of a strong Mexican national and cultural identity that they still treasure. The number of charreada competitions and charro associations with accompanying bailes and banquets in Texas increases annually. I can envision a time when charreada and rodeo mate and spawn new equestrian competitions and entertainments. That will be an interesting show!

Ab's father, Talbot Abernethy on a roundup.

Ab Abernethy on Boots.

WAGGONER'S COWBOYS

[Originally, photographs and text by Francis Edward Abernethy]

The cowboy is America's most representative and most marketable symbol. Stories about him and his songs and his styles are popular from the Ginza to the Champs Elysees, and in the modern mind he has taken the place of the mounted knight on horseback. The cowboy image, even though it is frequently projected as a professional gunfighter, has as sound a basis in history as his chivalric counterpart. He grew out of the working cowboy who came into being in Texas during the trail-driving days after the Civil War. He has come a long way since then and has made a greater impression on modern history and culture than has any other trade, craft, or profession.

The model for the modern cowboy symbol is not a complete figment of man's imagination. The best of his kind is alive with all the hoped-for virtues on the big ranches of West Texas. And some of the best of this geographically select group are on the six-county Waggoner ranch in north central Texas.

Dan Waggoner and his son Tom began building their herds in the 1850's, branding all the mavericks Dan and his men were tough enough to run down and throw. Dan and Tom and their cowboys fought Indians and drouths and competed with other stockmen for the accumulation of cattle and territory. In 1870 they trailed a herd to the Kansas railhead and made their first big financial profit, all of which they put back into a large spread and more cattle. They called this new ranch the Sachueista, after the Indian name for the tall grass that grew there. The Sachueista ranch is now over a hundred years old and getting stronger every year.

By the 1870's the boundary lines between cattle territories in West Texas had been pretty well agreed on, and it was up to the cowboys to see that the stock stayed on their own home range.

After a long hard winter when the cattle had drifted uncontrolled in search of food and shelter, the cowboys from every spread in the area would gather for the spring round-up, where they would cut out their own stock and then drive them back to their home range. Dot Babb, an old-time Waggoner cowboy, said that during the 1880's it was not unusual to see twenty-five to thirty chuck wagons on the roundup grounds, each chuck wagon accommodating thirty to sixty men. That adds up to 1800 cowboys, if one works with maximums, and most of them stayed in West Texas and passed their genes and traditions on to their grandchildren and great-grandchildren, some of whom are today's cowboys. The world's present-day cowboy culture was shaped by the men who worked for the Waggoners, for Burk Burnett, Charles Goodnight, and Lum Slaughter, for the Four Sixes, the Matador, JA, and Pitchfork ranches, and this culture is as natural to West Texas as the cattle that still graze there.

There was a strong spirit among these men that formed a new kind of life on the cattle range. Even in the midst of their time and work they felt that they were different. They felt the heroic stance of their lives, and they played it up and made the most of it. Their pride in themselves and their unique and adventurous sorts of lives made up for the hardships they had to endure.

The mechanics of being a cowboy has changed some since those early days of D. Waggoner and Son, but the spirit is the same as it was. Waggoner's cowboys usually sleep in a bunkhouse that has a television set, but it is still in the cold of a dark morning that they are rousted out, loaded in the "dog wagon," and hauled to the chuck wagon fifteen or twenty miles away for breakfast. Another departure is that the chuck wagon isn't pulled by a team of mules anymore, and the hands don't have to depend on their hat brims for shade and protection from the weather when they eat and sleep at the wagon. The chuck wagon is now mounted on a big six-wheeled truck, and they cover it and the eating and sleeping area with a big tarpaulin. The food, however, is still cooked over mesquite coals in a pit or on an iron woodstove, and the sounds that the cowboys hear at night when they sleep on the ground in bedrolls are the same sounds the old-timers heard—night hawks and coyotes, and the remuda as it grazes around them.

Getting ready to ride in the morning is the same as it always was. Two of the hands roll out before the rest, saddle up, and then drive up the hundred-horse remuda just as the day is lightening up. They push them into a holding pen that is made of one long rope braced waist high on stakes. These two hands then go to the wagon to eat, and two more cowboys rope out the horses to be used for the day.

These Three D horses are some of the best quarter horses in the world, all of them carrying the genes of carefully selected sires and dams. Each cowboy has a string of eight or ten horses which he is supposed to ride through fairly regularly and not wear out any one horse. They talk a lot about their horses and like them in direct proportion to how well they work. They aren't sentimental. They take care of their horses as a man takes care of his car, so they can get the most and best mileage out of them.

When Waggoner's cowboys are working a pasture many miles from the chuck wagon and a cattle truck is handy, they sometimes haul their horses to the work area in order to save time. Another thing that they have that their grandfathers didn't have is air support. When the pasture to be worked is extra large—and they sometimes call a two-thousand-plus-acre pasture a "trap"—the ranch foreman sends out a helicopter that herds the cattle from the back of the pasture up toward the pens where the cowboys are waiting. It would also surprise some of the old hands if they saw the cowboys roping from a jeep. But all that these modern methods do is to cut down on the number of cowboys needed to do the job. The work for each man is still the same. A cowboy on a horse ropes a calf and pulls him out of the bunch to be cut, notched, and branded in the same way as it has been since the beginning of cattle business.

No machine has been invented yet to gentle horses, either, and Waggoner's cowboys still break their own. Each January three or four hands are pulled off of cattle work to help the horse foreman break three-year-old broncs. These horses have spent their lives in the big pastures, and except for the times when they were branded and castrated they have never had a rope on them. Now they are roped, saddled, and ridden, and it speaks well for the bronc busters that a lot of horses go through with a minimum of acrobatics. Some do though and if skill can't keep the man on, then nerve has to get him up and make him get on again until he convinces the horse of the value of cooperation.

The Three D cowboys live a little better than the old hands did and they cover more territory, but essentially they are the same breed that worked with D. Waggoner and Son a hundred years ago. They have the skills, the nerve, the coordination, and endurance of professional athletes. Just about everything that a cowboy reaches for outweighs him and can run faster and hit harder than he can. It can hook him, tromp him, step on him, or kick a bone clean out of him, all of which it frequently does. The advantage the cowboy has is in direct proportion to the mastery of the skills of his profession.

This professional skill and their pride in it is one thing that separates Waggoner's cowboys from many other of the world's workers, most of whom do their jobs grudgingly or apologetically. The Sachueista men are cowboys because they want to be. Their pride and self-confidence is further bolstered by the knowledge that a large majority of the male population, young and old, USA-Europe-and-Asia, view them and their elite male-bond society with envy and admiration. Television, movies, literature, and advertising have pictured them as the national ego ideal, as symbols of the last line of battle against the depersonalization of the machine age and emasculation in an increasingly feminized society. An image which is that heroic can make up for long hours and low pay.

Bulldogging, back in the day.

Ab Abernethy, by James R. Snyder.

Cowboys at work.

Juneteenth Texas: Essays in African-American Folklore, the 1996
publication.

AFRICAN-AMERICAN FOLKLORE IN TEXAS
AND IN THE TEXAS FOLKLORE SOCIETY

Black people were a long time into Texas before the Anglos came to claim that territory as their own. Blacks of all hues and mixtures landed on the Caribbean islands with Columbus's expeditions, and they landed on the American mainland with Cortez, Pineda, and Narvaéz in the early 1500s. Black culture had been part of Spanish culture for over five hundred years of Moorish occupation, and black culture remained a part of Spanish culture in the New World.

And black people became a part of Texas folklore and legendry in these earliest of historical times.

Esteban (or Estevanico) the Moor was the first black man to set foot on Texas soil, as far as we know. He certainly became the most memorable of early black explorers. He was with Cabeza de Vaca when four survivors of the Narvaéz expedition walked for eight years (1528–1536) through Texas and Mexico, from Galveston to Culiacán. Esteban was not only a survivor; he was an adapter. He was a natural linguist, quickly learning Indian dialects as the small band of Europeans passed through one tribal territory after another.

As a consequence of his linguistic and social skills among the Indians, Esteban was chosen to accompany Friar Marcos de Niza's vanguard of Coronado's expedition in search of El Dorado in 1539. Esteban was a wily rascal, as keen after great wealth and fame as any Spanish grandee. On the journey north the Moor collected gifts and a large following of beautiful women and tribesmen who followed him in remembrance of times past with Cabeza de Vaca. It was Esteban who was the first European to discover Hawikah, the first of the fabulous Seven Cities of Cibolo. He found no City of Gold, only a large village of adobe buildings which glowed golden in the light of the rising and setting sun. And it was at Hawikah, in present New Mexico, that the Moor's luck ran out.

Esteban, with his retinue of women and loyal followers and baskets of goods to trade for things of gold and silver, found no

133

wealth in Hawikah. The City of Gold was made out of mud. The Moor was quickly and unceremoniously seized and flung into a cell. The elders of the village deliberated three days about the meaning of this intrusion. Then, fearful of such another invasion, they killed him. Friar Marcos, the appointed leader of this vanguard who was miles behind Esteban literally and figuratively, retreated and spread tall tales of the fabulous but well protected cities of gold. It is unfortunate that Esteban was not able to return with the truth. He would have saved Coronado a long wandering through the wilderness (Abernethy 1984, 6–10).

In 1791 nearly a quarter of the Spanish population in Texas was classified as Negro of some degree. Although free blacks could not hold government jobs, they were able to pursue any profession, marry whom they wished, and enjoy the freedoms of any Spanish citizen. The frontier allowed more racial latitude than did the city. Even so, slavery existed in Spanish Texas, and Indians and other unfortunates shared that condition with blacks (Campbell 10–12).

Bureaucratic Spain did recognize rank, and the Spanish conquistadors and nobility held social precedence over all others. Spain also recognized gradients of ethnicity—that is, of Spanish (Caucasian)-Negro-Indian-et cetera miscegenation—and filed its citizens under distinct categories. A catalog of those individuals who were drafted to accompany the Marques de Aguayo on his 1721 expedition to settle East Texas listed seventeen *mestizos* (Spanish father and Indian mother), twenty-one *coyotes* (unidentifiable Spanish-Indian mix), thirty-one *mulattoes* (Spanish-Negro mix), two *castizos* (Spanish mother and mestizo father), one *lobo* (Asiatic-Negro father and mulatto mother), one free Negro, one Indian, and forty-four Spaniards (Buckley 24).

Spanish rule ended with the Mexican revolution of 1821, and for the next fifteen years Mexico determined racial policy in Texas. Blacks had considerable social, occupational, and political latitude when Texas was under the Mexican flag. Blacks could hold political office under Mexican law, and slavery was legally banned. Mexico, however, realizing that prohibiting slavery absolutely would inhibit both the coming of Anglo settlers and the economic growth of

Texas, failed to enforce the ban. Also, incoming Anglos from the slave-holding Southern states circumvented the anti-slavery law by freeing their slaves on the east bank of the Sabine and "indenturing" them on the west bank (Campbell 23).

Three centuries and many black explorers and settlers after Esteban—during this Mexican period of racial ambivalence—an Afro-Texian of legendary proportions appeared on the East Texas scene. This man was William Goyens, whose life was not quite as dramatic as Esteban's but who has a large 1936 Texas Centennial marker on Goyens Hill near Nacogdoches to prove his historical worth. Goyens came to Texas around 1820 and established himself as one of Nacogdoches county's most successful (richest!) businessmen.

William Goyens' father had gained his freedom by serving in the North Carolina Militia during the Revolutionary War, so Goyens came to Texas as a freedman. Because of his high black profile, legends grew up about him, some erroneously describing him as a runaway slave. One tale tells how a white man walked into Goyens' blacksmith shop during the 1840s and identified himself as Goyens' previous owner. Goyens recognized his former master and asked him how much he was worth as a slave. The man told him $5,000. Goyens then went to the back of his shop, scraped some rubbish off an old box, and pulled out $5,000 in gold coins. The man took the money, gave Goyens a bill of sale for himself, and left.

That story is folklore. By 1840 Goyens had long ago quit working as a blacksmith. The real story is that some con man did come to Nacogdoches in 1826 with spurious evidence of Goyens' servitude and blackmailed him for 1,000 pesos—a bitter pill, no doubt.

William Goyens must have been a man of tremendous energy. He began his business life in Texas as a blacksmith and then became the gunsmith and armorer for the Mexicans stationed in Nacogdoches, which brings up another legend in Goyens' life. When Colonel Piedras was about to make his exit from Nacogdoches in 1832 he came to Goyens one evening for some secret blacksmithing. Piedras had two metal containers—each about the size a man could carry in his arms—and he wanted Goyens to weld a lid on them. He kept the contents covered, but Goyens got a glimpse of gold coins and other valuables before he sealed them up. According to reports Piedras buried this treasure in Ysleta Creek. Piedras lost the Battle of Nacogdoches and was killed in a later battle before he could return and retrieve his treasure. Goyens passed the story on but nobody ever found those two cans—unless Goyens himself did. He was a wealthy man.

Goyens was wealthy but he worked for it. In addition to being a blacksmith and gunsmith, he built and sold wagons and ran a freight line from Nacogdoches to Natchitoches—and was fined once when he was caught trying to smuggle goods past customs. He also had a sawmill and a gristmill, and operated a rooming-boarding house. He made most of his money, however, buying and selling land.

Goyens was a close friend of Sam Houston's, and during the Texas Revolution he spent much of his time as an intermediary between Houston and the East Texas Cherokees. He spoke Cherokee and Spanish and is considered to be responsible for holding off the Indians while the Anglos fought the Mexicans.

William Goyens had the respect and friendship of Nacogdoches. After the Republic of Texas disallowed the citizenship of freed blacks, Thomas J. Rusk, Adolphus Sterne, Elisha Roberts, and fifty other Nacogdocheans signed and sent a petition to the Legislature asking for special consideration for Goyens in light of his service to the Republic. It was granted, of course.

William Goyens died in 1856 leaving money, goods, five slaves, and 12,423 acres, none of which he had received in grants (Prince passim; *Handbook* I, 713–14).

During the Texas Revolution freedmen and slaves fought alongside their fellow Texians for independence. The first blood shed in the final series of battles was by a free Negro named Samuel McCullough, who was wounded in the capture of Goliad in October of 1835. Of the two soldiers cited for conspicuous bravery in Ben Milam's storming of San Antonio in December of 1835, one was Hendrick Arnold, a freedman and one of the two scouts, along with Deaf Smith. Arnold later married Deaf Smith's daughter. William Barrett Travis' slave Joe Travis endured the thirteen days of the Alamo and survived to tell the tale. Dick the Drummer set the march step that carried the Texians to victory at San Jacinto, and the black Maxlin Smith shared in the violence and the victory of that April 21st day in 1836.

The situation for blacks changed drastically under the Anglo government of the Texas Republic. The Constitution of the Republic of Texas ("General Provisions," Section 9) recognized the legality of slavery and prohibited freedmen from remaining in the country without congressional approval. Although most free blacks who had settled in Texas before the revolution were allowed to stay on, the spirit of this Draconic legislation became the same spirit that rushed the state into secession and the Civil War in 1861.

Many Texas slaves went with their masters to fight in the War Between the States. They suffered the same hunger and cold and disease that the rest of the southerners suffered. There were many instances of sacrifice and devotion and heroism among the blacks with the Confederate armies, but the most famous black Texan fought for the other side. Milton Holland had left Carthage, Texas, and moved to Ohio, and in 1861 he joined the Quartermaster Corp of the Union Army. As a sergeant-major he was wounded in the 1864 Battle of Richmond, where he led his troops in a gallant charge that won him a Congressional Medal of Honor.

The Emancipation Proclamation was delivered to Texas by General Gordon Granger on June 19, 1865—"Juneteenth"—and an already traumatized South changed for blacks and whites alike. After the initial shock, disbelief, and then jubilation, came the black experience of wandering loose in an antagonistic country with no means of support. This time of readjustment and reconstruction was long and harsh, and none can view the history of black and white relations during Reconstruction and the last years of the nineteenth century without dismay.

This does not mean that the black personality was completely subjugated after the War and Emancipation. Black communities and black leaders developed a segregated society and a rich culture around their own homes and schools and especially their churches. This period of segregation was an imposed system brought about by Klans and legislation and social states of mind that lasted for a hundred years. Because African-Americans lacked the former "protection" of the slave owners and later protection of civil rights legislation, during these Jim Crow times blacks were in a socio-legal limbo, subject to lynchings and other atrocities committed on their persons and property without any legal means of redress. Sometimes "to read history is to weep."

Nor does this mean that all black-white relations were bad. Many blacks and whites were bonded by love and mutual dependence during that time, and many survived because they helped each other.

The tattered times of Reconstruction had its own roll of dynamic Negro personalities. The efforts of such black legislators as George Ruby, Meshac Roberts, and Morris Cuney to effect a peaceful social change during Reconstruction was certainly the stuff of heroes, in spite of the overwhelming resistance which they met.

A notable group of African-Americans made their mark in West Texas. The western part of the state was opened to settlement through the protection of the black Ninth and Tenth Cavalries, the Buffalo Soldiers, so called by the Apaches because with their black curly hair they looked like bull buffalos, which, by the way, became their insignia. In an official report of an expedition against the Apaches, one of their commanding officers wrote, "I cannot speak too highly of the conduct of the officers and men under my command. They were always cheerful and ready, braving the severest hardships with short rations and no water without a murmur. The black troops know no fear and are capable of great endurance."

The opening of the west Texas range to cattlemen afforded blacks another occupation in which men of color achieved distinction. Mathew "Bones" Hooks was considered the champion bronc buster in a Texas full of busters. Al Jones went up the trail thirteen times, four times as the trail boss. "80 John" Wallace was a cowboy who bought land and stock and established a 7,600-acre ranch that his daughter has increased to 15,000 acres; Colorado City's integrated high school is named after him. One of the most famous cowboys of the West is Bill Pickett, who invented bulldogging. He later rodeoed—with Will Rogers and Tom Mix as his hazers—in

Madison Square Garden and became the first African-American in the Cowboy Hall of Fame.

In 1908 Jack Johnson of Galveston became the first black world champion heavyweight boxer. Scott Joplin of Texarkana gave the world ragtime. Huddie Ledbetter, "Leadbelly," disseminated the Brazos Bottom blues. Dr. J. Mason Brewer of Austin and the Texas Folklore Society became the nation's leading black folklorist.

These were the blacks of early Texas legend and history, the individuals whose personalities and activities were so dramatic that their stories became symbols, often larger than the lives they lived. Their names stood out in the Texas experience among people of all colors. Unfortunately, their names were unsung and their voices were silent in the academic records of their times and later. Texas textbook history was played out on a white, Anglo-Saxon, Protestant stage.

The study of African-American culture in Texas was from its beginning in 1909 an important province of the Texas Folklore Society. The Society's first publication was a 1912 pamphlet of Negro folk songs, and the first Publication of the Texas Folklore Society (PTFS I, 1916) contained a Negro folk tale. The first nineteen volumes, to 1944, contained thirty articles on Negro folklore. Many of these stories, songs, and beliefs were field-collected folklore that was published for the first time in Publications of the Texas Folklore Society. Field collections dropped off sharply after World War II, when Americans began to get more racially sensitive and self conscious. Thereafter the articles were usually studies about Negro folklore, as is this *Juneteenth Texas*, rather than illustrations of field collected songs and tales.

The twentieth century before World War II was a time of discovery of black culture and of blacks themselves, who had been slaves-chattel-aliens for many years and were just a few years beyond Emancipation. Their culture was only beginning to take shape as a growing, independent, and vital part of American culture. The study and appreciation of their folklore—their songs and stories, their culture and traditions and beliefs—were the first steps toward racial understanding and eventual integration.

On the national scene in the late nineteen and early twentieth centuries, Negro art forms—usually filtered though the white perspective—were becoming accepted fare in all levels of society. Joel Chandler Harris with his Uncle Remus tales might have done more than anyone to bring the richness of black life and culture into white consciousness. Harris was widely known, read, and loved throughout the United States, and his gentle, obedient, and unthreatening Uncle Remus was a comfortable character to come into white homes. Roark Bradford's *Ol' Man Adam and His Chillun,* from which Martha Emmons got her "Adulteration of Old King David" and Marc Connelly got his Pulitzer Prize winning *Green Pastures,* was written in the same spirit.

These paternalistic depictions of blacks, happily working for Ol' Massa on sunny Southern plantations, seem romantic and unreal to our present generation. They continue the slave-oriented Uncle Remus stereotype, and they proliferate other demeaning stock characterizations that hinder rather than help racial understanding. But, at the time, they began to narrow the gap between two cultures that were chasms apart.

The Fisk Jubilee Singers were international performers of Negro spirituals, and they impressed white audiences with the beauty, the seriousness, and the depth of feeling of a race which had long been singularly out of the framework of consideration.

Amos and Andy, Molasses and January, Hambone, and Rochester—all of whom were much loved by white audiences during the Depression Thirties—were in the vanguard of the civil rights movement, whether they were meant to be or not. Even post-Civil-War minstrelsy, with its stereotypes and romanticized "darky" songs, played a part in integrating black culture into the dominant white society. Hambone, of the syndicated newspaper cartoon "Hambone Sez," was quoted for his wisdom during the Depression almost as much as Will Rogers. One reason for the popularity of these entertainers was that their characters reinforced traditionally white-conceived stereotypes of always-happy, lazy, childlike blacks. This is not an acceptable concept by modern black activists—or white activists, for that matter. But these were positive images to white Americans during their times and were personalities who were fondly taken into white homes.

Blacks in popular culture are still stereotyped, and Jack Benny's Rochester becomes today's sardonic butler Benson. And Sanford and Son and friends at the junkyard take the place of Amos and Andy and Madam Queen at the taxi stand. No white man in his right mind would do a Step'n Fetchit imitation for Spike Lee, but hours of black television sitcoms present such characters as J. J. of *Good Times* and George Jefferson, the black Archie Bunker, both of whom are artistically flat, nondimensional characters. Attitudes and perspectives have changed over the past half century, but some of the results are the same.

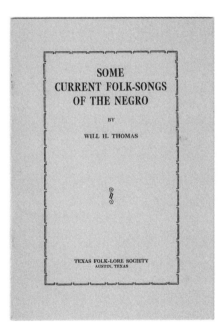

Some Current Folk-Songs of the Negro, the 1912 special TFS publication.

The Texas Folklore Society from its beginning to World War II was involved in the exploration and discovery of black culture. Its first publication, in 1912, was Will H. Thomas's monograph,

"Some Current Folk-Songs of the Negro." Dorothy Scarborough presented Negro folk music studies at meetings and published in *Coffee in the Gourd* (PTFS II, 1923), her important study of Negro blues as folk songs. This was before John Lomax began his serious work with black folk music. Spiritual singers regularly were featured performers at TFS meetings. And when Harvard's George Lyman Kittredge made his first visit to the TFS in 1913, Lomax took him to hear Negro preaching and singing at an Austin church (PTFS XXXIII, 6). Among later contributors, the best known collectors and tellers of Negro tales in the Society were Martha Emmons, A. W. Eddins, and J. Mason Brewer. John Henry Faulk studied and wrote about Negro church and religious life. Hardly a meeting went by before WWII without some presentation in the field of Negro folklore, and the Society regularly carried Negro folklore in its publications. Because Negroes' position in society was in a state of flux at the time, the attitudes of the presenters were similarly various (Abernethy, 1992, see chapter appendices).

Dobie recognized this variety of attitudes toward blacks in his preface to *Rainbow in the Morning* (PTFS V, 1926, 4) and said, "The editor disclaims any responsibility for the opinions and information set forth by the varying contributors on the subject of negro folk-songs printed in this publication. If one wants to spell negro with a capital N and another with a little n, the editor has nothing to say; if one considers the negro as a shining apostle of sweetness and light, another as a gentle old darkey, and still another as 'phallic kinky,' it is none of the editor's business" (PTFS V, 4). This is the same Dobie who in his political escapades twenty years later—and post WWII racial attitudes are different from pre-WWII—fell into disrepute among some Texans because of his liberalism, particularly because he espoused voting and education rights for Negroes and stated that they should be allowed into the University of Texas.

Editorial distancing such as Dobie's, especially in an academic journal, would be unacceptable in our present ethnically enlightened times, as would most of the attitudes toward blacks found in the Society's first thirty years of presentations. But we must not forget that we are talking about a different historical time, and social historians must never forget that they cannot judge past moralities by present-day standards. This is called generational chauvinism, the belief that only the values of one's own generation are valid. The old Roman Cato, who had lived beyond his conditioning over two millennia ago said, "It is not easy to render an account of your life to an age other than the age in which you have lived."

Dobie and most TFS readers and writers were the most educated and sophisticated people of their time and culture, but they were still products of their times. Scotus and Aquinas believed in a geocentric universe, Thomas Jefferson had slaves, and respectable western folk of the nineteenth century believed that society would collapse if women got the right to vote. Abraham Lincoln did not believe that slaves should be given citizenship, and he denied the doctrine of social equality for blacks (Randall, 118). And many educated ante-bellum southerners had no more guilty consciences about the presence of slavery than our own parents and grandparents of the Twenties and Thirties had about the presence of Jim Crow laws. Jim Crow was status quo, a fact of life, even though to some, sometimes, it seemed as peculiar as the previous stage of black servitude under that "peculiar institution."

Thus, much of that early writing in the realm of African-American folklore is perceived much differently today from the way it was seen and written over fifty years ago. Fifty years of racial social revolution has changed perspectives. The condescension and paternalism and stereotyping of those early folklorists are obvious and glaring in light of today's social and racial attitudes. But even today whites still have problems writing about black folklore. Much writing by whites about African-Americans is touched with racial romanticism. Some whites see blacks and their culture as they wish them to be, carriers of "pure" folk culture in black music and art, unsullied by the commerce and materialism of the more affluent white culture. Only the black world knows how close white writers are to reality.

Color does not separate individual members of the races; culture does. We are all children of Eve, the seed of some australopithecine mother of a million years ago. Those who sing the same songs, tell the same stories, worship the same gods, and dress alike and decorate their bodies alike are bound together by a cultural cement, color and racial differences notwithstanding. Those who say *crick* instead of *creek* and *you'se* instead of *y'all* are separated in spite of similarities of color, unless they can find compensatory folkloric and customary similarities. The purpose of this publication and of previous publications of the Texas Folklore Society is to acquaint members and readers with other cultures, to find the humanity that binds all children of Eve into a sympathetic and understanding people—to narrow culture gaps that can be as socially divisive as the Mason-Dixon Line.

I conclude with an animal tale in the Uncle Remus-style, black, folk tradition. Frank Dobie published this in his first PTFS (II) in 1923. This tale is typical of the African-American folklore that was collected and published in those early days of the Society. It was collected from the oral tradition and written down nearly seventy-five years ago by A. W. Eddins, a San Antonio school teacher and white writer who was following in the steps of white journalist Joel Chandler Harris. This is a classic dialect joke, funny because of its intellectual wit and its universal wisdom. The dialect personalizes it (at the same time that it stereotypes it) in the same way as do the Sut Lovingood tales or the José Jimenez monologues or Pat O'Brien's Irish jokes or Alan King's Jewish jokes. Black or white, any reader who has found himself as a goose in a den of foxes easily identifies with the teller of this tale. But in our society, then and now, the speaker must be a black man for the tale to have social significance.

> Ole Sis Goose wus er-sailin' on de lake, and ole Brer Fox wus hid in de weeds. By um by ole Sis Goose swum up close to der bank and ole Brer Fox lept out an cotched her.
>
> "O yes, ole Sis Goose, I'se got yer now, you'se been er-sailin' on mer lake er long time, en I'se got yer now. I'se gwine to break yer neck en pick yer bones."

"Hole on dere, Brer Fox, hold on, I'se got jes as much right to swim in der lake as you has ter lie in der weeds. Hit's des as much my lake es hit is yours, and we is gwine to take dis matter to der cotehouse and see if you has any right to break my neck and pick my bones."

En so dey went to cote, and when dey got dere, de sheriff, he wus er fox, en de judge, he wus er fox, en der tourneys, dey wus foxes, en all de jurrymen, dey was foxes, too.

En dey tried ole Sis Goose, en dey 'victed her en dey 'scuted her, en dey picked her bones.

Now my chilluns, listen to me, when all de folks in de cotehouse is foxes, and you is jes er common goose, der ain't gwine to be much jestice for a pore nigger.

J. Mason Brewer, Negro Folklorist, by James W. Byrd.

J. Mason Brewer.

BIBLIOGRAPHY

Abernethy, Francis E. *Legends of Texas' Heroic Age*. Boston: American Press, 1984.

—. *The Texas Folklore Society 1909–1943*. Vol. I. Denton: University of North Texas Press, 1992.

Buckley, Eleanor C. "The Aguayo Expedition into Texas and Louisiana, 1719–1722." *The Quarterly of the Texas State Historical Association*, XV, No. 1 (July 1911): 1–65.

Campbell, Randolph B. *An Empire for Slavery: The Peculiar Institution in Texas 1821–1865*. Baton Rouge: Louisiana State University Press, 1989.

Dobie, J. Frank. *Coffee in the Gourd*. PTFS II. Austin: Texas Folk-Lore Society, 1923.

—. *Rainbow in the Morning*. PTFS V. Austin: Texas Folk-Lore Society, 1926.

Handbook of Texas. Walter P. Webb, et al., eds. Austin: The Texas State Historical Association, 1952.

Prince, Diane. "William Goyens, Free Negro on the Texas Frontier." Thesis. Nacogdoches, Stephen F. Austin State University, 1967.

Randall, J. G. and David Donald. *The Civil War and Reconstruction*. Lexington, Mass: D. C. Heath and Company, 1969.

Sance, Melvin. *The Afro American Texans*. San Antonio: Institute of Texan Cultures, 1987 rev.

The Secretary-Editor, at home in the TFS Office.

PREFACE: IN WHICH THE AUTHOR ATTEMPTS TO JUSTIFY HIS VERBOSITY AND THE LENGTH OF THIS HISTORY

[from *The Texas Folklore Society: 1909–1943, Volume I*, PTFS LI, 1992]

━━

This book had a beginning that was simple enough, almost accidental. At the end of the 1984 Huntsville business meeting, Jack Duncan and John O. West asked that all the Society's programs be published in some upcoming miscellany. This was a simple enough request. They wanted to know what folklore topics members had been interested in and had been talking about since that first TFS gathering in 1911. When I returned to the Society's office I immediately set Marlene Adams, then the TFS secretary, to typing up all past TFS meeting programs for inclusion in the next PTFS.

The stack of programs made an impressive list and one that activated the typing of another list, the tables of contents of PTFSs that followed the programs. I was prompted to making this second list because I wanted to know the relation of the publications' contents to the meetings' contents.

That great flurry of list typing led me to wanting to know more about the people who made up these programs and tables of contents. And that was the beginning of numerous trips to the Barker Center at The University of Texas and days of sifting through the TFS files which are stored there.

Next step: I now had all of this data—the previously mentioned lists, the minutes of meetings, financial records, correspondence— which kept flashing pictures at me of people and meetings and tours and singings and dancings. Before long I had enough material to make a pretty good entry for each year. And really, this was all I had set out to do, to get in one place the records and happenings of the Society from 1909 to date.

I was next led astray by Leonidas Payne's pamphlet, "I Was Here When the Woods Were Burnt." Payne describes the seminal meeting between him and John Lomax so vividly that I was caught up in an atmosphere of social history that I felt compelled to continue. — And it is entirely consonant with the way I view life and literature: they are inextricably entwined. — Therefore, I have tried to inextricably entwine the goings on of the Texas Folklore Society with Gibson Girls and World War I and the Roaring Twenties and the Crash and Depression and World War II—and with the songs they sang and the movies they went to—and the clothes they wore and the cars they drove—and life. These were the settings in which all these meetings that Duncan and West were interested in took place.

The result, of course, was that considerably more space was required per year's entry than I had thought probable. In addition to which, I found myself sometimes waxing philosophical about the goings on within and without the Society and occupied a few more precious signatures.

All of this flurry of TFS activities has been very alive to me. I have seen the people listening and having singalongs and sight-seeings. I have labored with Dobie and Mody and Ransom as they struggled to put together an annual. I have read letters of anger and sadness and excitement and responded sympathetically to names that have come alive and let me listen to them and feel some of what they felt.

I have long loved the Society deeply, with the most dedicated and intense part of my professional life. By learning more of its heart's core, I love it now with a small part of wisdom.

The purpose of this history is to preserve for the Society its records and its story. The Texas Folklore Society is that important and that ancient that its progress can be a guide to other institutions and individuals. Some of the nation's most notable folklore scholars have passed through its portals, have had their professional beginnings in its meetings, and have sent their influence out to other folklorists.

I am doing this history in three parts, publishing each part as I go, because I recognize the flight of time and want to get something

completed and published in case I am abruptly called to my reward—
or whatever. Technically, however, the TFS history is just one book,
and I apologize for cluttering up the bookscape with three. A trilogy
really is presumptuous; we are not the Roman Empire.

But as it falls, the Society's history is logically divided into
three parts. This volume begins at the beginning in 1909, includes
the formative years up to its recess in 1917 because of WWI, and
then its reformation and its glory days under the leadership of
J. Frank Dobie. The volume closes when Dobie resigns and goes
to Cambridge in 1943. Volume Two begins with Mody Boatright's
assumption of the editorship and his tenure until 1944, then
Wilson Hudson's editorship until 1971. It concludes with the
movement of the Society from Austin to Nacogdoches in 1971.
Volume Three will be this editor's tenure from 1971 till now. I shall
be quite happy if I can complete the first two.

Icons of the Texas Folklore Society.

I doubt that I would have gotten this history done without the continual, tireless help of Carolyn Fiedler Satterwhite, the Society's secretary, office manager, and assistant editor. She has researched and organized and typed—and found things! She is uncanny about finding things, and she can read directions and understand them. She is a woman of acute intellect and delicate tastes and infinite patience, and I know that I have done something right in this life to be rewarded with her to run this TFS office.

I guess I would have gotten this done without a word processor—and Scott Meyers, who kept it running—but it would have taken longer and would have been ten times the trouble.

I want to thank Sarah Payne Foxworth—Leonidas Payne's darling daughter, born within a month of the Society's birth—who has given the Society letters and pictures, has provided personal information about the Society's early years, and has given generously to the financing of this book.

Surrounded by his life's work.

The editor sincerely thanks the generous others who helped in the financing: James Winfrey, Wilson M. Hudson, Mary Elizabeth Nye, Mrs. Howard Wilcox, Elmer Kelton, Paul Patterson, Kenneth Davis, Dorys Grover, Dick Bosse, Alton Hughes, Jack and Elizabeth Duncan, Johnye Sturcken, and Palmer Olsen.

To my editor-readers: My thanks to Allen Maxwell, once a TFS associate editor, director of SMU Press, *Southwest Review*, and the *Dallas Morning News* Book Section. Allen knows more about the literary history of Texas than anybody I know, and he has shared this knowledge (as well as rare books and photographs) graciously. I thank Martin Shockley, who reads with a rapier in hand instead of a red pencil; he always has my complete attention and respect. Nolan Porterfield of Cape Girardeau, Missouri, is writing a biography of John A. Lomax, and he saved me from some egregious errors. I thank James Ward Lee and Paul Stone. I thank my wife Hazel, who has generously proofread for style and structure and whose literary opinion I value beyond all others. And I thank Wilson M. Hudson, my mentor and fellow TFS Secretary-Editor, who has read with wisdom and has helped me the most in this and in all my TFS endeavors.

The Barker Center folk—Don Carlton, Ralph Elder, Bill Richter, John Slate, and others of the staff—bore with me and worked for me and helped immeasurably in my gathering of the TFS Archive materials which are stored there.

Ethel Ward-McLemore of the Texas Academy of Science and Rebecca Schroeder of the Missouri Folklore Society completed the historical connections between the TFS and their respective societies. Richard Holland of the Southwestern Writers Collection, Southwest Texas State University, researched TFS members at his university.

And my thanks to all those good folks who sent me programs and pictures and bits and pieces of the Society's history.

I'll see you when I get the next volume ready, if not before.

Francis Edward Abernethy
Stephen F. Austin State University
Nacogdoches, Texas
The fall of '91

PREFACE: TO VOLUME II, IN WHICH THE AUTHOR ATTEMPTS TO RECTIFY ERRORS IN VOLUME I

[from *The Texas Folklore Society: 1943–1971, Volume II,* PTFS LIII, 1994]

I open this volume two of the history of the Texas Folklore Society with the errata sheet for volume one because one must confess his sins and rectify them before he can cleanly enter the portals of the next world—and sin again.

Charles Hagelman—back in Houston, Texas, for over ten years but still writing on Northern Illinois University letterhead—pointed out that on page 144 I referred to April 21 as Texas Independence Day (really March 2) instead of San Jacinto Day. Hagelman also thought that the picture of the western star labeled "Wm. S. Hart" looked like Buster Keaton. It does, in fact, but that is illustrator Charles Shaw's area, and I will not take issue. Jack Burnett Kellam, artist-poet-musician of Zellwood, Florida, who has written a book on his longtime friend John Henry Faulk, noted that Frank Dobie Faulk was the child of John Henry and Lynne Smith, John Henry's second wife, not Hally Wood, his first wife (page 256). Wallis R. Sanborn II, San Angelo, Peggy Skagg's student, who wrote a grad-uate paper on Walter Prescott Webb, showed me that Webb's first publication was "Notes on the Folklore of Texas," published in *The Journal of American Folklore*, 28 (January-March 1915); I had erroneously placed his first paper in PTFS I, 1916 (page 80). Herbert Halpert, Folklore Professor Emeritus at the University of Newfoundland, wrote a "Dear Dr. Aberfeldy" salutation and explained that I had written his name three times on one page and had spelled it two different ways (page 208). To pile Pelion on Ossa, I misspelled it ("Hal*b*ert") in the index. Herbert C. Arbuckle III, the Society's bibliographer, noted that at the bottom of page 51 the reader could not distinguish between the president of the Society and the president of Southwest Texas State Normal College; Lillie Shaver was president of the TFS and C. E. Evans was president of SWT. I saw myself that I had entered "1944" instead of "1964" as the end of Mody Boatright's TFS secretary-editorship (page vii). And even though Mody continued in some of his duties until 1964, he formally resigned in 1963. Also, it has been pointed out that my parenthetical comments in Volume I were labeled "editor" rather than "author." I have chosen to continue that "error" here, and trust that the reader will understand that I am speaking both as author of these particular volumes and as editor of the TFS series.

These above errors, certainly, are not the only ones contained in *The Texas Folklore Society I*, but they were blatant enough to be seen. I do sincerely thank those who wrote me about the mistakes in the text. I know that they did read the book. And that is all that a writer can ask.

The Abernethys leaving on their honeymoon.

The years of this volume—1943 to 1971—are at the heart of my own life. I joined the navy in 1943, married in 1948, and made my own contribution to the baby boom with five children between 1950 and 1960. I began teaching in 1951, got my Ph.D. in 1956, and have been in academia ever since. My advent into folklore was an accident of time and place. Folklore broke into higher academics in the late Fifties. Charles Hagelman, my English department head at Lamar, decided he wanted a folklore course in his part of the catalog, and because of idiosyncrasies of background and personality I was appointed to create one. The course was a natural niche for me. My interests are wide (rather than deep?) and the field of folklore, I soon found, was as wide as the world and all mankind, and it was temporal back to the beginning. I have taught it for thirty years now, and I still get excited about it, and the horizons continue to stretch out invitingly before me. I have followed my own direction in the building of the course. I have never found anyone, outside of some of my students, who share my interest in my ethological approach to folklore, but my commitment to my discipline as I have learned it, is undiminished. And I became the secretary-editor of the Texas Folklore Society in 1971.

A dashing graduate.

I researched a lot of social history in preparation for these books, because I believe that the progress of the Texas Folklore Society cannot be understood without understanding the world as it was at the time. I discovered some fascinating reading in the process. For this particular volume, I relied most heavily on a book that I accidentally stumbled upon and have since read to the very last word. It was Rita Lang Kleinfelder's *When We Were Young: A Baby-Boomer Yearbook,* and it covers the years from 1947 to 1975. Because my children are the products of the baby boom, I gave them each a copy, as well as one to the Boomer assistant-editor Carolyn Satterwhite. To those of my own generation and to their children: "This book is your life!"

Stephen F. Austin State University Regents Professor of English.

I wish to thank Stephen F. Austin State University for granting me a semester's research leave so that I could get this volume to press on time for the 1994 Society publication.

I thank Mr. and Mrs. James Winfrey (with matching donations from Exxon) and Mrs. Howard Wilcox for financial assistance in the publication of this volume.

I thank all those members who sent in memories and memorabilia of their lives in the TFS between 1944 and 1971.

I thank the readers of this manuscript: Martin Shockley, Allen Maxwell, James Ward Lee, Charlotte Wright, and my wife Hazel. I particularly thank Charlotte Wright, the NT Press editor, for her meticulous editing and her valuable criticisms. These are people of wisdom and patience, with sharp eyes and acute judgments, and I hope that I have responded properly to their advice and criticisms. I was regularly in touch with Ernest Speck, John O. West, and Al Lowman, who together constitute an encyclopedic mine of information.

Carolyn Fiedler Satterwhite—the Society's secretary, comptroller, and office manager—is the assistant editor for this publication, and that title does not come close to describing the work she has done to get this book ready for the press.

If the reader requires further prefatory reading, he is directed to the preface in *The Texas Folklore Society I, 1909–1943.*

Francis Edward Abernethy
Stephen F. Austin State University
Nacogdoches, Texas
The Spring of '94

JANUARY 14, 2000

[from The Texas Folklore Society: 1971–2000, Volume III,
PTFS LVII, 2000]

Paisanos:

The best work that a future TFS Secretary-Editor can do for the future and the welfare of the Society is to take this three-volume history of the Texas Folklore Society and boil it down to one readable volume.

Honestly and truly I did not begin this project with the idea of writing the TFS history in three volumes. I envisioned a moderate sized book that future interested persons could turn to in order to learn more about the continuity of this Society. But my plans came apart at the beginning. I got so involved with Lomax and Payne and that first fall that they got together to begin planning that the most minute details of the TFS beginning took on significance that I felt that I could not neglect. I saw the UT campus and the game and the people and what they wore and what they were singing and reading about so vividly that I could not leave it out. And once I had set a precedent, I enjoyed the research into those times and people so much that the whole thing grew like a yeast. Researching and writing volume I was sheer pleasure. Volume II was enjoyable, but I began to lose aesthetic and historical distance between the happenings in the Society and myself.

This volume III was the hardest to write. The years were so close to me that I viewed them personally rather than historically. And I was very self conscious of using the personal "I" so much—and shifting back and forth between first and third person. I was always self conscious when I had to quote myself. And if I could have found anyone else to write this 1971 ff. story I would have put him or her on it. But nobody knows as much about the people and places and happenings of the last thirty years as I do. The Society has been the focus of my professional life since 1971. Not a day has passed that I have not been concerned with it and its paisanos. So I am the one to do this.

So, what you will notice about volume III of this history of the Texas Folklore Society is that it is a twenty-nine year newsletter from the Society's editor to the paisanos. The chapters are divided according to presses and publications, as much for equal time's sake as for their importance in the Society welfare. I hope that I have not left out too many significant people and important happenings.

Volume one of the history of the Texas Folklore Society was a tribute to our TFS grandfathers—John Lomax, Leonidas Payne, Frank Dobie, and their peers. Volume two recognized our folkloric fathers—Mody Boatright, Wilson Hudson, Martin Shockley, and their kin who taught us the way that we must go. Volume three is the history of a generation who came in wet behind the ears in academic folklore, became the fathers and movers and the shakers of the Society, and now find themselves as the grandfathers, watching a whole new world being created as they move to the sidelines. The process is as natural as birth and death.

The absolute and unquestionable pinnacle of my professional career has been my association with the Texas Folklore Society and its members. The Society has given me, as a member and as an officer, opportunities that I could never have had elsewhere. And its members have given me friendship and an education of a lifetime. I have prized both for forty years.

In your service,

F. E. Abernethy
Secretary-Editor

F.E. Abernethy, Texas Folklore Society Secretary-Editor, 1971–2003.

A sketch from *Built in Texas.*

PREFACE (In which the editor reflects upon his perambulations and peregrinations)

[from *Built in Texas*, PTFS XLII, 1979]

He was right, you know. You must be born again—and again and again, *ad infinitum,* or at least *ad cemeterium.* Those who aren't periodically reborn are like the snake who fails to shed his skin and is eventually squeezed to death by the narrowness of his old confines. Archer Fullingim, the ex-editor of *The Kountze News,* is a professed born-again Big Thicketite. Periodically he flings himself off into the wilderness of the Big Thicket and splashes around in Village Creek and wades through bay galls and pin-oak flats, and the Holy Ghost of the Big Thicket (and elsewhere, of course) takes a Pentecostal possession of him. He is born again and he talks in tongues that are almost as strange as some of his brass-collar-Democrat ravings. He rolls holily in the Thicket grasses and leaves, and he shakes and quakes through spasms of love and communion until he sheds his old, city skin and is born again to a new identification with the Thicket and the Great Spirit that it is a part of. Then he goes contentedly back into town to grow gourds and make mayhaw jelly, agitate the political conservatives of Hardin County, and wait for his next call to the wilderness.

Driving around Texas looking at gates and windmills and adobe houses was an experience for me similar to Archer's periodic assumption of the Holy Ghost of the Big Thicket. I have a visceral need to make seasonal pilgrimages about the state, to touch it and taste it and smell it, to see that the sage and prairie grass and the water that flows through the sandy creek beds and the winds that blow through the rock hills are still there. And they always are, no matter what the season. The leaves wither and fall or they turn glassy green—the water freezes in the stock ponds, or spills over under the watchful eye of a dragonfly, or settles down to a warm brown as the cows chug down the mud slope to drink—and nothing really changes. Archer's Holy Ghost is there too, in different, ever shifting shapes perhaps but always blessing the earth with its presence. It broods with warm breast and ah! bright wings over Texas (and, granted, elsewhere) and when you are close enough to it you feel that you can almost wrap the good earth around you like a great soft steer hide and feel its love and comfort.

I camped one night in the Palo Duro and awoke the next morning swallowed by a fog which filled the canyon so thick you could see it move, and every boulder and tourist and roadrunner became an ingredient in the thick, grey soup. I spent a bright night with a sweet moon behind a cotton gin on the Trinity and watched an old mammy coon and her young'un stroll by about a nickel's flip away. The old mammy waddled on down into the cotton rows barely acknowledging my presence, while the coon-child skipped and nosed the air and looked back over his shoulder. "Hey, Mama, I think there was somebody in that sleeping bag!" I trespassed one night in the mesquite and tall grass north of Ozona and figured I was about to get my plough cleaned by the ranch foreman, who relented and took me where the grass was shorter and less combustible, and who later, around midnight, rousted me out to help him fix a float valve on a water trough in the next pasture.

My best camp was in those rocky hills south of Marfa, just before they drop off into the Rio Grande valley and Presidio. I pulled in around sundown, pitched camp, fixed an ailing clutch spring, and then poked along the trails for a while looking for snakes. I got back to the pickup at good dark and stirred around considerably fixing supper, which consisted of frying a steak I had picked up at Alpine and opening a can of fruit cocktail. After supper I cleaned up meticulously, wiping out the skillet with a Scott Towel, burning my paper plate, lipping my fork, and cleaning my pocket knife on my boot. But with all this activity I still wasn't tired enough to relax and go to bed, and I recognized that I was feeling lonesome and bored. The radio didn't help and neither did several cigarettes and an Old Charter nightcap. I glumped around, sitting on the tailgate, then lying on my bed roll, till I finally gave up, put on my headlight, and started walking along the ridge road. I guess I walked a mile, stopping to look at crawling things, seeing a baby diamondback coiled in a circle no bigger than a silver dollar, before I finally got to the edge of the hill, where it falls off into the valley below. I found a throne rock there, where somebody put it so that you could sit and lean back and look down at the lights of Presidio and Ojinaga and at the little yellow lights shining from the people of the long river valley and watch the lights from the cars and trucks as they rolled off the high places and sailed almost silently down the long road to the bottom. I sat and watched and breathed in all the sounds and sights, and soon everything went easy, and I wasn't lonesome or bored or anything that you sometimes are when you are feeling alone. There are rare and magic times when the distractions of the flesh fade and the body relaxes enough for the soul to slip out and take communion with whatever broods over the bent world with its bright and silent wings. I wrapped around me all those rocks and chiming stars and the sounds of trucks whining down the mountains—and all those night walkers that start little rock slides and rustle through yucca stumps and dead bear grass—I wrapped all this gentle pulse around me and walked back to camp to lie down and thread my eyebeams with the stars.

The next day at Presidio the temperature was 108°, and I damn near fried.

I bathed in rivers and stock ponds, usually well off the road, but once in sweaty desperation and the heat of mid-August afternoon I performed my ablutions in Live Oak Creek near Fort Lancaster while traffic sped over me on the highway bridge. Now I can't drive over a highway bridge without wondering what's going on underneath. One evening south of Blanco a bunch of old nosey mama cows came to watch me as I lay immersed in a spring pool trying to bring down the body's temperature and to flush off the dust of the road. Much refreshed, I arose like a skinny Proteus from the sea, and off they ran, tails lofted indignantly in the air, shrieking, "Run away, run away—it's a nekkid man!" They eyed me from the security of a patch of live oak, still wary of my intentions, as I dried off in the sun and put on my clothes. By the time I got back to the road they had walked to the pool and were looking suspiciously around to see what else might come out of the water.

I drove through Hale Center when the sirens and radios were screaming the town's population into their storm cellars, and rain poured out of an angry cloud that sat down over us like a black-iron skillet lid. Little tails funneled down out of the dark clouds to the west, and there wasn't ditch number-one to get into in case one of the twisters had gotten serious and cut off my retreat to the south.

On my first trip, up through the blacklands and the Cross Timbers to the Panhandle, I carried enough camping gear to support a safari. Thereafter I cut down to essentials and during the day grazed on cheese, milk, and oatmeal cookies. Most of the time I had a cot to sleep on, but I enjoyed the ground when I wasn't in rocks. The one night I got caught in the rain, I tied my lariat to the front bumper, ran it over the cab and back past the tailgate to a mesquite tree. Then I hung the tarpaulin over the rope, letting it hang down on both sides of the truck bed. That makes a good tent. By the time I got it up I was wet and the rain had begun to slacken and soon stopped. I went to bed under the tarp anyway and got hot and hoped it would start raining again to justify my discomfort. Buzzing and whirring things flew out of the prickly pear and into the tent and couldn't find their ways out. I finally roused myself enough to gamble that the rain was over and to strip back the tarp. Breathing came easier under the open sky, and it didn't rain.

I saw a world of barns and fences and bump gates, I mean really saw them with fresh eyes, and looked at worn wood grain and saddle-notches and rubble and specks of shiny gravel in adobe, and saw how stone fences have thin shims between the big rocks on both sides of the fence so the rocks will slope into the middle and support each other. I admired the good standing houses built in the traditional style and ways, but I learned more from the old-timers that were crippled over to one side with their ribs showing and their blank eyes staring. They were houses unadulterated, with all their sins and blemishes apparent, showing how the maker put them together in the beginning. Sometimes the chinking still showed the marks of fingers and palms, and old worried boards revealed bent square nails with cuss words still on them.

Remnants of folk architecture.

Old houses—decayed, crumbling, propped—are not dead things when you sit down and visit with them. Their lives might be over as far as providing comfort and cover, but their past is rich in all the life and living and sinning and dying that they had sheltered. They've seen the elephant and heard the owl. When they finally do go, the old chimney stands for a while like a tombstone over the house place till time and vines drag it, too, into the dust from whence it came.

Deep East Texas and the Hill Country were the richest in traditional houses. I could have worn my camera out taking pictures of East Texas log barns. That part of the state still has a lot of traditional building, because people were still building with logs and in the old styles through the 1930's and 1940's. And those log buildings that were built in the nineteenth century out of fat pine will be there till somebody pushes them over. The Germans of the Hill Country built the best and sturdiest houses, mostly rock, some out of cedar logs, and one could spend a lifetime savoring the work of those master builders. I didn't find many old houses and farm buildings in the Panhandle. They were probably used up during the Depression and the Dust Bowl. While I was there I wound my way through pastures to our old ranch house on the Washita, and all that was left was the blacksmith shop, the concrete horse trough, and my grandmother's Great Majestic wood cook stove. I looked for a piece of myself among the debris, but nothing was there except the sound of the wind that dusted the old place out in the thirties.

The old things are usually kept where land and property are handed down. People that belong to an area keep the things of their families' and their culture's past; new people clean out for a fresh start.

A preface should be placed at the end of the book rather than at the first because the editor writes the preface after he's built the book, and he's usually mulling over the whole job to see what he learned and whether it was worth all the fuss. It was worth it. I discovered the new and revisited the old and learned again the deep love I have for this land and the life upon it. I'm too much in love with the present to worship the past, but I do respect it mightily. The old folks have planted the vines from which we gather the grapes, and the stock is still strong and the fruit is sweet.

The Texas Folklore Society got a lot of help from its friends with this volume. The contributors, of course, are the stars of the production and we genuinely appreciate their labors.

Because of the size of this book and the ever increasing production costs, we had to have financial assistance from the outside. We thank the following foundations and individuals for their help, and we want them to know that we couldn't have made it without them: the Moody Foundation, the George and Mary Josephine Hamman Foundation, Southland Paper Mill Foundation, The Harris and Eliza Kempner Fund, Buddy and Ellen Temple, Time Incorporated, and a generous Society member. And I could not have run all over the state looking and taking pictures without a much appreciated faculty research grant from Stephen F. Austin State University. The Society is ever in debt to those foundations and individuals who have come to its aid and made its spending less deficital.

For their continuing support of the Texas Folklore Society on the Stephen F. Austin State University campus, the Society thanks President William R. Johnson and Roy E. Cain, head of the department of English. And may the sun and moon shine ever brightly on the Society's secretary and assistant editor, Mrs. Martha Dickson, who does the hard work that turns ideas into realities.

Francis Edward Abernethy
Nacogdoches, Texas
April 19, 1979

Built in Texas, the 1970 publication.

BUILT IN TEXAS

Man is naturally and genetically a builder, continually struggling to plumb and square life into an order that he can cope with. He builds books out of words, songs out of sounds, and he goes into the big woods of his old beliefs, cuts and dresses the logs, and dovetails them together into new religions. He takes whatever is in the lumber pile of his culture and shapes it into traditional forms. His folk art and philosophies and religions are shelters he has constructed to protect himself from the harsher elements of life and from the slings and arrows of the fortune that rages out about him. He builds his barns and bungalows and material needs for survival from the same sorts of sources and for the same reason, for protection from the disorder that nature and life subject him to. Walling, fencing, and impounding are fundamental to life and fundamental to preserving the order that is necessary for survival. The walls might be individual or social, chain-linkly literal or morally figurative, but they constitute bounds within which life began and within which society was able to continue. And they are our folklore.

Everything begins with walls. The nervous, throbbing life that we evolved from and still relate to began with a walled-off cell of impounded protoplasm, fenced in so that it could not escape. Then the cell wall became a wall of cells and later a chitin-plastered house sheltering a family of cooperating cells. As life became more affluent it shingled the roof and walls with scales and later thatched the house with feathers or finished it with fur. And there we stood and still stand, unadulterated and slightly embarrassed, before our bathroom mirrors in a house fine enough for a god. The modesty imposed by our culture and the raw sport of nature require that we cover one wall with another; so, like the old German that sophisticatedly plastered over the original limestone rock of his house or the Anglo that framed his log cabin in with more fashionable board and batten, we veneer our originality with Hart, Schafner and Marx.

The lower animals are the primal "folk builders," instinctively rather than traditionally using the materials and methods and following the forms of their ancestors. Like the folk, they build utilitarian structures of naturally available materials to provide a place to produce and protect their young and to shelter them from the elements. The dirt dauber builds his neat little house out of mud. Beavers cut and stack sticks and logs into island huts. Roadrunners throw a stick nest together like the poorest type of white trash, while the fashionable oriole meticulously hangs and weaves its scrotum-like home out of the finest sorts of horse hair, moss, and leaves. That which the animal builds is purely functional, every angle and corner of roof and wall and floor. This satisfies a basic characteristic of folk architecture.

Man in his dim beginnings lived in much the same way as did his animal kinsmen, crawling into holes and caves for shelter, stacking rocks across a cave entrance for protection, burrowing down in the deep grass like deer, living as a part of his environment, sometimes barely softening it with walls. But he became what sociologists refer to as the folk and became a folk builder, constructing his walls with what was at hand, rocks into huts, skins and hides into teepees, posting logs side by side, like trees growing, to make a palisade wall, and covering all with palmetto leaves. The Bushmen of the Kalihari have a way of teepeeing a clump of tall grass by twisting it together at the top that will wall out some of the night's cold. A Mexican with a machete can quickly build a shelter out of a few sticks and banana leaves that will roof out the rain. And an Eskimo, almost as quickly, can cut and stack blocks of ice, sealed with snow, into an igloo that will keep out some of the bone-chilling cold.

The early builders in Texas followed the same patterns of living and building. The Morrises, moving from Mississippi to Fisher County in the 1860's spent their first winter in a cave on the bluffs of the Clear Fork of the Brazos. Ben Abernethy proved his claim in Old Greer County living in a dugout. Those settlers who tarried on the timbered lands of East Texas built with the readily available pine logs in the traditions of their fathers; those in the Western Cross Timbers used oak. European migrants into central Texas stacked rocks into houses in the fashions learned in the Old Country. West Texans of the Pecos, who had neither rocks nor logs to build with, mixed mud and grass, made adobe brick, and built in traditions borrowed from the Mexican-Indian population already settled there. These were the folk, building out of the environment, wasting nothing, building forms to suit their needs.

This purest type of folk building blends with its surrounding as closely as the homes of the animals the folk lived among. The log house with stick-and-mud chimney and puncheon floor was as natural to the forest world that it was a part of as the nest of a bird. The sod shanties and dugouts of the plains were as much a part of the landscape as prairie dog mounds, and both men and dog shared his home with the rattlesnakes and spiders and centipedes of the prairie.

A variety of materials and structures.

Those early Texas settlers were conscious of their primitive homes and their vulnerability to nature, and they certainly were not living in the primitive manner just to be colorful. If given a choice between a log house and an aluminum-sided trailer house, they would probably have chosen the latter. They planned to do better as soon as possible. They left us some of their reflections in the folk music they sang about themselves and their surroundings. The legendary Tom Hight sings about his home in Old Greer County, Texas, in a traveling folk song sung to the tune of "The Irish Washerwoman." Tom reportedly went to Greer County in the 1880's, suffered much under trying circumstances, and then resigned his claim and returned to civilization. Tom probably lived in a half-dugout. That is, he dug a room down about four feet, built walls from ground level up two or three more feet, covered it with boards or logs, and sodded it over with turf.

> My house is built out of natural soil,
> The walls are erected according to Hoyle,
> The roof has no pitch but is level and plane,
> And I always get wet if it happens to rain.

Tom also commented on his closeness to nature and to the creatures of nature that he shared his home with.

> How happy am I when I lay down to bed,
> A rattlesnake hisses a tune at my head,
> A gay little centipede all without fear
> Crawls over my pillow and into my ear.

One particular city-bred Easterner who came west in search of fame, fortune, and adventure sang his song about "The Little Old Sod Shanty" to the tune of "Little Old Log Cabin in the Lane," a popular minstrel song of the 1880's and '90's. The distance that lay between the dream and the reality was emphasized by the contrast between the pastoral and ideal Log Cabin in the Lane and the starkly uncomfortable and lonesome sod shanty on the claim on the Texas frontier.

I'm getting mighty weary now just holding
down my claim.
My vittles are not always of the best.
The mice creep shyly round me as I lay me
down to rest
In my little old sod shanty on my claim.
The hinges are of leather and the windows
have no glass,
And the board roof lets the howling blizzard in.
I can see the hungry coyote as he creeps up
through the grass
In my little old sod shanty on my claim.

Housing was easier to come by in East Texas where tall, straight, rich pine grew, ready for hacking and hewing and being laid into walls. But the log house, as romantic as it might seem to be now, was not so to the people of the settled and civilized South who had graduated to houses of brick and milled lumber. A come-all-ye that had as its burden a warning to all young ladies who were considering going west with a Texan is called "Louisiana Girls." The song begins with a warning about Texans generally, about their uncouth manners and dress, and then describes the living conditions.

They'll take you to a house with hewed log walls,
And it ain't got no windows at all,
An old board roof and a puncheon floor,
It's that way all Texas o'er.
It's that way all Texas o'er.

The journals of early Texans give an even more graphic description of the folk building of the early settlers, many of whom had never built any kind of housing before. They were able to get help and do better or, discouraged, return to the Old Country.

One group of Polish settlers who came directly from their homes in Upper Silesia to Texas arrived in December, 1854, and during that first winter, as one settler put it, "We lived in burrows covered with brush and stalks."[1] The Poles continued to live close to nature and the wild life that they shared it with even after they built their first year's huts in Panna Maria. Father Leopold Moczygemba tells about entertaining friends in his home and a rattlesnake falling through the grass roof and landing on the dinner table.[2]

Caroline von Hinuber tells about her first home in Industry, which her German family occupied through the winter of 1831–32:

> After we had lived on Fordtran's place for six months [Charles Fordtran, a tanner from Westphalia], we moved into our own house. This was a miserable little hut, covered with straw and having six sides, which were made out of moss. The roof was by no means waterproof, and we often held an umbrella over our bed when it rained at night, while the cows came and ate the moss. Of course, we suffered a great deal in the winter. My father had tried to build a chimney and fireplace out of logs and clay, but we were afraid to light a fire because of the extreme combustibility of our dwelling. So we had to shiver.[3]

Ferdinand Roemer described the first houses of the New Braunfels Germans in 1846 as hovels made of cedar posts set side by side, palisade style, and roofed with tent cloth or buffalo hides.[4] Frederick Olmsted described the German-Alsatian settlement of D'Hanis in Medina County as

> a most singular spectacle upon the verge of the great American wilderness. It is like one of the smallest and meanest of European peasant hamlets. There are about twenty cottages and

hovels, all built in much the same style, the
walls being made of poles and logs placed together vertically and made tight with clay mortar, the floors of beaten earth, the windows
without glass, and roofs built so as to overhang
the four sides and deeply shade them, and covered with thatch of fine brown grass laid in a
peculiar manner, the ridge-line and apexes being ornamented with knots, tufts, crosses or
weathercocks.[5]

Father Claude-Marie Dubuis, a Catholic missionary came to
Castroville in 1847, and wrote a letter home describing his first
rectory.

. . . I was solemnly installed in the house set
apart for the Missionary. Without delay I will
describe it to you. The walls consist of several
stakes driven into the ground and the little
grass thrown above formed the roof. No need
of doors or windows, the whole building was
pervaded by daylight. A few dozen scorpions
mingled with myriads of insects had been do-
miciled there and formed the only furnishings,
with the exception of a cowhide on which I
could expect the repose of a sybarite.[6]

Life and building methods improved, and Carl Urbantke tells
about building a house in later, more settled times. He built his first
Texas home near Millheim, Washington County, in the mid-1850's.

At last everything was prepared for the building of a house. Logs, rafters, boards, all dressed
with the ax; also several thousand shingles,
made from logs of the Spanish oak. My friend
Wilm let me use his wagon and mules, with

which I hauled it all to my building site. In
the erecting of the house we helped each other. Logs, sixteen feet long, were notched at
the ends and joined together. In this manner
the four walls were made, into which open-
ings were cut for the doors and windows.
The cracks between the logs were filled with
a mixture of clay and dry grass. The floor was
two feet above the ground and was built, like
the walls, of wood and clay. In this manner a
strong log house was erected, sixteen by sixteen feet, with a porch on the south side, and I
had no expense whatsoever except what I paid
for the nails I used on the roof.[7]

The first houses, especially of the European settlers, were poorly
primitive because the people had neither the skills nor the individual
traditions to build with. They soon were able to adapt to their new
environment, use the traditional forms and building methods from
some of their own craftsmen, blend with the Anglo and Mexican
traditions which they encountered, and establish ways of building
that provided comfortable and enduring shelters.

Man builds because he has to. He has to have a den to protect him
from the elements and from predators, a warren in which he feeds and
breeds and shelters his family. Like the lower animals, he requires order.
His order, however, is not just a familiar place to flee to, but one that
reflects and satisfies his culture's traditional forms and fashions. His
house must be comfortable to the eye as well as to the body. He also
has a need for symmetry. Balance of form, whether round or rectan-
gular, satisfies this need for order. This drive, or instinct, is stronger in
some than it is in others, but in the true builder a violation of plumb-
ness and squareness, of straight, true, and round in his own work is a
continuing aggravation, like an old sin committed but never paid for.

A simple log home.

Folk building is still going on, though not always in the ways of our ancestors. Early Texans lived in dugouts only as long as they had to. When lumber became available they moved out of the ground and into houses with floors and shingle roofs, still built, however, in a traditional style. The old log and rock houses became barns when people could afford something better or when transportation facilities allowed them to move into towns. As the old slipped or began to decay, the useable materials were used to build other out-buildings. The Texas countryside is covered with homes that were demoted from housing people to housing hay. As the buildings deteriorated further they were patched with whatever tin was handy (Old Prince Albert cans and license plates are considered to be the best patches for rat holes.), with parts of other buildings, or shored against further decay with asbestos shingles or composition siding. The owner does whatever is necessary to keep a shelter in service a few more years. When the building finally groans and falls under the weight of ice or snow or the force of a strong wind, the useable material is pulled to make hog pens and chicken houses or to make patching for other buildings suffering the inevitable vicissitudes of old age. A man keeps building with old materials just as rats and mice take parts of old nests to make new ones.

Folk building is primarily utilitarian, and keeping a building functional as long as possible is as much a part of the folk building process as hewing the logs or quarrying the stone for the original structure. Sealing wall cracks with split-out cardboard boxes and papering the walls with newspapers is part of the continual building process that is done in a traditional manner. Door hinges made from the leather of old shoes and porch posts wired at a crack with baling wire is a part of the continuous process of folk building. A home is never finished. Like the body, it starts breaking down almost as soon as it is born, and the responsibility of the man of the house is to keep it wired, propped, and patched as long as it is useful. The folk process is in operation as long as he is using available materials. This doesn't mean available from the hardware store, lumber yard, or mail-order catalog, but from the materials that naturally accumulate around a house place: old telephone poles and railroad ties—cables, chains, and baling wire—combine belts, binder twine, and tin.

People know about building things from tradition and experience. They know to put the wire on the inside of a fence post so that an old cow leaning through to graze on the other side won't spring out the staples. They know, because their elders told them, to put the boards on the inside of a crib's stud wall so that the weight of the corn or the grain won't pop the walls off. They know by observation to put the fireplace on the north wall so winter's norther will ease the heat south through the house. And experience taught them to build their outhouses far enough from the house— but not too far—and to station the wood pile by the well-worn path so that one trip could serve two purposes.

Most folk building is found in the country and in small towns or on the urban margins, because that is where a person can build without reference to his peers. There he does not have to conform to building codes, zoning laws, or the tastes, standards, and styles set by urban neighbors. Plastic urbanity limits traditional building not only by style and space but by economics. The urbanite works steadily so that he can hire somebody to house him with newly purchased and pre-fabricated materials. The rural or outskirts man with no regular income or time-limiting occupation builds and maintains because he has to.

Deciding who the folk are sometimes poses a problem and the term "folk" is often used with condescension. But more likely, they are those who are tossed into nature and can survive, those who can cope and make do with what they have to live and build with. They are those who don't have to send out for a plumber or electrician or carpenter everytime something breaks down. They are those who never throw away a piece of Strong Barn or a 2 x 4 because they know they will need it and use it eventually. The folk are also those who are kin to the land both in sympathy and ancestry, and they use the products of the land and the remnants of its past uses as naturally and comfortably as they use their hands.

A man knows that those things which he does for himself provide him with the richest rewards and the most satisfaction. The food he raises, the game he hunts and kills, the barn he designs and builds with his own hands—the products of these occupations are the offspring of his energy and his imagination. They are parts of his life and of his and his forefathers' traditions and are continuing proofs of his ability to survive. His building is a result of his own conception and is a tangible result of himself. And a shed that he builds for himself will always mean more to him and to his people than the prefabricated aluminum garage hauled in and jointed together by strangers.

Noah must have been mighty proud of the Ark.

Notes

1. T. Lindsay Baker, "Panna Maria and Pluznica: A Study in Comparative Folk Culture." *The Folklore of Texan Cultures,* PTFS XXXVIII (Austin: Encino Press, 1974), 206.
2. Ann Carpenter, "O Ty Polshi!," *The Folklore of Texan Cultures,* PTFS XXXVIII (Austin: Encino Press, 1974), 206.
3. Caroline von Hinuber, "Life of German Pioneers in Early Texas," *Texas State Historical Association Quarterly,* II, No. 3 (Jan., 1899), 229.
4. Ferdinand Roemer, *Texas,* Oswald Mueller, trans. (San Antonio: Standard Printing Co., 1935), p. 93.
5. Frederick Law Olmsted, *Journey Through Texas* (Austin: Von Boeckmann-Jones Press, 1962), p. 170.
6. Claude M. Dubuis, "Texas Recollections: A Letter from Castroville: 1847," *The Kountze News (March* 1, 1978), p. 6.
7. Carl Urbantke, *Texas Is the Place for Me* (Austin: The Pemberton Press, 1970), p. 24.

Building log homes in the 21st Century.

I'll Sing You a Song

Album cover for the East Texas String Ensemble.

PREFACE

[from *Singin' Texas*, Texas Folklore Society Extra Book #18, 1983]

Singing is as natural to some people as scratching a tick bite—and just as compelling. They catch the rhythm of their walk and hum or think a song to go with it. They sing to the click-clack of windshield wipers. And a mood switched on by a beat or a breath of wind or a good looking woman yearns for expression in a howl or a moan or a shout. Some people have to sing. They don't have to sing to somebody; they sing to and for themselves. They sing to express joy and to get a little beauty in the monotony of their lives or to jack themselves out of despair or to make the blues bearable. They love and they want to groan because of the ache of it, but they sing "Born to Lose" instead. This is why, like the poor, music will always be with us, and folk music has been with us longer than any other.

Theoretically folk music could go back to man's animal beginnings and to his animal kinfolk. The rooster crows the message that he is in control of his territory. The coyote howls out his challenge to other dog coyotes that might be considering moving in on his ground. And the range bull rumbles and bellows his warning to those who might be thinking about invading his harem and domain. The sounds that these male animals make when they are announcing their mastery of their territories are not the sounds they make under ordinary circumstances. These are their songs, and they have a recognizable structure and some melodic variation. The male animal sings "This Is My Country!" and tells the world that he is the king of his mountain; the female who is sexually ready sings back "I'm in the Mood for Love," and like Nelson Eddy and Jeanette McDonald they are in business. Man, in his own bestial beginnings, probably had a special sound, a song, which announced to the world that he had staked his claim. The female who was prepared to join him sang a reply. The sounds they made evolved with them into songs, and because these animals became folk, these were folk songs.

Technically speaking folk music is that large repository of tunes, beats, songs, and ballads that take their origins in the forgotten or dimly remembered past and that have been shuffled along from one generation to another until they have arrived at our time. Nobody knows who wrote the song, and how it got to this point in time and space is interesting but irrelevant. The main thing about a folk song is that it is a survivor. It has qualities that have given it a lasting power. Its importance does not lie in the fact that it is old, but in the fact that it has survived all the changing tastes, moralities, and movements to reach us at this time.

Folk song is alive and always growing, and it is continually being reinterpreted by its singer, to whom the song belongs. Its opposite is the copyrighted art song, which is static and unchanging. The music, the arrangement, and the lyrics of an art song are more important than a singer's interpretation. An orchestra plays art music, with each instrumentalist following the score down to the last printed note. A jazz band plays art music in the folk style and takes the music away from the author and the score and makes the song its own, each musician playing in and around the notes, slurring, bluesing, giving it the beat to suit his own personal feelings about the song. Order is maintained by a general agreement about the tune the musicians are playing. This tune that stays in the back of each player's mind keeps the music from being what a purist would define as folk music, because the latent tune is an ordered and unchanging form, always remaining the same. The handling of the music, however, is folk, because it is dynamic, seldom the same twice, always the expression of the interpreter, not the author.

The songs in this book are folk songs of one degree or another. Some are unquestionably folk songs because they are so old that there is no historical way to tell the who-what-when-where-and-why about them. Others can be traced back to a single source, but their history has been their evolution in the hands of the people after that. A few of the songs are relatively new and are still in the process of being absorbed.

Therefore, the dialogue "Is that a folk song?"—"Well, I never heard a horse sing it!" is apocryphal and doesn't answer the question, but it is relevant. Folk music includes songs that the folk sing so long and so much that it becomes theirs. They don't sing away a copyright or a man's name on a piece of printed music, but they eventually sing away the exact tune and the exact words and begin substituting notes and words that more accurately describe their feelings. The last rendition will be something different from what the original author intended and will be the property of the folk. The songs in this book are the property of the folk of Texas and the Southwest.

This is a personal book because folk music is personal. The folk sing a personal expression of some part of their lives, and the song is a part of their own pasts and their people's past. Most of the songs in this collection are mine because I inherited them from my people and from my part of Texas.

The purpose of this book is to show that folk music is a strong part of our history and of the continuity of our own lives. Much of it is trite and maudlinly sentimental and some appeals to our basest interest in blood violence and the sensational, but all of it is a reflection of the values of our own history. The study of song is the study of the singer, and both bind us inextricably to a past that is still as operative on our lives as our livers and lights.

Singing at a hootenanny.

I got more folk music from my grandfather, Ben Abernethy, than from anyone else. I don't mean that he taught me music. But he was walking music. Grandad was short and gentle with a big black hat and high topped shoes, and he had a ranch on the Washita River in the Texas Panhandle. He wore his shirt buttoned at the collar and his sleeves rolled down even during the summer. This was during a time when I wore only a pair of pants or overalls, so I considered it a strange phenomenon. And he whistled and sang. His whistle was usually kind of light and dry and windy, but it could be stacatto sharp, and he could and did whistle everything he had ever heard fiddled, favoring "Black-Eyed Susie" and "Cotton-Eyed Joe." I don't guess I ever heard him sing a song all the way through, but he would cut into the chorus of "Rosin the Beau" or "Willis in the Ballroom" or maybe sing the first couple of lines to "Sally Goodin" and then whistle—or wind whistle without really making a whistle—the rest of the tune. Sometimes we would be walking down one of the pasture trails and he would be thinking a song and go into a shifty little dance he called the pigeon's wing. Grandad had all kinds of music working in him, and it rubbed off on the people around him.

Grandad and a two-foot stack of Victrola records were my earliest musical education. Those records had gone through no telling how many Panhandle dust storms, and I don't ever remember buying new needles, but they would play. We had a lot of Vernon Dalhart records. "The Wreck of the Old 97" was my favorite. The Skillet Likkers—Gid Tanner, Riley Puckett, Fate Norris, and Clayton McMitchan—led the rest both in quantity and quality. They had the same strength and vitality in their "Crow Black Chicken" and "Prettiest Little Gal in the County" that one can find in the best bluegrass and country music nowadays. And there were a goodly number of weepers in the stack, songs like "The Vacant Chair" and "I's Gwine Back to Dixie."

Most of the folk music I have collected in the field hasn't been of this Victrola quality. It wouldn't sell. I play some of it for students in folklore classes and their reaction is amusement first, then boredom. Most of the singers who can be classified academically as "folk" have very little trained talent. They sing for their kids and their kinfolks and their friends, and everybody thinks they are great because they love them, and anything they did would be good. But they won't make it in the entertainment world.

I haven't known a lot of real folk singers but I have known some, and the main thing I have always felt about their singing was that they were singing about experiences that they and their people had had or could have had. When John Radcliff sang "Raise Big Taters in Sandy Land" at a Josey party near Fred, Texas, I felt that he had done just that and knew what he was singing about. When Ada Williams sang a sad old love ballad about a lady standing in her garden and meeting a man who turned out to be her long-lost lover who was supposed to have died in the Civil War, I felt that this was an imaginary part of her own life or of her dreams that had become a part of her life.

Folk songs don't always come out that way, however. A student where I used to teach left our college for the more exciting atmosphere of The University of Texas. One year and several guitar lessons later she returned to East Texas and tried to impress the locals by singing mountain ballads and songs with a hillbilly twang.

After that she switched to blues rock and did well, but her mountain music was bad. She and the Kingstons and the Brothers and the Peters and Pauls can do what they want to with the traditional songs. That is one of the perils in a folk song's life, to be strangely handled. But they are not making folk music; they are just singing folk songs. Their experiences, education, and cultural levels are too far from the content of the song for it to have real meaning for them. They are trying to be somebody else, to sing like somebody else, and the result is phony. Folk music is a sincere and personal statement, and nothing kills the spirit of folk music as much as a showbiz personality turning on the charm for a dilettante audience. It lacks maturity, and folk singers, like folk songs, have to get ripe.

I've come by most of the songs in *Singin' Texas* honestly. That is, they are either songs I've grown up and lived with or they are songs that I have collected from folks who have. I knew some of the songs all the way through. I had to go to friends and books to piece out others. Nearly everybody knows the first verse to "Little Joe the Wrangler" and "When the Work's All Done This Fall," but a slim few can sing those songs to their ends—and there are slim few audiences that will happily sit through all those verses. What I was trying to do in putting this book together was to get the best known or most representative or the most classically Texas traditional songs and set them in some social and historical framework. I wrote what I thought was most interesting about the songs and hoped that others would feel the same way.

I grew up with all kinds of music, mainly the big band sound of the Thirties and Forties—Miller, James, the Dorseys, Woody Herman—and like most of my generation I "forgot" the country music that had been my earliest education. Religion kept me honest, however, and I thank the Baptist Church for conditioning me with the long standing traditional Protestant church music and harmonies, which like the Bible and Shakespeare are foundations for Southern culture. During high school Bobby, Perry, Blondie and I learned the joys of four-part barbershop singing. We had a big reunion after the war on Thanksgiving in 1946 and listened to the Army-Navy game and drank heavily and sang long and re-bound ourselves together for life. We swing band enthusiasts of the early Forties looked down on the honky-tonk hillbilly music that was the sound of the Depression, but like church music it was a conditioner, and those exciting sinful times in countyline honky-tonks were always drunk to the tune of a hillbilly song. During the war we all got nostalgic to country music because for some reason the old country songs sounded more like home than the sound of Stan Kenton.

I bought a Stella guitar with money I made shrimping in the summer of '46, and the only songs that would go with the C, F, G7 chords that I made were country songs. I started fresh because my generation didn't play stringed instruments and sing along; we listened to records and danced. During graduate school a group of us gathered periodically and blew off steam with a little pickin'. I started playing regularly, along with other folk song revivalists, during the Fifties and Sixties, both for ballad lectures in classes and for programs. I played and sang the old songs I had long known or church music, along with the ballads and folk songs that were included in every college text. Pickers and singers gathered regularly to play at the Tap Room of Beaumont's King Edward Hotel and we swapped a lot of songs. Climaxing the folk music revival for me was my association with the Texas Folklore Society and its annual hootenannies. I heard a lot of traditional music on those Thursday and Friday nights from Brownie McNeill, Americo Paredes, John Q. Anderson, John Lomax, and Hermes Nye, to name a few. What academic interest I have in folk music sprang from these associations.

The largest factor in my musical life and education has been the East Texas String Ensemble (pronounced "in-symbol") in which I have sung and played dog-house bass for the past fourteen years. After a lot of party pickin', four of us liberal arts faculty members fortuitously jelled in 1968 into a sound that we enjoyed making. Charles Gardner was the focus. He had picked up stringed instruments from his father and played anything and knew all the old songs. Charles played lead fiddle and mandolin. Stan Alexander played a strong guitar and sang a wealth of traditional folk and country songs. Stan had started a folk music club at North Texas that included such modern musical lights as Steve Fromholtz and Michael Murphey. When he was at The University of Texas he was a Threadgill regular along with Janis Joplin and Bill Malone. Tom Nall played banjo and guitar and was just getting into traditional music. Tom had been raised on big bands and cool jazz, which he still plays, and moved into a new world with country and western.

The East Texas Strings have been together for fourteen years now and have and still are weathering personality traumas and menopause, but the musical times we've had together have been some of the richest moments of our lives. We've played everywhere—churches, schools, country clubs, art museums, honky-tonks, rock festivals, back yards, front porches, a spate of festivals from Galveston to El Paso, and topping them all we've played the Texas Folklife Festival in San Antonio every year since its beginning. We entertained the Chinese ambassador, played the Fourth of July party at the American Embassy in Guatemala City, and did a State Department tour of Honduras. We can play five hours with damn few breaks and never repeat a song. The band is a continuing education.

A lot of East Texans were involved in my musical education. Brother Woodrow Wilson of Vidor and his daughter Neda introduced me to Sacred Harp music and I've loved those old sounds since the first time I heard them. The students of Kirby High School in Woodville introduced me to Josey parties and the songs of the play party tradition. The Williamses of the Big Thicket—Miss Ada and her daughter Lois Parker and Aunt Minnie—are all gone now but I can still hear them singing "Sweet Bunch of Daisies" and the old songs that were so close to their lives, which they made close to mine. Nowadays, any time I need to take a short course in traditional music, I drop in at Steve Hartz' Old Time String Shop on the square in Nacogdoches. If Steve and his partner Tom Cornett haven't struck up a tune, somebody will soon be along who will.

Dan Beaty, Regents Professor of Music at Stephen F. Austin State University, wins the gold star for assistance given in putting *Singin' Texas* together. Dan is a classical concert pianist who doubles in jazz and boogie and presently is involved in mind-boggling musical experiments in computer composing. He wrote this music from my singing, and the bad—but natural—thing about singing these songs is that you don't sing them the same way twice. Dan is a man of infinite patience and energy and he has my long-lived gratitude for these and other labors he has performed in my behalf.

I thank the research centers at Stephen F. Austin State University and Lamar State University for grant money to pay for tape and equipment and a lot of time driving and looking for singers and songs in East Texas. And I thank my wife Hazel and my children—Luanna, Robert, Deedy, Maggie, and Ben—for being the sweetest music in my life.

This book is dedicated to my grandfather, Benjamin McCluskey Abernethy, because he sang the songs I first remember. And it is dedicated to those who have given my life music by singing to me or with me—to all those who have kept the beat and have sung the close harmonies.

Francis Edward Abernethy
Stephen F. Austin State University
Nacogdoches, Texas

Ab Abernethy and Twitchy, his squirrel.

Men singing Sacred Harp music.

SINGING ALL DAY & DINNER ON THE GROUNDS

By the time we got to Harris Chapel the singing had already started. The Sacred Harp singers of this part of East Texas, near Marshall, had gathered for their one hundredth annual all-day singing and dinner on the grounds. The meeting house was large, white, many-windowed and frame, and it sat in a clearing near the community cemetery where old cedars stood. The parking area was shaded by post oaks, and surrounding all were the pines. Sam Asbury pretty well described the sound of a full house of Old Harp singers when he recalled, "The immediate din was tremendous; at a hundred yards it was beautiful; at a distance of a half mile it was magnificent." We parked somewhere in the "beautiful" range and could feel the music roll over us before it flowed away into the surrounding woods.

We went in with the guilt a city man feels from violating a time schedule, but there was no need to worry. There is no body of people more casual in their comings and goings than Sacred Harpers. Children wander about among their aunts and uncles, and there is frequent rotation among the members on the singing benches. They are as comfortable and unselfconscious with their singing as they are at their own supper tables.

We got ourselves situated and there was no doubt about it; we were, according to Asbury, in the "tremendous" range and those mighty Old Harp singers were pounding out their songs to the greater glory of the Lord.

Sacred Harp music—named from the 1844 songbook *The Sacred Harp*—has been preserved mainly by the Primitive Baptists, although in the beginning most of the lower churches in the South sang the same music. Even now many regular Sacred Harp singers are from denominations other than Primitive Baptist. The survival of the music and the tradition, however, has been dependent upon the beliefs and attitudes of the Primitive Baptists. They are fundamentalists who have followed their selected portions of the Bible to the letter and have arrived at a belief in predestination. For that reason they don't have revivals and they don't send out missionaries, and they are easy to be with. You don't have to worry about their trying to save you or get you to join the church. They leave matters of the soul to God, and a man is either saved or he isn't. To me this is a chancy philosophy that puts man's afterlife in the position of a pig in a poke, but the results of their belief in the doctrine of the elect is impressive in them. They move with a serenity that is born of confidence in a life to come that is more than the usual mouthings of the wishful thinkers, and I guess I envy them some.

Primitive Baptists are also called Hardshell Baptists because of the uncrackable shell of their beliefs, and foot-washing Baptists because of their observance of that little practiced ritual. Foot washing sounds sort of odd when you first think about their doing it in church. And I never will forget how one fine old lady down in the Thicket would rock and chuckle about how her mother used to wash her feet with bleach, trying to get them presentable for foot washing. But it's not funny when you are there. It is very moving and impressive. They kneel and wash their brother's feet and then embrace and ask forgiveness for the sins they might have committed against each other. At Appleby one Sunday toward the end of foot washing, everybody began singing "Amazing Grace," softly and with the characteristic Sacred Harp minor chords, and there wasn't a dry eye in the church.

The Hardshells don't have paid preachers or Sunday schools and they don't take up offerings and they don't have musical instruments. But they get along well enough without these adornments. The pastor sometimes preaches at as many as six different churches during the month's circuit, and he doesn't get a salary for it; he works at his regular job during the week. Instead of having Sunday school, the heads of the families are supposed to teach their children about the Bible. When the church needs money the elders let it be known how much and what for and the congregation scrapes it up among themselves. Or, if the church needs repairing, the members show up with their hammers and nails and fix it. And the main thing they don't have is a piano or organ or some other kind of mechanical music box. The Lord be eternally praised that they decided that "Singing with grace in your hearts to the Lord" meant that they were supposed to sing *acapella*. Otherwise some of the strongest and most beautiful music in the world would have been marred beyond measure.

The Harris Chapel Community, singing and eating.

The south end of the Harris Chapel meeting house was a raised platform with a pulpit or speaker's stand, depending on what the building was being used for at the time. The thirty or forty main singers sat two or three deep in a hollow square just below the platform, and the leader stood in the middle. They were divided into four groups. The altos sat with their backs to the platform. The basses sat to their right. Across from and facing the altos sat the leads (the soprano line), backed up by the audience, most of whom sang the lead with them. On the leads' right sat what they call the "tribbles" (the tenor, or treble, line). Except for the basses, all the singing parts were integrated, male and female. If some female were to show up, however, who sang a pretty good bass, she would probably be welcomed to that section.

The Harris Chapel singers were following the tradition: everybody got to lead two songs. The song leader finished his pair and called on his successor. A man arose from the bass section and asked whether number eighty-two had been "used" yet. It had not, so a stout gentleman in the "tribbles" sang the note names for the four parts: "Faw, sol, law, faw!" Everybody got his note, the leader's hand came down, and they began their musical march through "Bound for Canaan" as strongly as Cromwell's Puritan Roundheads descended on Charles' Cavaliers at Marston Moor, singing only the old Elizabethan fasola notes the first time around and then going into the words.

Compared to Sacred Harp singing, First Church music is water to wine. They sing with a power and a vitality and involvement that makes the song a living work of art. The sound is strong and the beat is regular and heavy, and the leader and most of the singers pound and saw the air in time to the beat. This is singer's music, not listener's. Those in the audience who don't sing, follow the song attentively, and many of them follow the words in their books. The singers don't sing to entertain or to pass a few minutes from the hour's meeting time. They sing their pleas and prayers directly to their God.

W. B. Yeats, in his poem "Sailing to Byzantium," said that when he died he wanted to come back, to live again, as a work of art. This to him was Nirvana, the highest point that man could reach. Old Harp singers are close to becoming a work of art. They blend themselves so completely with the sound and sense of the music that the singers become the song.

When the leader has lead his two songs he calls on another. Everybody gets to lead; it's both a duty and a privilege. Old men who can hardly sing any more are helped into the square by their loving fellows who help them once again make their musical affirmation of the grace that is their personal gift from God. The strong men sing stronger for them, and the old-timers sit down feeling that they are still helping roll the world along.

As to the music, beyond the fact that the doleful and Asiatic minor chords cause the music to differ from the conventional First Church sound, the tunes have an ancient heritage and the words have a definite philosophical cast of their own.

Most of the tunes are English, Irish, Scottish, and Welsh folk melodies. They originated somewhere in the lost past and have been handed down from one generation to another for hundreds of years. The tunes have shifted and changed with the times and the singers and have carried the burden of all sorts of secular songs before some preacher used them as the vehicle for his message.

Sacred Harp had its beginning during the time of the Great Revival on the southern upland and lowland frontiers at the end of the eighteenth century. The people involved were for the most part rural and illiterate, and they were reacting against the austerity of New England Calvinism and the tunelessness of Calvinist Psalm singing. Like the Wesleys in England, the frontier ministers had large and emotional congregations of Presbyterians, Baptists, and Methodists but no songs to sing. And they had to bolster their faith that there would be a better world hereafter if they could just get through the here and now. So the preachers and the versifiers took the tunes that the people did know, the folk songs that their ancestors had brought with them from the old countries, songs like "Barbara Allen," "Lord Randall," or "The Blue-eyed Stranger," and put holy words to the sinful songs. A Sacred Harp song that illustrates this parodying of folk music is called "Plenary," or "Hark! From the Tombs." It is still used by some Masonic groups as a funeral dirge, and is sung as a dead march to the Scottish folk tune of "Auld Lang Syne."

> Hark! from the tomb a doleful sound,
> Mine ears, attend the cry:
> "Ye living men, come view the ground
> Where you must shortly lie.
>
> *Chorus:*
> Where you must shortly lie,
> Where you must shortly lie,
> Ye living men, come view the ground
> Where you must shortly lie.

The words to "Plenary" are not over 150 years old, but the folk tune goes back several hundred years, and the *memento mori*, remembrance-of-death theme was old in the Middle Ages.

This *memento mori* theme is characteristic of Sacred Harp music, and that separates it as much as anything I can think of from modern music, church or otherwise. The only ones who keep reminding us of our eventual and inevitable trip to the grave are the insurance salesmen. We don't concern ourselves much about the hereafter, and we think as little as possible about the death that every man owes life. As a result, maybe we have lost some of life's seasoning. Eternal night or a live-long day would be as boring as thoughts of an everlasting Paradise. What makes October so sweet and beautifully mellow is our knowing that the year is nearing the end of its time. And life is precious in a direct ratio to our knowledge of its ephemerality. You have got to know death if you want to give life its due.

The words of the Old Harp songs are often sad and mournful. The verses, many of them, were written by people who knew too much of this world's suffering because they lived on land that was barely subdued. They weren't romanticizing when they wrote, "Time . . . Swift as an Indian arrow flies." The Southerners who formed the Sacred Harp tradition were those strong and violent natures that made up the first waves of all frontiers. They were emotionally forceful or they wouldn't have started out in the first place, and they couldn't have stuck in the second. As a result of the harsh land they lived in, the death that roamed swiftly among them, and their own tumultuous spirits, they lived lives that teetered on the edge of catastrophe. They felt themselves buffeted in a world where they seemed to have very little control, so their philosophy became fatalistic. "Whatever will be, will be," they said, repeating the philosophy of their Anglo-Saxon ancestors in the time of Beowulf; and because they had no control over the awful powers of nature and life, they handed the responsibility over to their God. They decided that since they had a hard time winning in this world, they had better start counting heavy on the next.

SWEET RIVERS

A few more days or years at most
My troubles will be o'er,
And I shall join that heav'nly host

On Canaan's peaceful shore.
My happy soul will drink and feast
On love's unbounded sea;
The glorious hope of endless rest
Is pleasing news to me.

There are some Hallelujah songs like "When the Roll Is Called Up Yonder," most of which came in as part of the camp meeting revivals, but even these are shouts of joy because of the pleasures of the expected world to come.

About eleven o'clock some of the throats tired and a lady in the altos sent her daughter up on the platform to get a sack of Christmas candy to pass out among the singers. The little girl, who was small and solemn and about four years old knew the way. I had camped by the pulpit with my tape recorder, and she had already made about thirty trips to the candy sack, each time getting just one, poking it in her mouth like a chipmunk, and very seriously handing me the cellophane wrapper to dispose of.

We sang till noon and then moved out to the long tables that were situated in a pine grove just north of the meeting house. The women had been drifting out to the tables before the singing stopped, so by the time we got there, the boxes and baskets had been unpacked and the tables were spread with food. I have as yet to go to a dinner on the grounds where there wasn't enough food to feed the multitudes four times over, but if you are a visitor the ladies all worry that you won't get your plate filled soon enough: "You better hurry yourself or they'll eat it all up from you." The tables at Harris Chapel looked about a hundred feet long, and there wasn't a bare spot on them, to start off with at least.

We ate and stood around under the pines talking till after one o'clock. Small family groups wandered through the cemetery visiting their folks who had already crossed the sweet river. They'd stop by a long-gone uncle or aunt, talk about them, and lovingly pull the weeds from the grave site. One family settled under the shade of two huge cedars near the front of the cemetery and talked easily of the business and gossip of their kin. Finally, eight or ten of the singers drifted back to the meeting house and began singing, and they all followed the sound back inside, formed the square and started again as strongly as ever before.

Somewhere around three o'clock they began to taper off, and as we got to the end everyone became more reflective and personal about the songs. The leaders dedicated songs to their parents who slept among the old folks, or would comment how much they had enjoyed the singing that day. The presiding elder took the center as the last leader. He was an old man who had more friends and kinfolks on the other side than he had here. He said, "I'll welcome you back next year if I'm still here and if your health holds." Then they all stood and sang their final hymn, "Longing for Heaven," with hope and sadness. A prayer that humbly accepted all the workings of God, good or bad, closed the singing, and the brothers of the band embraced each other and the women hugged their sisters and children, and the sense of kinship was strong.

You probably won't be able to like this music the first time around. It's too different from the First Church sound that we are accustomed to. In time, its roots go back beyond our own musical training. And an understanding and appreciation of Sacred Harp requires something that our society plays down, and that is an understanding of suffering as a natural and endurable part of life. The marketplace would have its customers believe that they can avoid suffering if they have the right kind of car or if they keep smelling good and stay slim. And if things still go wrong they can take a tranquilizer or write Abby. The Old Harper believes that suffering is as much a part of life as sundown, and the only thing that helps is to recognize it and sing about it.

Promoting gospel music.

GIVE THE WORLD A SMILE EACH DAY

[Originally, photographs and text by Francis Edward Abernethy]

I've been doing some serious looking around in the world of religious music, and I believe that modern gospel music is pulling ahead of the rest. University campuses are fielding large groups of young people singing modern up-beat religious songs that have a cool sound and a lot of youthful exuberance, but both the songs and the singers need some seasoning before they can be considered as influential factors in church singing. My favorite religious music, Sacred Harp, hangs on with celestial tenacity, but it is rare and hard to find. I gave up on First Church singing years ago. Singing there is a formality presided over by huge multi-throated monsters of braying brass that drown out all attempts at human singing and the making of joyful noises. That leaves the field to gospel music and its singers, whose numbers are considerable and increasing.

Gospel music is hard to define for the non-gospel listener, but the Sunday singers know exactly what the music will be when they read that the county singing convention "urges all lovers of gospel music to attend" the fourth-Sunday singing. They know that gospel music is not "a passage from one of the four Gospels, chanted at Mass in monotone with inflections," as it is defined in the *Harvard Dictionary of Music.* And they know that they won't be singing spirituals "developed by the Negro during slave days" and in the repertoire of Mahalia Jackson, as explained in the *Encyclopedia of Popular Music.* The music of modern gospel singers had its beginning in Southern fundamentalism and is in the white singing tradition. Gospel doesn't have the soul that its old Granddaddy Sacred Harp has, but it has spirit and enthusiasm, and its message is one of happy optimism and the joy of God in this life.

Gospel music, like jazz, is easier to recognize than it is to define and describe. A sweet old lady asked Fats Waller to explain jazz to her, and he supposedly replied, "Madam, if you don't know by now, don't mess with it." That might apply to gospel, but you would miss some good sounds and enjoyable singing if you didn't mess with it. And the place to get acquainted with it is at a gospel singing convention.

The tradition of the gospel singing convention goes back about two hundred years to the "graduation exercises" of the late eighteenth-century singing schools. The singing schools, which began around 1770, were a reaction against the rather tuneless droning of the Puritan singing tradition. The singing school teachers set out to show just how much soul-stirring pleasure singing could be. The schools used religious songs in their practice, and after two or three weeks of intensive study, the participants met in the church on Sunday for one final all-day singing and dinner on the grounds.

The custom of meeting periodically for all-day singing continued, especially in the rural areas, after the popularity of singing schools waned. This custom was fostered in the nineteenth century mainly by the Baptists, Methodists, and Presbyterians, who in mid-century still used the four-note, singing school system (fa, sol, la, mi: an Elizabethan musical notation). The music they sang, which is now called Sacred Harp after the song book by that name, was mostly folk music with religious words. This music was fatalistically sad and was dominated by minor keys.

There was another kind of song in this Sacred Harp book which was to point the way to modern gospel music. This was the fuguing (fleeing) song, which is identified most closely with William Billings, a singing-school master before the Revolutionary War. The fuguing songs were songs whose melodic lines were based on traditional rounds, each singing part beginning and repeating a set phrase at a different time, but all parts concluding together. This play with notes and timing was like musical gymnastics and it was fun. It not only gave musical pleasure to the ear but afforded a certain amount of technical satisfaction also. Unlike the slow and mournful religious folk songs with which they were bound in the book, the fuguing songs were joyful and optimistic. They were also usually in a major rather than minor key.

Another step away from the original Sacred Harp tradition in singing was the introduction of the French seven-note scale (do, re, mi, fa, sol, la, ti, do) into religious music. Jesse Aiken in Philadelphia published his *Christian Minstrel* in 1846 with the seven-note system. The book became popular in the rural areas of the South and with it the seven-note system and a further movement away from the sad minor keys of Sacred Harp. But even though the music did change some, the custom of singing all day and having dinner on the grounds did not.

In the last half of the nineteenth and early twentieth century two religious song writers appeared who were to bring religious music one step nearer modern gospel music. These men were Ira Sankey and Aldine Kieffer. Like William Billings a hundred years earlier, they were concerned with the joy and play of tune and tempo. Under the influence of these two men and others who were moving in their direction, religious music in the early twentieth century became more optimistic and joyous.

This new mood in religious music was not brought about by the music. The music was merely the result of a more optimistic outlook than that which was held by the early pioneers and settlers of the mountains and the South. Those old timers had a hard time staying alive, and it is reflected in their music. Living was a lot easier by the turn of the twentieth century and the music showed it. Add to this the development and influence of popular music and jazz in the first twenty-five years of this century and the increasing use of musical instruments in the church and you have gospel music. You also have the beginnings of singing "conventions," which differ from the traditional all-day singing now held primarily by the Primitive Baptists.

The two men who were responsible for the spread and popularity of gospel music in the South were Virgil Stamps and J. R. Baxter, who organized the Stamps-Baxter Music Company in 1926. Their early publications had songs in the old style and in the regular First Church style, but the new gospel style became the most popular. This new music was joyful and easy to sing. It was lively and bouncy with a ragtime, syncopated off-beat; and it was accompanied by instruments, usually a piano. Guitars, bass fiddles, drums, and accordions show up frequently nowadays. Singing schools and quartets sponsored by the Stamps-Baxter Company were all over the Southwest, and anybody living in Texas in the 'thirties who listened to radio will remember the Stamps Quartet singing "Give the World a Smile Each Day."

The company began publishing what they called convention books in 1928. The first one was *Harbor Bells No. 1*. By 1933 they were publishing two books a year to be used by gospel singers in their conventions throughout the South. Although there are now many other gospel music publishing companies, Stamps-Baxter is still the dean. They continue to publish two convention books a year, and there is a gospel singing convention somewhere in East Texas just about every Saturday night and Sunday. Most of the songs in the convention books are new, and when people get together for a singing right after publication time the songs will be on their first time around. The dedicated singers frequently get together and woodshed some of the new songs before meeting time.

Although gospel music is in the Southern tradition it has been moving north rapidly since World War II with nomadic Southerners, and in its expanding popularity is taking its place alongside country-and-western music, a similar white Southern export. It is sung regularly in such Protestant churches as the Assembly of God, the Church of God, the Nazarenes, and Pentacostals. And it is the regular singing fare at homecomings and family reunions.

One of the most memorable musical evenings I ever spent was with the Big Thicket Gospel Singing Convention at Honey Island several years back. The singers met in a big white frame church house that by music time was packed to the walls and back to front. Gospel music invites and expands with musical accompaniment, and on this particular evening every gospel singer in the Thicket who had a stringed instrument was jockeying for space on the platform down front. There were four guitars, two of them amplified, an amplified bass and an oldtime bull fiddle, two accordions and a piano, and somebody had passed out tambourines to those who didn't know what to do with their hands. The sound of it all was loud enough to split a board, and if the Lord was listening to the first three or four numbers, He probably walked into the other room. About then, though, the musicians and the leader on stage began to get it all together and the singing audience began to get their second wind and confidence and thereafter they made many joyful sounds. I was stirred also by the fact that the amplified bass hit the resonant frequency of my church bench.

I like the sound and singing of gospel music best at the small county conventions that meet in rural schools or churches. I like the size and the personality of them. They, like most conventions, begin on Saturday night, open again around 9:30 or 10:00 Sunday morning, shut down for dinner on the grounds, and then close out with an afternoon session. They get in about eight hours of singing that way, which satisfies for awhile.

The Nacogdoches County Quarterly Singing Convention met at Martinsville this January under favored conditions. I guess that there are prettier places in the world than that country between Swift and Martinsville, but right off I don't know where they are. This January "fourth-Sunday singing" was a holy one. January Sundays, blessed or not by singing conventions, can be bone-chilling cold or windy or soggy with rain. This Sunday had been washed the night before and shone as brightly and warmly as that first morning in Eden's garden. And the promise of spring and new life was as strong as the hope for resurrection.

Small conventions are fairly loosely conducted, and that is another reason I prefer them to the large area conventions. They usually don't start on time. People get there around time, but this is a gathering of friends and kinfolks and people from the same part of the country with the same love of God and His church and His music. There is a lot of community here, and before singing the people have to greet each other and swap descriptions of the latest illnesses and infirmities and crops and cattle and who had babies and who got married and who died—all the solid information about the most important things that happen to people in a culture.

We met that morning in a small grade-school auditorium, around seventy-five of us. There was a sound system with four singing mikes and a piano mike, that might have helped some, but what made the music was the people. They came to sing because they liked to sing. Singing was as natural to them as talking and praying. And they came to sing because singing was a more fervent way to communicate with God than praying or testifying. Three or four women were the piano players, and they took time about or came up on invitation to accompany the singing. The piano, though, was there just to help out. It wasn't the main sound and it never was overbearing. I think that's usually the case with instruments and gospel singing. The sound of people singing is always more important than the musical instruments accompanying them. At the Big Thicket singing, no matter how loud the instruments were, the voices of the singers were always on top and always dominant.

The opening prayer that Sunday at Martinsville recognized the fact that many singers were attending their own churches and couldn't be there, and justified their own attendance (and consequent absence from their own churches) by the belief that they were worshipping Him just as devoutly in song as were their church-attending brethren. Then the president of the convention started the singing and continued it by calling up members to lead a song apiece. The songs they sang were pretty new to the singers because they were in the periodically published song books that had just lately come out. We used three books that morning in Martinsville, the latest Stamps-Baxter book and two more from a Cleveland, Tennessee, publisher. The Stamps-Baxter book, *Golden Songs of Glory,* was their golden anniversary (1926–1976) edition and was the most used of the three. That company has been publishing two books a year since 1933, with three-hundred-plus songs per book. That means that there are a lot of gospel songs still faintly vibrating on the air waves. Many of the singers could sight read. Most sang relatively; that is, they could tell by looking at the notes about how far to go up or down. And the parts were pretty traditional. After you've sung a bunch of gospel you know pretty well what your part is supposed to sound like.

There was little time between songs that morning. The leaders—young folks, middlers, and old—marched down to the front, announced which book they were using and what page the song was on, and they sailed into it. Sometimes the leader would call up another pianist or he might call up friends who would take parts and sing behind the mikes. Sometimes the leader would testify about what the songs meant to him or what God and the gospel had done for his life. Singing was a religious experience for most of them there, and the singers and the songs expressed an intense seriousness along with the joy and hope of their faith.

Everybody sang and the acoustics were good and I enjoyed it all. If I had a criticism of conventions, large and small, it would be that they seldom sing the old gospel standbys. It has been a long time since I heard "On the Jericho Road," or "I'll Fly Away" or "Just a Little Talk with Jesus" or "Take My Hand, Precious Lord." The next time I get called on to lead a song I'll spring one of those oldies on them.

The morning session at Martinsville concluded with specials by groups and individuals. The audience didn't sing. They just listened and enjoyed. When they finished we had prayer and then adjourned to the school cafeteria for dinner.

Gospel singing for everyone.

Although gospel music might be best sung and appreciated at the small county conventions, it reaches the most people in the cities and at the statewide conventions. Gospel concerts regularly pack in large audiences at the big city auditoriums to listen to "battles of song" between such groups as The Blackwood Brothers, The Singing Christians, The Happy Goodmans, the Four Galileans, and perennial editions of Stamps Quartets. During these concerts the audience listens, except when asked to join in or to rise and clap along with the music.

East Texas' main gospel convention is the Tex-La Neches Valley Singing Convention, which became forty years old in its third-Sunday meeting at Woodville in January, 1976. The convention was organized in 1936 and in the beginning consisted of gospel music singers from the seven counties along the Neches River, from Angelina County to Jefferson County. Other counties soon began joining and sending singers until all of Deep East Texas was represented. By 1941 gospel singers were drifting in across the Sabine from Louisiana, so the Convention added them to the membership and "Tex-La" to the title. At first the Neches Valley Singing Convention met four times a year, but the organization soon became so large that it had to reduce its schedule to meeting only twice annually. According to its press it is now the largest single gospel singing convention in the world. As many as 15,000 singers have attended and the average attendance is well over 5,000.

The several thousand who met in Woodville's ultra-modern high school auditorium for the Neches Valley Singing Convention have come a long way from the old-time all-day singing under a brush arbor. Conventions are a part of a big business, and in the foyers at the larger conventions the booksellers and record pluggers have their wares on display. There are electric cords everywhere running from microphones, speakers, tape recorders, radio hook-ups, electric organs, and amplified guitars. And the music comes out in all the recognizable modern beats. Some of the finest eight-to-the-bar boogie bass I have ever heard came from behind gospel music. Amplified guitars move from modern sweet love-ballad styles through country-and-western to rock-and-roll, taking Jesus on a modern gospel trip.

Unlike the Sacred Harpers' all-day singings or the small country conventions, much of the big-time gospel convention is entertainment with the audience looking up at the performers on stage.

During a particularly spirited piece or when some quartet hits an especially strong passage, the audience will show its appreciation by applause. Quartets and combos, family groups, robed choirs, combinations both professional and amateur have their time on the stage. At Woodville signs were noticeably posted warning the participants to make their remarks and book and record plugs short, and only at the time when they had the stage for a song. The gospel movement is modern and big because of its ability to incorporate the modern musical idiom into its religious framework.

Although the individual songs will go the way of all pop music, gospel music as a kind is here to stay. Or, it will stay as long as we are getting by as well as we are now. The music reflects the singer's joy in the good life that God gave him and in the life hereafter that He promised. It is optimistic and ebullient, and the singers almost dance in their chairs to the infectiousness of the beat.

But the basis of the pleasure is religious. One song leader began with the following remarks, which I think typify the gospel music mood and its religious appeal: "When you come to sing gospel music, you're supposed to be happy. Or if you aren't, the music will make you happy. It's happy because we're happy in the love and mercy of Jesus. We know that he has given himself so that the world can be a happy place when we love and believe in him. So let's sing about the joy and happiness Christ has given us."

And they do.

Hallelujah!

Lonnie Guerrero.

LONGINO GUERRERO'S CORRIDO ON J. FRANK DOBIE

The Texas Folklore Society met at the Driskill Hotel in Austin on April 16–17, 1965. This was a memorable meeting for me because I was president of the Society that year. My family and I were accorded the Jim Hogg Suite in honor of the occasion, and the children were much impressed. I remember the Saturday morning session very well because John O. West gave a paper on Jack Thorp and John Lomax that indicated that the latter had borrowed significantly from the former. John Lomax, Jr., was in the audience, and everybody got real quiet during the reading. Academic objectivity was maintained, however and fortunately, and no enmities were incurred.

The other thing I remember about that session was that Américo Paredes was accompanied by two of his corrido singing friends, Longino (Lonnie) Guerrero and Frank Rios. Américo gave brief introductory remarks on the corrido as a continuing and modern folk tradition and introduced the two musicians. They concluded the Saturday morning session singing two of Lonnie's latest corridos, "La Tragedia del Presidente Kennedy" and "El Corrido de J. Frank Dobie," also called "Homenaje a J. Frank Dobie." Kennedy had been assassinated in 1963 and Dobie had died in 1964, so these events were still fresh on members' minds.

During the 1960s Lonnie Guerrero wrote and recorded thirty-five songs. He continued his work in music, and in 1983, when he was sixty-seven years old, was inducted into the Tejano Music Hall of Fame as a singer and composer.

Américo Paredes.

The Frank Dobie corrido was not commercially recorded in 1965 but was taped and deposited in the folklore archives at the University. The tape has since disappeared, but I was able to locate Lonnie through Américo. Lonnie was seventy-four when I wrote him in 1991, and he was still picking and singing. He wrote on November 26, 1991, that he had read Dobie's stories of the Mexican border and wrote the corrido, with some help from Frank Rios, as a memorial to Dobie. Lonnie Guerrero very graciously allowed the Society to use his words and music, transcribed by Dan Beaty, in this publication.

EL CORRIDO DE J. FRANK DOBIE

by Longino Guerrero

Año del sesenta y cuatro, desde la altura del cielo,
Se recibio la noticia que conmovia al pueblo.
Herido de sentimiento, y sollozando he venido
Porque murio en Austin, Texas, un escritor conocido.

Refrain:
Una oracion en su nombre, pro el descanso de su alma;
Ha muerto Francisco Dobie, un hombre de mucha fama,
Un escritor renombrado por su lectura divina,
Y su cancion favorita fue siempre "La Golondrina."

Era costumbre de Dobie andar por los chaparrales,
Y conoció las espinas del mezquite y los nopales.
Entre los montes y valles su vida habia pasado
Fue partidario del campo como hijo de Coronado.

De muchos pueblos de Texas, el conoció los paisajes,
Y anduvo en muchas haciendas del valle del Rio Grande.
Allá en su rancho bonito, que le nombraba El Paisano,
Alli escribio muchos libros recordando al Mexicano
estribillo.

Refrain:
En sus novelas y hazañas el conocio mucha historia,
Desde la flor de la tuna, hasta la flor de magnolia;
Los Hijos de Coronado tendre mos en la memoria
Gratos recuerdos de un sabio, que semerece la gloria.
En el panteon del estado situado en la capital
Alli descansan los rostos del escritor inmortal.

THE CORRIDO FOR J. FRANK DOBIE

by Longino Guerrero

In nineteen hundred and sixty-four, from Heaven on high
There came the news that deeply moved everyone.
Full of sorrow, sobbing have I come
Because in Austin, Texas, a well known author has died.

Refrain:
Say a prayer in his name, for the repose of his soul;
Francisco Dobie is dead, a man of great renown,
A writer who was famous for his divine learning,
And his favorite song was "La Golondrina."

It was Dobie's custom to go about in the chaparral,
He was acquainted with the thorns of mesquite and cactus.
Among mountains and valleys he spent his life;
He loved the open country like a son of Coronado.

He knew the features of many Texas towns,
And he visited many haciendas in the Rio Grande Valley.
Down on his pretty ranch, which he called "El Paisano,"
He wrote many books in remembrance of the Mexican.

Refrain:
In his novels and his deeds he saw much history,
From the flower of the prickly pear to the magnolia blossom;
We children of Coronado will keep in our memory
Pleasant recollections of this wise man who well deserves his place in Glory.
In the state cemetery, located in the Capital,
There lie the remains of the immortal writer.

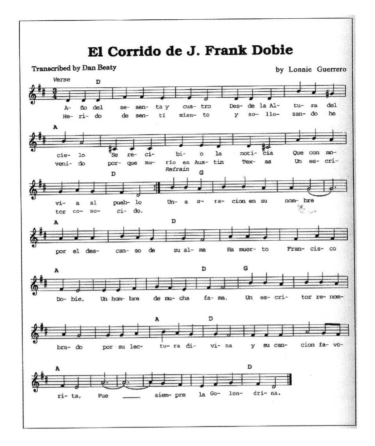

Guerrero's corrido for J. Frank Dobie.

A "Yellow Rose" songsheet.

THE ELUSIVE EMILY D. WEST, FOLKSONG'S FABLED "YELLOW ROSE OF TEXAS"

The purpose of this paper is to show how a haunt has crept into the hallowed halls of history and hopefully to exorcise it.

I am not an iconoclast. I love the old Texas traditions, its songs and legends. I was raised on the old tales and tunes, and I have made a decent living and had a happy profession teaching and talking about Texas folklore for the past thirty-five years. So I'm going to dance with the gal that brung me till this party is over.

However, even in the realm of Texas legends, one has to draw a line somewhere (Just as Travis "undoubtedly" did at the Alamo!), and I would like to draw some parameters around the so-called and lately created legend of the Yellow Rose of Texas, both the song by that title and the subject of the song. The folklore has gotten out of hand: medals have been struck, hotels named, novels written. Who knows what lies ahead!

We have the beginnings of the story from William Bollaert, a traveler in Texas in 1842. Bollaert got his information first hand from none other than General Sam Houston:

> The Battle of San Jacinto was probably lost to the Mexicans, owing to the influence of a Mulatta Girl (Emily) belonging to Colonel Morgan, who was closeted in the tent with General Santana, at the time the cry was made "the enemy! they come! they come!" and detained Santana so long, that order could not be restored readily again (Hollon 108).

According to legend, Santa Anna fled the battlefield clad only in his drawers and slippers, in which he was captured the next day.

225

The mulatto girl's name was Emily, and she had been appropriated by Santa Anna from the effects of one Colonel Morgan. Emily was made famous over a hundred years later because there were those who jumped to the conclusion that Santa Anna's Yellow Rose became the Yellow Rose of Texas, the subject of one of the most popular minstrel songs of all time.

I do believe that Emily was a mulatto, a light-skinned Negro, and that to Santa Anna she very well might have been *his* Yellow Rose of Texas. But I have *never* believed that Santa Anna's Rosey Emily was the one who showed up every time Mitch Miller struck up the band in the late 1950s and played his version of that old minstrel tune, "The Yellow Rose of Texas." Emily West (Her name was not Morgan, and she was not a slave.) was an indentured servant living in Connecticut, who hired out to Colonel Morgan in May of 1835 for $100 a year and returned to New York in 1837 (Hollon 83), probably because Texas would not allow free Negroes within its borders after it became a republic. Emily's tryst with Santa Anna had repercussions beyond which she could imagine, but the song was not one of them.

But a funny thing happened on the way to the forum—a piece of misinformation slipped into the academic mainstream and drifted along unnoticed. Of course, it is impossible for scholars to scrutinize every bit of esoterica that floats their way; they are just not interested in some things, and there is too much of it. So this piece of flotsam drifts along, attaching itself to the river's natural accumulation, and before long toleration of its presence becomes acceptance. And it becomes a basic premise.

We all get caught some time.

And *mea culpa:* in the dispersal of this popular misinformation linking Emily and the YRT song, I also have sinned and fallen short of the glory of academe and editorial veracity. I sinned editorially three times: once for fun (in *Observations and Reflections*), once for necessity (in *Legendary Ladies*), and once out of curiosity (in *Juneteenth Texas*). I fear that I have added much to the obfuscation of the lines between fact, fancy, and folklore.

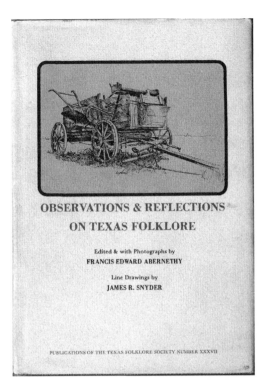

Observations & Reflections on Texas Folklore, the 1972 publication.

I shan't flagellate the deceased equine, but allow me to give it a couple of pokes as I trace the peregrinations of this legendary license.

Here is what happened in the history of the "The Yellow Rose of Texas." To begin with, YRT is not a folk song, as it is often called; it is a published, commercial art song. It was printed as sheet music in 1858 by Firth, Pond, and Co. on Broadway *in New York!* The tune *might* have been taken from a current folk tune, but we have no record of it before the 1858 musical notation. The title sheet states that the song was "Composed and Arranged [that usually means words and music] Expressly for Charles H. Brown by J. K." J. K.'s identity remains in the same realm of mystery as W. H.'s of Shakespeare's sonnets. Charles H. Brown, however, was a bookman and a publisher in Jackson, Tennessee, who was obviously involved in the popular music business and might have been involved in vaudeville and minstrelsy. The tune we sing YRT to now is the same as it was in 1858. Except for the usual "darky" substitution, the words have not changed, unless you were corrupted by Mitch Miller's version in the 1950s and 1960s.

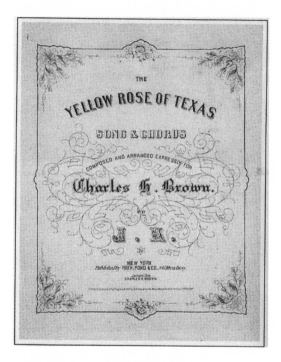

Charles Brown's "The Yellow Rose of Texas."

The following version is from a facsimile copy of the 1858 Firth, Pond, and Co. copyright contained in *Popular Songs of Nineteenth-Century America* (254–257).

THE YELLOW ROSE OF TEXAS

There's a yellow rose in Texas that I am going to see,
No other darkey knows her, no darkey only me;
She cried so when I left her, it like to broke my heart,
And if I ever find her we never more will part.

Chorus:
She's the sweetest rose of color, this darkey ever knew
Her eyes are bright as diamonds, they sparkle like the dew,
You may talk about your Dearest May, and sing of
Rosa Lee,
But the yellow rose of Texas beats the belles of Tennessee.

Where the Rio Grande is flowing, and the starry skies
are bright,
She walks along the river in the quiet summer night;
She thinks if I remember, when we parted long ago,
I promis'd to come back again and not to leave her so.

Oh! Now I'm going to find her, for my heart is full of
woe,
And we'll sing the song together, that we sung so long
ago;
We'll play the banjo gaily, and we'll sing the songs of yore,
And the yellow rose of Texas shall be mine for evermore.

YRT became a standard minstrel song early on, was played on both sides of the Atlantic, and was included in the *Christy's [Minstrels] Plantation Melodies* (many editions) and in *Haverly's Genuine Refined Minstrel Songster,* and numerous other song books of the nineteenth century. That is, the words and music of the song were passed along intact by commercial publishers, not folklorically by word of mouth.

YRT was a minstrel song sung by black-faced white men. Pre-Civil War Minstrelsy was filled with songs about yellow roses, "yaller gals," Dearest Maes, Rosa Lees [song titles], and belles of Tennessee, and with songs about romantically sad separation stories, where the singer yearns to go back to some part of Dixie ("I'se Gwine Back to Dixie," "Dixie," et al.). I have perused many collections of songbooks of both pre and post Civil War, and YRT is typical in subject, references (to other minstrel songs), and wording and phrasing ("playing banjos gaily," "singing songs of yore"). I cannot find *anything* that makes me think that YRT is anything more than a successful generic minstrel song of its time. I conclude that the song was written for a particular show or occasion by a white composer and that it refers to no particular individual. This first-person "darkey" singer is a typical white creation of the Pre-Civil War black-faced minstrelsy tradition.

I certainly have never found anything to tie the song to the Texas Revolution, San Jacinto, or Emily West-Morgan.

Also, consider the song's wording. For one thing, the historic Emily was in Texas, according to retrievable documents, from September 1835 until the summer of 1837 (July passport), about twenty-two months. If this man-singer is going back to Texas to see his YRT (They "parted long ago," remember.), he had better hurry because she wasn't there long. If anybody left anybody in Texas, it was Emily who left him.

And the river she walks along in the song is the Rio Grande, *not* Buffalo Bayou nor the San Jacinto, the two waterways nearest the battlefield.

After the song's publication in 1858, Charles Brown and his followers and borrowers so spread the YRT that by Civil War times it was a tune to march to, like Dan Emmett's "Dixie," and was well enough known to be parodied. The YRT was a favorite marching song of Hood's Texas Brigade, and they retreated to Georgia from the disastrous Tennessee campaign of December 1864 singing:

> And now I'm going southward and my heart
> is full of woe;
> I'm going back to Georgia to find my Uncle
> Joe [Johnson].
> You may talk of General Beauregard and sing
> of Robert Lee,
> But the gallant Hood of Texas played Hell in
> Tennessee. (Silber 56)

After the War, the YRT remained a popular song, and even after the minstrel shows were on the wane the song was popular. YRT's first publisher, Wm. A. Pond, published the song again in 1906 in English and German ("Die Gelbe Rose von Texas") and in four parts for a barbershop quartette. The arrangement this time was by William Dressler, but the composer was still cited as the mysterious J. K.

American concert composer David Guion, who incorporated popular music and folk songs into his compositions published a Texas Centennial commemorative edition of the YRT in 1936, dedicated it to President Franklin D. Roosevelt, and was invited to play it for him at the White House.

YRT became a standard along with "Home on the Range" and "The Last Roundup" for choruses and glee clubs. During WWII it was included in all singalong books. Just about everybody knew it and liked it, so when Mitch Miller recorded Don George's arrangement of YRT in 1955, it went to the top of the Billboard charts and was number seven for the year. Burl Ives, folk music, and guitars were popular during those late 1950s, and along with "On Top of Old Smokey," guitar pickers were supposed to know YRT.

And I am convinced that it was the omnipresence and popularity of the YRT, superimposed on the discovery of the Emily West-Santa Anna linkage in Eugene Hollon's *William Bollaert's Texas* that got us into this mess. The only person I can point to as the perpetrator is Frank X. Tolbert of the *Dallas Morning News*.

Frank Tolbert was a prolific writer for the *DMN*, and the column "Tolbert's Texas" was his vehicle. Frank had an easy, readable style, knew Texas history, and because of his large newspaper audience was a popular voice—along with Frank Dobie—in Texas history. Frank, who had discovered Bollaert after 1956, took literary license with Emily in his 1959 *The Day of San Jacinto,* describing her person and appearance more than Bollaert would have allowed (76). But in 1961, literary license became creative fiction. Covering my own derriere, I recognize that Frank might have found primary sources that he never informed us about, but these (as of now) are lost to history.

As far as I can tell, here is the passage in Frank's 1961 *Informal History of Texas* that started it all:

> While the dictator [Santa Anna] dallied in the champagne atmosphere of the silken marquee with a decorative servant girl on the afternoon of April 21, 1836, he was losing an empire.
>
> And what became of Emily? She lived to tell her story to her master, Colonel Morgan, and to inspire a wonderful song. Musical historians seem to agree that the folk song "The Yellow Rose of Texas" was inspired by a good-looking mulatto slave girl. And in one set of original lyrics—not the ones popularized by Mitch Miller—the girl of the song is called "Emily, the Maid of Morgan's Point." (95–96)

—And Frank leaves it at that.

We have several problems songwise with Frank's statement, but can we bring him to court on this? He never directly says that Emily inspired YRT. He said she "inspire(d) a wonderful song" but does not commit himself to naming the song. Then he says, "Musical historians [what "musical historians," no basis for this statement] *seem to agree* that the folk song [not a folk song] YRT was inspired by a good-looking mulatto slave girl [In this line he does not specifically name Emily.]. "And in one set of original lyrics—not the ones popularized by Mitch Miller [of whom he was conscious—and he never locates or documents the "original lyrics"]—the girl of the song is called 'Emily, the Maid of Morgan's Point" [Folklorists have been combing songbooks and sheet music for over three decades since then and have as yet to come up with this reference.].

But of course, Tolbert did not have to make the connection between Emily and "The Yellow Rose of Texas." Those who came afterward helped make the connection in the public mind.

Henderson Shuffler, the founder and director of the Institute of Texan Cultures, might have been the first. Henderson and Frank

Tolbert were long-time buddies, visited frequently, and talked a lot; and I cannot imagine the subject of Emily and "The Yellow Rose of Texas" *not* coming up in their discussions. I met Henderson in 1968 and visited with him regularly while we were trying to get the first Texas Folklife Festival off the ground in 1972. Sometime during those years he and I discussed the Emily-YRT story, which by that time he had crafted into a speech, primarily for men's clubs. When I became the editor of the Texas Folklore Society publications in 1971, I told him I wanted to print his speech in a TFS publication. Henderson was hesitant, insisting that it was non-scholarly and was for the sake of fun and not academia. And he was right. "San Jacinto, as She Was: or, What Really Happened on the Plain of St. Hyacinth on a Hot, April Afternoon in 1836" was loaded with factual errors and fictional people; but it was hilariously prurient and double entendrish and was a good read and a great after dinner speech. For a sample, Henderson closes his speech with a tribute to a band of Texas history buffs who formed "The Knights of the Yellow Rose" (130).

> Some moonlit April night [the Knights of the Yellow Rose] plan to meet beside the towering monument which marks the battlefield of San Jacinto. . . . There they will plant a small patch of pussywillow, encircling a garden of yellow roses. And in the center, a modest stone, on which will be engraved this legend:

> In Honor of Emily
> Who Gave Her All for Texas
> Piece by Piece

Shuffler throughout uses the Yellow Rose imagery referring to Emily, and twice he cites the possibility that Emily was the Yellow Rose of Texas—saying "there is some indication" and she "may well have been." He also refers to the Tolbert's *Informal History,* which "mentions old lyrics of 'The Yellow Rose of Texas' which sing of 'Emily, the Maid of Morgan's Point.'" Henderson went out on a limb with his free associations, but he hung on to the trunk.

As did Judge Thomas Stovall, another public speaker, who incorporated Emily and the YRT into his after dinner speeches. Judge Stovall was the founder of the *Sons of* the Knights of the Yellow Rose of Texas, known by its acronym SKYRT. Members wore small embroidered yellow roses on their coat lapels, gathered periodically to discuss and imbibe, and shouted their internationally know motto, "Up With the SKYRT."

As *un*serious as these two men were, the connection that they *implied* was made flesh and moved among men by Martha Anne Turner, a professor of English at Sam Houston State University. [Professors of English frequently get in trouble when they meddle in history. They lack a certain discipline.]

We must never forget that these three people—Henderson Shuffler, Judge Stovall, and Martha Ann Turner were part of a historical gossip mix that was going on throughout the 1960s. The Bollaert account of Emily in Santa Anna's tent hit the book stands in 1956. Frank Tolbert incorporated that information with his fictional addenda in 1961. These things take time to gestate. And really, Martha Anne is the first one *whom I have found* to go formally, historically, and academically public with the Emily-Yellow Rose connection.

Martha Anne made the Yellow Rose connection at a meeting of the American Studies Association in College Station on December 5, 1969. The paper was published in the Association's journal in 1970. Unlike Henderson and the Judge, Martha Anne was as serious as a dug grave, and also unlike the other two, she had been doing research. As did the others, she followed Tolbert's *Informal History of Texas* by asserting as a basic premise that an early version of YRT had Emily, the Maid of Morgan's Point in it. That copy has still not been found.

In the Archives of The University of Texas Library Martha Anne found a handwritten copy of YRT which she solidly maintained was the earliest version of the song. The handwritten copy follows the copyrighted copy closely enough to be kin; the only thing wrong is that Martha asserts that this was probably written soon after the Battle of San Jacinto. The problem is that there is no date on the copy and absolutely no way to verify an early date—or any date for that matter. It is just an old handwritten copy of YRT. To compound the felony, she later says that "The lyrics of this printed [1858] version are almost identical to the aforementioned curious manuscript copy . . . and signify that the composer [J. K. of the 1858 sheet music] was the same person, further confirming its [the ms's] authenticity" (1970, 29–31).

Martha Anne expanded her 1969 speech into a monograph, *The Yellow Rose of Texas: the Story of a Song* for the Southwestern Studies Series in 1971. She expanded it even further in 1976, the year she published her findings in a book entitled *The Yellow Rose of Texas, Her Saga and Her Song*. Her book contained added information about the history of the song and, of course, staunchly maintained the Emily-YRT connection. But in spite of her enthusiasm for the subject, she had no new evidence beyond Frank Tolbert's unsubstantiated statement that an early version of YRT refers to the Yellow Rose as "Emily the Maid of Morgan's Point," a version that we cannot find.

The above references are the main ones in academia that were involved in the Emily-"Yellow Rose" connection. The controversy was brief but heated, and as yet we have no documented evidence of a connection between the song "The Yellow Rose of Texas" and Emily West of San Jacinto fame.

But most folks, I-god, never let the truth stand in the way of a good story!

The Emily-YRT connection was good copy and journalists jumped on it like a duck on a June bug in feature stories and Sunday supplements. Martha Anne's opinions were sanctified when James Michener in his epic *Texas* said, "Immortality was visited upon the least likely participant of the battle [of San Jacinto]. Emily Morgan, who had diverted Santa Anna's attention that hot afternoon just before the charge of the Texicans, became celebrated in song as 'The Yellow Rose of Texas' and few who sing it in romantic settings realize that they are serenading the memory of a mulatto slave" (Michener, 418). Anita Bunkley wrote a whole novel, *Emily, The Yellow Rose,* on the subject. A medal with a yellow rose on one side and YRT song verse on the other was struck during the Bicentennial Year. And, from a hotel brochure—"for the ultimate San Antonio Experience," the Ramada chain invites you to stay at their Emily Morgan Hotel near the Alamo Plaza.

And all of this tempest in academia does make one wonder— just how many angels *can* dance on the head of a pin!

BIBLIOGRAPHY

Bunkley, Anita. *Emily, The Yellow Rose: A Texas Legend.* Houston: Rinard Publishing, 1989.

Harris, Trudier. "'The Yellow Rose of Texas': A Different Cultural View," *Juneteenth Texas* (PTFS 44), F. E. Abernethy, ed. Denton: University of North Texas Press, 1996.

Hollon, W. Eugene and Ruth Lapham Butler, eds. *William Bollaert's Texas.* Norman: University of Oklahoma Press, 1956.

Jackson, Richard. *Popular Songs of Nineteenth-Century America.* New York: Dover Publications, 1976.

Michener, James A. *Texas.* New York: Random House, 1985.

Shuffler, Henderson R. "San Jacinto as She Was: Or, What Really Happened on the Plain of St. Hyacinth on a Hot April Afternoon in 1836." *Observations and Reflections on Texas Folklore* (PTFS 37), F. E. Abernethy, ed. Austin: Encino Press, 1972.

Silber, Irwin. *Songs of the Civil War.* New York: Columbia University Press, 1960.

Tolbert, Frank X. *The Day of San Jacinto.* Austin: Pemberton Press, 1959.

—. *An Informal History of Texas from Cabeza de Vaca to Temple Houston.* New York: Harper & Brothers, 1961.

Turner, Martha Anne. "Emily Morgan: Yellow Rose of Texas," *Legendary Ladies of Texas* (PTFS 43), F. E. Abernethy, ed. Dallas: E-Heart Press, 1981.

—. *The Yellow Rose of Texas: Her Saga and Her Song With the Santa Anna Legend.* Austin: Shoal Creek Publishers, 1976.

—. "The Yellow Rose of Texas': The Story of a Song." *Journal of the American Studies of Texas* 1 1970.

—. "The Yellow Rose of Texas': The Story of a Song." El Paso: *Southern Studies Series,* 1971.

Ab Abernethy performing songs of The Depression
at a hootenanny, 2007.

SONGS OF THE DEPRESSION

BEANS, BACON, AND GRAVY

I was born long ago, in 1894,
And I've seen lots of hard times, that is true;
I've been hungry, I've been cold,
And now I'm growing old.
But the worst I've seen is 1932.

Refrain:
Oh, those beans, bacon, and gravy,
They almost drive me crazy,
I eat them till I see them in my dreams,
In my dreams,
When I wake up in the morning,
A Depression day is dawning,
And I know I'll have another mess of beans.

We have Hooverized our butter,
For blued our milk with water,
And I haven't eaten meat in any way;
As for pies, cakes, and jelly,
We substitute sow-belly,
For which we work the county roads each day.

There are several advantages to living a long time, one of which is that you become historical. You begin to find the commonplace times of your life in history books. The Depression was a distinct part of my life, and I talked to my father about these years and it was even more distinctly a part of his.

Every generation is the product of its parents. The Depression was the offspring of the Roaring Twenties. Will Rogers said of the

Depression: "We're the first nation in the history of the world to go to the poor house in an automobile." So, you can better understand a child by knowing its parents.

And speaking of parents, traditional mothers in the *early* Twenties, before it was in full roar, still required their daughters to wear the restrictive foundation garment of the day, corsets that were equipped to hold up black hose. Traditional daughters hastened to restrooms and removed such impediments to the Charleston, Black Bottom, and the Shimmy. An illustrative classic of the Jazz Age was sung, "I wish I could shimmy like my sister Kate./She could shimmy, she could shake it like jello on a plate." For those of you who are interested, the word "shimmy" comes from the French *chemise*, and the full name of the dance was the Shimmie Shewobble.

The Twenties were soon in full roar, and the culture shock suffered by that decade's elders must have been massive. Few times, standing so close together, has there been such a sharp line of distinction as that which existed between pre- and post-WWI. The world before WWI had been Jeffersonianly rural with all the conservative moral values of that way of life. The post-war Twenties were urban and in direct reaction against all relics of Victorian morality. The Twenties continued with a material prosperity such as ordinary Americans had not known before. With jobs to be had and good wages, the American people were able to buy cars, radios, phonographs, and a host of labor-saving electrical appliances. They paid to see professional sports. They went to college—and Europe. They borrowed money and they bought things on credit, and this is what will come back to haunt them. They lived better than any pre-WWI American society, and they tried to be everything their parents had not. As a parent during the Hippy Sixties and Seventies, I can sympathize with my own grandparents who had the rearing of their children in the Twenties.

By the mid-Twenties female style had achieved the asexual flat look, bustless and buttless, that announced that recreation, not procreation, was the purpose of sex. Ironically, the young Flappers who had earlier divested themselves of their corsets to free their bodies for the Shimmy and the Charleston, by 1926 were wearing tube-like foundation garments to flatten out their curves. The generation announced through its worldly ways that pleasure was the purpose of life.

And do you realize that the Roaring Twenties are the first years in recorded western civilization when women wore skirts that revealed their legs and cut their hair short or wore *flesh*-colored hose—and pants! This was the world of our now-sainted mothers and grandmothers, we must remember.

We came to the end of that roaring, fast changing time, in 1929, with Americans singing the theme song of that entire decade, Irving Berlin's "Blue Skies":

> Blue skies, shinin' on me
> Nothin but blue skies
> Do I see.
>
> Blue birds, singin' a song
> Nothin but blue birds
> All the day long.
>
> Never saw the sun shinin' so bright
> Never saw things lookin' so right.
> Oughta see the days hurryin' by
> When you're in love
> How time does fly.
>
> Blue days, all of them gone.
> Nothing but blue skies
> From now on.

The prosperity and boundless optimism of the Twenties *almost* made it through that decade; there would be "blue skies from now on." America had seen eight years of an expanding Stock Market and believed in its continuation. Proving the investor's optimism, the stocks went up in what was called the Great Sleigh Ride of the summer of '29 to an all-time high on September 3. After that there was no way to go but down.

On October 24, Black Thursday, the Market tumbled. A group of bankers rushed in and bought stock and restored some of the trust, but confidence faltered over the weekend, and investors came back Monday morning ready to sell. Tuesday, October 29, was The Day of the Crash. The financial world of the Twenties and everything that was a part of it turned upside down on that Black Tuesday. Savings and investments were lost, and the financial dominos began a tumble that soon would reach down to the least of persons in this bountiful land of ours. The Great Depression came to Texas, the U. S., and the world. It stayed until it was rescued by the World War II economy, and the effects were felt by everybody before it was over.

I move into an autobiographical mode, not to regale you with the details of my childhood, but to reveal how one family lived through the early years of the Depression.

Talbot and Aileen Abernethy, Ab's parents.

In 1929, Dad had the Dodge agency in Shamrock, Texas, but lost it within a year of the Crash, and we moved back to Grand-dad's ranch in the Panhandle. Mother did not last long in the high lonesome of that place. The ranch was five miles from the mailbox and nearest neighbor, and seventeen miles from the nearest town. Mother was an East Texas girl, and the wind and the treeless space of the high plains depressed her considerably. A mockingbird in a bush outside her bedroom window afforded her some relief, some piece of beauty in that bare expanse. Then, one morning as she watched him sing, a cat sprang upon him and reduced him to feathers. That was the end. Mother had them drive her to Childress, where she caught the Fort Worth and Denver back to Dallas, where her parents lived. Dad and I stayed on the ranch.

Families lived together and held together during the Depression just to survive. Dad's three brothers, and Mother's two brothers and sister helped each other. When I started to school in '31, I was moved to my maternal grandparents' home in Dallas, where it took four people working to support six, my grandmother and I the only ones not working. Granddad Cherry, who had been the contractor for several major buildings in Dallas, and who owned his home, an apartment building, and a farm, had lost everything and was reduced to maintenance and repair work. My Uncle Francis, who was a mechanical genius, lost a car one year because he could not make a $7.50 payment. Mother worked in a ladies' ready-to-wear store in downtown Dallas selling dresses on commission. Dad worked on the ranch when the seasons required, and between crops and roundups sold shoes on commission or helped Grand-dad Cherry and worked at anything he could find. Until he died he would still shake his head in wonder when he remembered how it was to have nothing and not have any idea where he was going to find work. When school was out, he and I would hitchhike the 350 miles from Dallas back to the ranch.

A Dustbowl family.

Dad wandered all over Texas and Oklahoma looking for work—as did thousands of other men. He did not get a steady job until 1934. One of the folk songs circulating during the Hoover years described the drifting, hopeless situation of the wanderers of the Depression.

WANDERIN'

I've been wanderin', early and late
From New York City to the Golden Gate.
Looks like I'm never gonna cease my wanderin'.

I've been wanderin' far and wide,
I go with the wind and ride with the tide.

Been workin' in the army, been workin' on the farm,
And all I've got to show for it is the muscle in my arm.

Ashes to ashes, dust to dust,
If the Republicans can't help us the Democrats
must.

1930 was the year of the apple sellers. A bumper crop of north-western apples for a short while provided the Depression's unemployed with an opportunity at capitalism. The ambitious jobless could buy a crate of seventy-two apples for $1.75, sell them at a nickel apiece, and make a profit of $1.85, which was a good day's pay. This lasted until the competition increased and wholesalers kicked the price up to $2.25 a box and higher. But as short-lived as it was, selling apples became a symbol of Depression entrepreneurialism. One of the enduring comic strips began in 1938 as "Apple Mary," about a Depression woman who was reduced to selling apples on the street corner to support herself and her crippled grandson. The strip evolved into our present "Mary Worth," with little or no resemblance to the Depression ancestor.

Calvin Coolidge, at the time an editorialist, had said, "When more and more people are thrown out of work, unemployment results." By 1931, over eight million people had been thrown out of work and there was nationwide unemployment. Every city had its bread lines and soup kitchens managed by individual charities. President Hoover was not yet convinced the nation was in a depression, or if it was, it was caused by the Europeans. Hoover also believed that federal relief would rob the people of their dignity. Thus, the national government did little for the welfare of the jobless and the homeless, and the result was a new generation of panhandlers, men who had once been self-supporting, who had fought for their country in WWI. Out of this common experience came the theme song of the Depression.

BROTHER, CAN YOU SPARE A DIME?

They used to tell me I was building a dream,
So I followed the mob—

When there was earth to plow or guns to bear,
I was always there—right on the job.

They use to tell me I was building a dream
With peace and glory ahead—
Why should I be standing in line
Just waiting for (a piece of) bread?

Once I built a railroad, made it run,
Made it race against time.
Once I built a railroad, now it's done.
Brother, can you spare a dime?

Once I built a tower to the sun,
Brick and mortar and lime.
Once I built a tower, now it's done.
Brother, can you spare a dime?

Once in khaki suits, Gee, we looked swell,
Full of that Yankee Doodle Dum.
Half a million boots marched into hell—
And I was the guy on the drum!

Hey, don't you remember me; they called me Al.
It was "Hey, Al" all of the time.
Don't you remember; I was your pal.
Hey, Brother, can you spare a dime?

Herbert Hoover was packing for a move in 1932, and his last year was not a happy one. Banks and businesses were failing, unemployment was rising, and a spirit of hopelessness was on the land. Americans blamed the president, and the dispossessed called their shanty towns "Hoovervilles." The poor ate "Hoover hogs" (armadillos) when they could catch them, and slept in the cold, sheltered by "Hoover blankets," or newspapers. Wanderers, hobos, and bums became a visible part of American life, and living off the land and handouts became a way of life for many. An amazing number of songs grew out of this new element of society.

HALLELUJAH, I'M A BUM

Oh, why don't you work
Like other men do?
How the hell can I work
When there's no work to do?

Hallelujah, I'm a bum,
Hallelujah, bum again,
Hallelujah, give us a handout,
To revive us again.

I went to a house
And I knocked on the door;
The lady came out, says,
"You been here before."

I went to a house,
And I asked for some bread;
The lady came out, says,
"The baker is dead."

When springtime does come,
O won't we have fun,
We'll throw up our jobs
And we'll go on the bum.

Visionary songs—some cynical, some resigned—appeared, including parodies.

SWEET BYE AND BYE (a parody)

You will eat bye and bye,
In that glorious land in the sky.
Work and pray, live on hay,
You'll have pie in the sky when you die.

Definitely not a children's song, "The Big Rock Candy Mountain" was the hobos' classic fantasy song, describing a perfect world for the Knights of the Open Road.

THE BIG ROCK CANDY MOUNTAIN

In the Big Rock Candy Mountain
You never change your socks,
And little streams of alcohol
Come a-trickling down the rocks.
The box cars are all empty
And the railroad bulls are blind,
There's a lake of stew and whisky, too,
You can paddle around in a big canoe
In the Big Rock Candy Mountains.

Chorus:
O—the buzzing of the bees in the cigarette trees
And the soda-water fountains,
And the bluebird sings by the lemonade springs
In the Big Rock Candy Mountains.

In the Big Rock Candy Mountains,
There's a land that's fair and bright,

Where the hand-outs grow on bushes
And you sleep out every night,
Where the box cars are all empty
And the sun shines every day,
O I'm bound to go, where there ain't no snow,
Where the rain don't fall and the wind don't blow
In the Big Rock Candy Mountains

The most famous Hooverville sprang up in Washington, D.C., when the Bonus Expeditionary Force arrived that summer of '32 lobbying for early payment of their WWI bonus. They camped on the Potomac until July 28, when the President sent troops under General Douglas MacArthur (with Major Dwight D. Eisenhower in the ranks), who very unpolitically rousted them out with fire and sword. Veterans remembered the bonus marchers that November when Herbert Hoover met Franklin D. Roosevelt at the polls. There was no way that the glum, Depression-ridden Hoover could beat a man who smiled like sunshine and whose theme song was "Happy Days Are Here Again!"

Incidentally, several songs of optimism illustrated the hope that was—and is—always a part of life: "Let a Smile be Your Umbrella on a Rainy, Rainy Day," "Let's Have Another Cup of Coffee" ("Just around the corner, there's a rainbow in the sky, / So let's have another cup of coffee and let's have another piece of pie"), and "Life is Just a Bowl of Cherries" ("Don't make it serious; life's too mysterious / You work, you save, you worry so / But you can't take your dough when you go go go. / Life is just a bowl of cherries, so live and laugh at it all").

Back to "Happy Days": The nominating committee had planned to play "Anchors Aweigh" to welcome Roosevelt, who had been Assistant Secretary of the Navy, but the tune sounded so glum after the nominating speech that his campaign manager suggested "Happy Days," a pop song from the 1929 musical *Chasing Rainbows*. In the musical, the song was sung in the trenches when the soldiers heard about the Armistice.

Happy Days are here again,
The skies above are clear again
Let's sing a song of cheer again,
Happy Days are here again.

All together, shout it now!
There is no one who can doubt it now,
So let's tell the world about it now,
Happy days are here again.

Your cares and trouble are gone.
There'll be no more from now on—

Happy days are here again,
The skies above are clear again,
Let us sing a song of cheer again,
Happy days are here again.

Enough people were looking for a new way of life—a New Deal!—to overwhelmingly elect Franklin Delano Roosevelt as the President of the United States. He took office on Saturday, March 4, 1933, announced a bank holiday for Monday, March 6, and on March 9 began a Hundred Days of restructuring the socio-political system of the U.S.A. He told Americans that "the only thing we have to fear is fear itself—nameless, unreasoning, unjustified terror which paralyzes needed efforts to convert retreat into advance." In his first Hundred Days, between March 9 and June 16, Roosevelt fought that fear with action. He called for the legalization of beer and the abolition of the gold standard and created an Alphabet Soup of agencies—AAA, CCC, TVA, NRA, PWA, ad infinitum—designed to help Americans regain financial control of their lives. He started America on a course of government involvement in citizens' lives that the nation is still following. But mainly,

Franklin D. Roosevelt was taking decisive action to help a struggling people, and most Americans thanked him for it.

In 1932 Will Rogers said, "Last year they said things couldn't go on like this. They were right: they didn't—they got worse." Particularly so for the farmers. Farm prices had not been good since WWI, and they fell even more after the Crash. Roosevelt established a Bureau of Farm Relief, which established a commission to study the plight of the farmer. Will Rogers said: "They won't take the farmer's word for it that he's poor. They hire men to find out how poor he is. If they took all the money they spend on finding out how poor he is and give it to the farmer, he wouldn't need any more relief." Cotton hit the bottom in '31 and '32 at 6¢ down to 5¢ a pound. It wasn't worth the picking.

SEVEN CENT COTTON, TWENTY CENT MEAT

Seven cent cotton, twenty cent meat
How in the world can a poor man eat?

Flour up high, cotton down low
How in the world can we raise the dough?

Our clothes worn out, shoes run down
Old slouch hat with a hole in the crown
Back nearly broken, fingers all wore
Cotton goin' down to rise no more.

Seven cent cotton, twenty cent meat
How in the world can a poor man eat?

Then, on top of the bottom dropping out of the cotton and grain market, the boll weevil hit in '33 and '34 and destroyed what little cotton the farmers could pray up out of the ground. The following is a black blues song. Blacks were worse off than whites.

BOLL WEEVIL SONG

De first time I seen de boll weevil,
He was a-settin' on de square.
De next time I seen de boll weevil, he had all
of his family dere.
Jus' a-lookin' foh a home, jus' a-lookin' foh a
home.

De farmer take de boll weevil,
An' he put him in de hot san'.
De weevil say: "Dis is mighty hot, but I'll stan'
it like a man,
Dis'll be my home, it'll be my home."

De farmer take de boll weevil,
An' he put him in a lump of ice;
De boll weevil say to de farmer: "Dis is mighty
cool and nice,
It'll be my home, dis'll be my home."

De boll weevil say to de farmer:
"You better leave me alone;
I done eat all yo' cotton, now I'm goin' to
start on yo' corn,
I'll have a home, I'll have a home."

De merchant got half de cotton,
De boll weevil got de res'.
Didn't leave de farmer's wife but one old
cotton dress,
An' it's full of holes, it's full of holes.

An' if anybody ever axes you
Who it was done writ dis song,
Jus' tell 'em was a poor old cullud man wid a
paih o' blue duckin's on
Ain' got no home, ain' got no home.

And then, on top of the Depression, a crashed market, and boll weevils, the Drouth hit, and the crops dried up and the land blew away. The farmers plowed again, all up and down the Great Plains, and the soil stayed dry and loose. The winds blew, as they always do on the Plains, and Kansas ended up in the Panhandle of Texas. And the Panhandle of Texas became the Dust Bowl.

Lubbock's C of C advertised that it was The Land of the Five-inch Rain—the drops were five inches apart. It was so dry in the Panhandle that cows gave evaporated milk, and chickens plucked themselves to escape the heat. The dusters came in so hard that one hen got caught with her tail pointed north and had to lay the same egg twelve times. The crops were so bad that the crows had to lie on their stomachs to steal corn—and ducks and frogs fell into buckets of water and drowned. It got so dry that the Baptists started sprinkling and the Methodists just used a damp cloth. And one Panhandle cowboy got struck by a drop of rain, and the shock was so great it took two buckets of sand to revive him. The Waggoner ranch needed water so bad that they offered to swap oil for water, barrel for barrel. That's supposed to be true. They drilled for water and got oil.

Woody Guthrie, who lived in and around Pampa town, was Texas' Dust Bowl troubadour. He wrote this song about dusters, particularly Black Easter (April 14, 1935) in Gray County in the Panhandle during the Depression.

DUSTY OLD DUST

I've sung this song, but I'll sing it again.
Of the place that I lived on the wild windy plains.

In the month called April, the county called Gray,
Here is what all of the people there say:

Chorus:
So long it's been good to know you,
So long it's been good to know you,
So long it's been good to know you,
This dusty old dust is getting my home
And I've got to be drifting along.

A dust storm hit, and it hit like thunder.
It dusted us over, and it covered us under.
Backed up the traffic and blocked out the sun.
Straight for home all the people did run—
singin'

Chorus

The church it was jammed, and the church it
was packed.
And that dusty old dust storm it came up so black
That the preacher could not read a word of
his text,
So he folded his specs, and he took up
collections—and said

Chorus

Dish towels in the windows, dust on the horse trough and in the milk house, food was always gritty.

Back in the cities many businesses and industries went under with the Crash, and those that were left struggled to survive. The way many industries survived was at the expense of the working man. They cut wages and stretched the hours, and there were plenty of people desperate enough to work that they would take any job for just about any wages—and work from can to can't for a meager day's pay. The industries that took advantage of the Depression to hire cheap and work long, found themselves in the mid-Thirties facing the rising power of the unions. Unions were never generally popular and were equated by many with the breakdown of traditional capitalism and the rising power of world Communism. Lenin had said, "Workers of the world arise! You have nothing to lose but your chains." They were now arising and singing their own songs.

UNION TRAIN (COMING AROUND THE MOUNTAIN)

I see that Union Train a comin,
I see that Union Train a comin,
I see that Union Train a comin,
Git on board, git on board!

It will take us all to freedom—It has saved many a thousand

Here is another, asking for just bare necessities:

I DON'T WANT YOUR MILLIONS, MISTER

I don't want your millions, mister,
I don't want your diamond ring.
All I want is a living mister;
Give me back my job again.

Think me dumb if you wish, mister,
Call me green, or blue, or red.
This one thing I sure know, mister:
My hungry babies must be fed.

We worked to build this country, mister,
While you lived a life of ease.
You've stolen all that we built, mister;
Now our children starve and freeze.

By the end of the Thirties Roosevelt had instituted some reforms and was trying to help people get by. Young men joined the CCC, made $30 a month, of which $20 had to be sent home to their folks. The WPA (We Piddle Around) put a lot of men to work building dams and paving roads. The Tennessee Valley Authority (TVA), brought about through the Public Works Administration, rescued a large part of seven states and created a public power system. And for the first time, the old folks who couldn't work anymore received an old age pension check.

THE OLD AGE PENSION CHECK

When our old age pension check comes to our door
We won't have to dread the poor house anymore
Though we're old and thin and gray
Good times will be here to stay
When our old age pension check comes to our door.

When her old age pension check comes to her door
Dear old grandma won't be lonesome any more
She'll be waiting at the gate
Every night she'll have a date
When her old age pension check comes to her door.

With a flowing long white beard and walking cane
Grandpa's in his second childhood, don't complain
His life began at sixty
And he's feelin' very frisky
And his old age pension check is what to blame.

The Depression wasn't over by the end of the Thirties, but the worst was, and the nation had survived. A lot had happened since the Crash: bread lines and hobos and *The Grapes of Wrath*—a change from a capitalistic to a socialistic government—Shirley Temple, *Gone With the Wind* and *Snow White and the Seven Dwarfs*—Huey Long— Big Band swing, Glenn Miller, and "Star Dust"—John Dillinger, Pretty Boy Floyd, Bonnie and Clyde. During the Depression you could get a hamburger and a cup of coffee for fifteen cents; milk was ten cents a quart (nobody bought gallons), bread five cents a loaf, eggs twenty cents a dozen. A package of cigarettes was fifteen cents, a gallon of gas the same. You could buy a Pontiac coupe for $585, a gas stove for $24. And a peanut pattie and a big orange were a nickel apiece.

The trouble was that not many people had the nickels. College teachers were making around $2500 a year; public school teachers half that—if the state had the money to pay. A doctor made about $3500, a lawyer maybe $500 more. Steelworkers and textile workers were making about $400 a year. I worked on a ranch as late as the summer of 1940 for 75 cents a day, room, and board. A generation that is raised around those kinds of prices has trouble paying a dollar for a candy bar or a coke.

During the Sixties, when *The Graduate* was filmed, this Depression generation was satirized as "materialistic" because of their consuming consciousness of income and outgo, and jobs and the general cost of things. They were still very conscious that dollar bills put food on the table, clothed the kids, and paid the rent. They were still trying to get over the Depression. Some never have.

Reflections

The Abernethy family.

THE FAMILY SAGA: A COLLECTION
OF TEXAS FAMILY LEGENDS

an introduction

[from *The Family Saga: A Collection of Texas Family Legends*, **PTFS LX, 2003**]

From the beginning of man's time, from our be-figged first parents Adam and Eve, the family has been the basic social unit. The family clung together, tightly knit, for simple survival.

The old father, the patriarch, called his bickering sons together, and they sat in the light around the fire. He waved his hand about him, indicating all the points of the compass, and said, "Out there in the darkness lies our destruction. Outside of this firelight stand both man and beast, and they can destroy us one by one if we do not travel together as each other's protection." Then he took a stick and gave one to each of his sons. "Break them," he said. They did so, easily. Then he took the same number of sticks as he had sons and bound them in a bundle. "Break this," he said. None could break the bound bundle.

The old father held up the bundle (called a *fasces* in Latin) in the firelight. "We are as these dry and brittle sticks," he said. "Each of us alone can be quickly broken and tossed into the fire. Only bound together as a family can we survive and not be broken." So they stayed together and grew from family to group to tribe to community to society and finally to a nation that still had a drop of the old man's blood running in its veins. And they continually told the tales of their ancestors and their history.

Of all the family sagas, the Bible—particularly the Old Testament's collection of stories of the Children of Abraham—remains the longest, best written, most complete of all the sagas in existence, from the Judeo-Christian point of view, at least.

By the twelfth century B. C. the Jews were no longer nomadic. They had found a fertile land held by a weaker people; so, blessed by the family gods, they took the land and settled down to enjoy their first permanent home.

Writing was not yet a part of their Hebraic culture, but storytelling was, and their stories of the family formed a saga, a group of related family legends, that went back to what they knew as the beginning of time, to their Eden. Their tales went back to the first parents, to the family in the old country, to their migrations and the wars they had fought. The stories they told went back to the fires and floods and catastrophes that they had endured, to the feuds within the tribe, to the miracles they had known, the animals they had hunted, the treasures they had won and lost. And most of all, the tales they told were stories of the great Jewish personalities—the singers and hunters and fighters—the heroes and heroines who had dominated generations, whose tales still excited wonder and admiration. And the most holy of their men, the priests, were responsible for the survival of these legends of times past.

Likewise, a family's most treasured of kin is the one who knows the stories of his family's past and can relate these tales around the diningroom table to the delight of young and old, no matter how many times the tales are told. My grandad's brother, the last of his family, every Thanksgiving told how in the winter of '98 they were snowbound in a dugout in old Greer County. They had run out of food, but were saved when Uncle Sterle, the eldest brother, came riding through the drifts with a pair of gallon jugs of molasses tied to his saddle horn. Uncle Arthur could never tell that story without getting choked up.

If a family is blessed with enough good storytellers down through the generations—scops, bards, or minstrels who can turn an episode into an *Iliad*—the legend will eventually take on the shape of a short story. The best stories have a natural beginning, middle, and end; it is a matter of natural selection.

The title and the idea for this book began in 1958, when Mody Boatright first published his essay, "The Family Saga as a Form of Folklore." What Mody identified was a long established form of folklore that was firmly entrenched among people everywhere. We would not presume to improve on Mody. We have merely further defined and categorized where Mody left off.

Mody went back to early medieval Icelandic and Norse family sagas for his pattern. Those old sagas, passed along in the oral tradition, told stories of the gods on earth, the adventures of heroes, and the lives of kings. They were an accumulation of heroic legends about one family or hero, brought together and eventually written down in a unified saga.

The family saga—as Mody and this collection defines it—is made up of an accumulation of separate family legends. These are the stories of the old folks and the old times that are told among the family when they gather for funerals or Thanksgiving dinner. These are the "remember-when" stories the family tells about the time when the grownups were children. Families with strong identities and strong bonds eventually have a library of legends, treasures passed along in the oral tradition. Because of shared humanity and common family experiences, the legends of these old families follow a recognizable pattern of topics, some of which are contained herein. A large and chronologically extended collection of family legends brought together under one cover, or one roof, is a family saga.

Only some of the many kinds of family legends are contained herein, but not all. I could have had a chapter on hunting and fishing tales from the families I encountered that believed that these sports were at the core of their family's identity. I gave a talk about family legends to a group of genealogists, and the topic of outhouses came up. I could have done a chapter on family tales that involved adventures in outhouses, like the time Dad and I walked in on a bull snake, for instance, or when my aged aunt was greeted by a skunk. I met with a three-generation family of doctors, and one of them told about putting a football bladder in a patient during some emergency. Mercifully, I have forgotten the details.

A family legend is a type of folklore. It is a traditional prose narrative that has a historical setting and real people as characters. The legend is passed down in the family through the oral tradition, by word of mouth, from one generation to another. As with all folklore, the story exists in variations, its author or first teller is anonymous, and it fits a formula in being true to the spirit of the family but not necessarily to the facts of history.

We recognize that family history is more complex than the isolated legends contained in this book. Each story is told in a particular context, sometimes by a particular person. We also realize that family-story traditions frequently begin their journey through time in the form of letters, diaries, memoirs, and journals. For that reason we vary from the absolute and include some first-person narratives, recognizing that they do not fit the formal definition of a traditional family legend. We also know, however, that first-person narratives—stories one tells about one's own experiences—are honed over the decades by that first person to make a better story and to fit his forever-growing and changing attitudes about life. The personal tale is an example of personal folklore and is a personal legend. When it falls into the flow of tales a family tells, it becomes a family legend.

The family saga, therefore, is *not* history. It is *not* an accumulation and an evaluation of factual and documented details, because most families have few facts and very little documentation. But even though the stories are not history, they are shadows of history, which in one sense is more important than the details. A list of ancestors and how long they lived and whom they begot and how long they lived is important factually, but it does not interpret; it does not reveal a family's spirit nor what it believes nor how it thinks. A genealogical list tells *what*, not *why* and *how*; and the *what* is the beginning, the first step, the introduction. The *why* is the reason for being. And the *whys* of a family are revealed in the family's legends.

The literature of a culture is the key to understanding the mind of that culture and its place in time and history. The legends of a family reveal the same things on a smaller scale. The family keeps and tells the stories that reflect the family's culture and beliefs—how the family sees itself—and it binds them together. It keeps the stories that reflect what that family feels are the strengths of its people or the characteristics that the family still honors. When times and attitudes change, the stories change, or they disappear all together. What we have in *The Family Saga* is a collection of stories that, one way or another, have survived the passage of years and migrations, fires, and floods—and most importantly, of changing attitudes. These stories remain to remind their families that they are a part of a history that goes far back in time, and if the pattern holds, will continue far into the future.

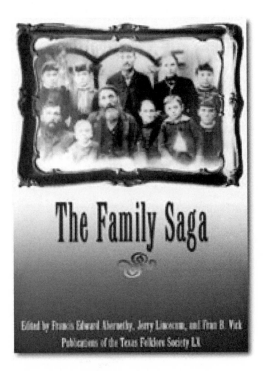

The Family Saga, the 2003 publication.

The Talbots.

DUSTING OUT

Dallas Times Herald

Sunday, November 28, 1982

During the early years of the Depression the Jim Talbots lived in a two-room shack on Grandad's Washita River ranch in the Texas Panhandle. Jim was Grandad's cousin and he helped out on the place and he was peg-legged. He was a big strong man and he wore this regular strap-on peg leg, and I would have given my toy tractor to have seen him take it off and put it on again. As I remember the story—or imagined it—Jim Talbot got caught in the crossfire in a train robbery at a railroad station and stopped the bullet that eventually cost him his leg. That scene is as vivid in my mind now as it was fifty years ago.

Jim's family consisted of Jim and Pearl and their three kids—an older girl and a little boy, and Frances, who was seven years old and my age. Girl that she was, she was the only child to play with for miles and miles of Panhandle plains, and she helped to keep away the high lonesomes that always hung over the prairie. Frances was red-headed and completely freckled and ready to explore the far reaches of any barn or plum thicket or rat's nest. Neither of us could imagine a world without the other, and I loved her dearly.

The Jim Talbots dusted out in 1932. The bottom had already dropped out of the cotton and grain market, and a harvested crop barely paid for the seed. Then the drouth hit. Grandad cut back on his stock and there wasn't any work for Jim and no money to pay him with. The ranch was on its way out, even though we didn't know it at the time. The Jim Talbots were the first to go.

It hadn't always been that way. At first the land had been filled with life. Dad said that when they first moved out on the Washita the grass brushed the bottom of his stirrups as he rode. He and his brothers used to ride fenders and shoot prairie chickens and race greyhounds after coyotes, and in the winter the tanks were covered with ducks. We killed hogs in the chill of late fall mornings, and great flocks of blackbirds fanned and circled by the lot gate where we threw out feed for the cattle. But by 1932 the grass was short and spare, and the hot ground showed bare and caked, and the tanks were bogs of mud, or cracked dry. It was a land of horned toads and tumblebugs and killdeers, and the hot wind harried its surface without mercy. It would not support much life. It could not support the Jim Talbots.

A lot of dusted-out farmers went to the valleys of California during those bad years. Jim Talbot decided to stick with Texas. He moved south to work for another cousin, and to live in another two-room shack, on a farm near Taylor.

It didn't take long to load the family. Two rooms holding five people do not have much space left for extra furniture. They had a small four-hole wood stove with a stove-pipe oven, five chairs in all, a table, kitchen safe, and two beds, and that was about it. Jim had a few tools but he had always sharecropped or worked somebody else's place so he had no plows or harness.

It must have been a grim afternoon when Dad helped them load all their worldly possessions in the back of an old Chevy bob-tailed truck. But for Frances and me it was a time of excitement and expectation—a time of people talking and moving—and we were filled with thoughts of traveling and seeing new places and rolling merrily down the highway in another adventure together. While the grownups loaded the truck, we played Annie Over with a black sock stuffed with rags. We thought our world would always be the same.

They finished loading a little before sundown, that time of the day when the prairie took on a gentler countenance. The last things loaded were the two mattresses. The men laid them on top of all the furniture and made the back of the truck look like a big soft bed. Frances and I crawled up on top and played and rolled around till Dad hollered up at us to calm down. When we left the shack Pearl got in the cab and held the boy in her lap. He was squalling because he wanted in the back with us. The girl climbed up on the mattresses in the back of the truck. She sat in a corner by herself, kind of drawn up in a knot. I think she was crying.

We drove back to the ranch house at dusk, leaving the shack sitting empty and forsaken in the middle of the prairie space. Tumbleweeds were already slipping under the fence and huddling against its weathered walls.

Nobody talked much in our family anyhow, and there was even less talk that night at supper, even though Frances and I poked and giggled through the meal, and Frances knocked over her milk. After supper we played with Frances's doll on the back porch while Jim and Dad and Grandad sat on the steps and talked. They spoke in low tones with long pauses between sentences. A coyote gave a few yaps somewhere out on the prairie and the windmill creaked and rattled. Otherwise for them it was a place of silence.

At bedtime Frances and I slept on a pallet in the front hall. We talked about the fun we were going to have on the trip and that maybe we would eat at a cafe. A mockingbird sang late into the night from the windmill top.

The next morning Dad put bows on the truck bed and tied a big wagon sheet over them, and the truck looked all the world like a covered wagon. It was cool and dark under the tarp, and even before it was tied down, Frances and her doll and I had circled up to play in the back corner. I had a boy doll with overalls but I never got it out when Frances was there. While we were playing, Jim's wife pushed in a cardboard box that had their traveling clothes in it. It was tied with binder twine.

Dad pulled the truck up by the windmill to top off the radiator and sent Frances and me after some drinking water. We got a couple of jugs to fill from the tank in the milk house. They were big, gallon vinegar jugs with towsacking wrapped around and sewed on for cover. As long as the towsacking was wet, the water stayed cool, and the jug had a good musty wet smell when you raised it to drink.

Grandmother and Pearl came out of the house. Pearl was carrying a shoe box of fried chicken and biscuits. Frances and I had filled the jugs and had crawled up the windmill ladder and were walking the crossbraces. Jim and Grandad stopped talking and shook hands. Pearl and Grandmother hugged each other, and as she turned to leave, Grandmother reached into her apron pocket and handed her a tin of snuff. Pearl got up in the cab and Jim told Frances to get down from the windmill and get in the truck. The other girl and the boy were sitting back in the corner under the wagon sheet when Frances and I crawled in and started wrestling around on the soft mattresses. We were anxious to begin this new game together.

We were doing somersaults when Dad told me to get down out of the truck. I climbed down and waited for him to send me after something for the trip, when he hugged me against his leg and told me to help Grandmother with the milking while he was gone. Then he crawled up into the cab and Jim pegged around to crank the truck. He jerked around till the engine coughed and popped and finally started running. Then he got up in the cab and they pulled out of the yard and rolled down the hill to the pasture road that led out to another world.

I stood and watched part of my life driving away and I couldn't move. I could not believe it. I couldn't believe that they—Dad and Jim Talbot and Frances—could drive off on this great adventure and leave me behind. I couldn't believe that Frances would go away and leave me in this lonesome place without anyone to play with.

Then a kind of panic struck me, and I ran after the truck as it bumped and swayed on the road that skirted the cow-lot fence. It slowed to cross the cattleguard that led to the next pasture and I almost caught up with it. But then the old truck started making dust and I stopped. I could see Frances sitting with her legs hanging over the back edge of the truck and the mattresses. She held up her hand for a wave and the tears rolled down her cheeks. I leaned against a fence post—aching and empty—and cried as I watched the old truck with its wanderers drive away through the prairie-dog town that was the top of the farthest hill I could see.

I never saw the Jim Talbots again. The dry prairie wind that blew the water out of the chicken troughs and sucked the moisture from the soil and the grass and any green thing that grew—crop or weed—blew away Frances and the Jim Talbots and that part of my life that they occupied.

The land got drier after that. The sand drifted deep against the fence rows, and the tumbleweeds rolled back and forth across the scorched prairie. The everlasting winds shifted around the compass, never bringing rain, always dust. The grasshoppers came and the government passed out "hopper bait," but they still rose in waves as you walked along the stripped and tattered rows of cotton. The elm trees in the yard and all the fruit trees died, and we chopped them into firewood. The only tree left on the place was one lone cottonwood. Finally the windmill could no longer bring up water and the sucker rods rattled dryly in the pipes. The land died, and we moved away and left it lying there on the prairie.

The Depression ended, and it did finally rain again on the Washita but the hard times and the hot winds had dusted us out by then, and we weren't there to see it. I know it rained because I went back about thirty-five years later and looked at the old place, and I saw the grass.

I finally found the house place. I wound around through pastures and tied gates and cattleguards and came on it kind of unexpectedly. But there it was, or what was left, still sitting on the wind-swept hill, some frame barns and out buildings, looking down to the Washita River, a mile away. A cow lot was left, the red grain barn still had a fence around it. A long building that had two seed barns, a garage and a blacksmith shop, all joined, was still there. The cottonwood, not much bigger, was still there, but the house was gone, wrecked and hauled off. All that was left were three concrete steps leading up to nowhere and my grandmother's old Great Majestic iron stove sitting in what was once a daily-swept yard.

The Farm, painting by James R. Snyder.

BLOWING AWAY IN THE PANHANDLE

During the good times of the 1920s, Grandad bought a large ranch on the Washita River in the Texas Panhandle. His dream was to have his four sons living near him and working on the ranch. Between the hard times of the Dust Bowl and the drouth, his dream for his family came apart in the process. Dad lost his car business in Shamrock in 1929, and we joined Grandad for a while.

I do not know how long Dad and Mother stayed on the ranch. It was less than a year. The main story to come out of that time is Mother's time of departure. As a city girl, she had not wanted to move to the ranch in the first place, and the ranch was five miles from the mailbox and seventeen miles from Canadian, the nearest town. Mother told this story; Dad never mentioned it.

The bright time of her day, as she remembered, was early morning as she lay in bed and watched a mockingbird in its nest in a wild plum tree near her window. She watched the bird build its nest, lay the eggs, and eventually hatch them. She always stayed in bed through the baby birds' early morning feeding time. This was her only escape, she says, from the high lonesomes of the barren plains of the Panhandle.

Then, one morning as she watched and before she could do anything to save the biddies, a cat made a quick climb and a pounce and ended the mockingbird family. To hear Mother tell that story, before that day was over she was on her way to Childress to catch the Fort Worth and Denver back to Dallas.

Mother came back to the ranch to visit, but she never stayed very long. I spent much of my early life there and thought that it was the greatest place on earth. But drouth, Dust Bowl, grasshoppers, and the Depression were more than the old place could bear. We lost the ranch in 1935.

That last winter on the ranch a terrible blizzard snowed in Grandmother and Grandad and their invalid daughter for over a week. Grandad was sick and Grandmother was chopping up furniture and the flooring to keep a fire going. She used to tell of having to go out and dig down through the snow to get to the stable where the milk cow was kept. Those were hard times.

Ab as a boy, holding wild ducks.

The story the family remembered and continued to speculate about was the moving of the Jim Talbots from the ranch. Jim was Grandad's cousin, and Grandad had built Jim a two-room house on the ranch. But by 1932 the drouth had hit, the bottom had dropped out of the cattle, grain, and cotton market, and there was no way that the ranch could support Grandad's family plus Jim Talbot and his wife and three kids. "Seven-cent cotton, forty-cent meat/How in the world can a poor man eat!"

Dad loaded everything those five people owned in the back of a bobtailed truck, covered it with wagon bows and a wagon sheet and took the Talbots to South Texas. It was as close to *Grapes of Wrath* as you could get and not be in the movie. The exodus of the Jim Talbots was one of the most dramatic episodes of our family's life during those hard times of the Depression. Their story is still a part of the fabric of our family.

Ben and Louisa Abernethy, Ab's grandparents.

The Abernethy family, with Ab standing (in white pants) to the left of Aunt Vergie, with his grandfather, Ben Abernethy, seated in front.

RURAL CUSTOMS IN "THE SPECIALIST"

[Paper presented at the Seventieth Annual Meeting
of the Texas Folklore Society, Jefferson Texas,
March 28, 1986]

Periodically I stumble across an old piece of vaudeville-style humor bogged down in the morass of my office files under the "Miscellaneous" label. I always discover it with pleasure and surprise, as if I've found an old friend of my youth. It is Chic Sale's classic "The Specialist," and I read it again with laughter and run off copies to send around to my friends, some of whom remind me that I sent them copies on my last discovery. "The Specialist" is two-generations-old outhouse humor, so a truly appreciative audience, one with first-hand experience with this venerable institution, becomes increasingly hard to find.

One reason for my continuing enjoyment of this semi-scatalogical outhouse humor is that it was an indelible part of my own growing up, not only because it was there that I first discovered strange and what turned out to be everlasting internal murmurings as I studied the ladies' underwear section in the Sears & Roebuck Catalog, but as it figured in other dramatic incidents during what I considered then to be very uneventful times.

Our own little house behind the house stood a discrete distance away—it seemed miles at the time—and was silhouetted sharply against the Panhandle prairie skyline. One refinement was a mounted path that dad had built with a slip and team that ran, with a branch off to the milkhouse, right up to the door. Another was a large bullet hole right below the ventilator star that focused a moving beam of sunlight with which one could during his philosophical meanderings mark the inevitable passage of time.

Grandad was responsible for the bullet hole. He was sitting on the back steps one evening looking over his old Marlin .44–40. He had the rifle across his knees, and when he levered it to test the

277

action, it went off and sent a lead slug the size of your finger flying through the wall of the outhouse, which at the time contained Carl Giddens, one of the hands. Carl jerked open the door and sprang forward like he was catapulted. He managed to clear the threshold but hobbled as he was, he stretched his full six-and-a-half feet before the door like a multi-colored carpet. The bullet had angled through the side wall and had gone out the back. It had scattered a world of splinters, but it missed Carl a good three feet, four if he had his elbows on his knees. Grandad was appalled at what he had done and was immediately by Carl's side. He was greatly concerned with Carl's welfare and asked first if he had been hit and then asked if the bullet had come before, after, or during.

An invalid aunt who walked with the aid of a cane-bottom chair made the trip one morning and encountered a skunk just inside the door. They both became terribly agitated, and like Carl, Aunt Vergie retreated faster than her impaired means of locomotion would accommodate. Like Carl, also, she found herself stretched out on this well mounted path, she without her chair, which she had thrown with a sudden burst of energy some eight or ten feet away. Grandmother found her some time later, and the strongest statement of mother love I know of is her getting Vergie's odoriforous self up and back to the horse trough and bathed. The smell of skunk long hung in the corners and crevasses of the outhouse, and it was only the fact that the skunk odor had strong competition that it didn't remain forever.

Dad and I stopped by one evening after milking. In a state of enthusiasm or emergency I ran ahead and swung the door in on a very large bull snake. I haven't heard a bull snake blow in many a year but in my memory that one sounded like a train whistle. Much panic ensued with granddad running out with his pistol, which he was always trying to find a use for. By the time forces were mobilized the snake had slithered off somewhere underneath, secure in the thought that no one was coming under after him.

The spirit of that monstrous bull snake, or Vergie's skunk, of various birds and varmints that got trapped inside, and an assortment of wasps, dirt-dobbers, and spiders became a part of the ambiance of that particular place and always added an element of suspense and expectation to a visit. This could probably be said of most privies. My wife, who grew up with indoor plumbing, set some sort of record for not going when we visited an uncle's ranch. On her first reluctant trip out back she found that all the corners were frequented by large colonies of daddy long-legs spiders who clung together and pulsated rhythmically in her direction. I tried to assuage her fears by explaining that they were not poisonous and would not hurt her even though they did walk across her as they regularly migrated from one corner to another.

All of which brings us to Chic Sale's "The Specialist." Chic was a vaudeville actor in the Nineteen 'Teens and Twenties, who was good enough to play the Palace and who later acted in Broadway musical comedies and in movies in Hollywood. He was a talented actor and mimic and could assume a multitude and a variety of roles from a staid and serious Abraham Lincoln to a bouncing village schoolboy. Chic became Lem Putt, the carpenter who specialized in building outhouses, when he delivered "The Specialist." The monologue was not a part of his vaudeville routine but was created for presentation to Rotary clubs, with which he was closely associated. He presented the routine before other men's clubs but never before a mixed audience. In 1929 during a presentation he saw someone writing it down, so he promptly published it under his own aegis in order to copyright it. It is still in print and copyright and the illustrated booklet can be purchased for $5.00.

I present excerpts from "The Specialist" not only to remind us all of the joys of indoor plumbing, but because—even though it was written with humor—it is based on traditional and customary wisdom and practices. Lem is a specialist. He knows his privies. And what he tells us about their construction and their uses is an accurate depiction of a very necessary and universal part of life two or three generations ago.

Much of Lem's wisdom is imparted to a prospective customer who is planning to build a modest two-holer as a necessary addition to his farm's out buildings. The customer had wanted it near a large apple tree. Lem cautions against it:

There ain't no sound in nature so disconcertin as the sound of apples droppin on th' roof. Then another thing, there's a crooked path runnin by that tree and the soil there ain't adapted to absorbing moisture. During the rainy season she's likely to be slippery. Take your grandpappy—going out there is about the only recreation he gets. He'll go out some rainy night with his nighties flappin around his legs, and like as not when you come out in the morning you'll find him prone in the mud, or maybe skidded off one of them curves and wound up in the corn crib.

Lem has other very pragmatic/practical and well thought out ideas about the placement of his customer's privy. He advises the prospect that the path to the privy must, by all means, go by the woodpile for some quite practical reasons:

Take a woman, fer instance—out she goes. On the way back she'll gather five sticks of wood, and the average woman will make four or five trips a day. There's twenty sticks in the wood box without any trouble. On the other hand, take a timid woman, if she sees any men folks around, she's too bashful to go direct out so she'll go to the wood-pile, pick up the wood, go back to the house, and watch her chance. The average timid woman—especially a new hired girl—I've knowed to make as many as ten trips to the wood-pile before she goes in, regardless. On a good day you'll have your wood box filled by noon, and right there is a savin of time.

Now, about the digging of her. You can't be too careful about that, I sez; dig her deep and dig her wide. It's a mighty sight better to have a little privy over a big hole than a big privy over a little hole. Another thing; when you dig her deep you've got 'er dug; and you ain't got that disconcertin thought stealing over you that sooner or later you'll have to dig again.

Lem goes into the construction of the house itself in elaborate but thoughtful and revealing detail.

I can give you a lean-to type or a pitch roof. Pitch roofs cost a little more, but some of our best people has lean-tos. If it was for myself, I'd have a lean-to, and I'll tell you why.

A lean-to has two less corners for the wasps to build their nests in; and on a hot August afternoon there ain't nothin so bothersome as a lot of wasps buzzin round wile you're settin there doin a little readin, figgerin, or thinkin. Another thing, I sez, a lean-to gives you a high door. Take that son of yours shootin up like a weed: Don't any of him seem to be turnin under. If he was tryin to get under a pitch roof he'd crack his head everytime. Take a lean-to, Elmer: They ain't stylish, but they're practical.

Lem also gives us considerable insight into the interior furnishings of a well built outhouse.

Now, about her furnishin's. I can give you a nail or hook for the catalogue, and besides, a box for cobs. You take your pa, for instance; he's of the old school and naturally he'd prefer the box; so put 'em both in, Elmer. Won't cost you a bit more for the box and keeps peace in the family. You can't teach an old dog new tricks, I sez.

And as long as we're on furnishin's, I'll tell you about a technical point that was put to me the other day. The question was this: What is the life, or how long will an average mail order catalogue last, in just the plain, ordinary eight family three holer? It stumped me for a spell; but this bein a reasonable question I checked up, and found that by placin the catalogue in there, say in January—when you get your new one—you should be into the harness section by June; but, of course, that ain't through apple time, and not countin on too many city visitors, either.

An' another thing—they've been puttin so many of those stiff colored sheets in the catalogue here lately that it makes it hard to figger. Somethin really ought to be done about this, and I've thought about takin it up with Mr. Sears Roebuck hisself.

As to the latch for her, I can give you a spool and string, or a hook and eye. The cost of a spool and string is practically nothin, but they ain't positive in action. If somebody comes out and starts rattlin the door, either the spool or the string is apt to give way, and there you are. But, with a hook and eye she's yours, you might say, for the whole afternoon, if you're so minded. Put on the hook and eye of the best quality 'cause there ain't nothin that'll rack a man's nerves more than to be sittin there ponderin, without a good, strong, substantial latch on the door.

Now, I sez, what about windows; some want 'em, some don't. They ain't so popular as they used to be. If it was me, Elmer, I'd say no windows; and I'll tell you why. Take, fer instance, somebody comin out—maybe they're just in a hurry or maybe they waited too long. If the door don't open right away—and you won't answer 'em, nine times out of ten they'll go round and look in the window, and you don't get the privacy you ought to.

Now, about ventilators, or the designs I cut in the doors or walls. I can give you stars, diamonds, or crescents—there ain't much choice—all give good service. A lot of people like stars, because they throw a crooked shadder. Others like crescents 'cause they're graceful and simple. Last year we was cuttin a lot of stars; but this year people are kinda quietin down and runnin more to crescents. I do cut twinin hearts now and then for young married couples; and bunches of grapes for the newly rich. These last two designs come under the head of novelties and I don't very often suggest 'em, because it takes time and runs into money.

I wouldn't take any snap judgment on her ventilators, because they've got a lot to do with the beauty of the structure. And don't over-do it, like Doc Turner did. He wanted stars and crescents both, against my better judgment, and now he's sorry. But it's too late; 'cause when I cut 'em, they're cut. And gentlemen, you can get mighty tired, sittin day after day lookin at a ventilator that ain't to your likin.

Now, how do you want that door to swing? Openin in or out? He said he didn't know. So I sez it should open in. This is the way it works out: Place yourself in there. The door openin in, say about forty-five degree. This gives you air and lets the sun beat in. Now, if you hear anybody comin, you can give it a quick shove with your foot and there you are. But if she swings out, where are you? You can't run the risk of havin her open for air or sun, because if anyone comes, you can't get off that seat, reach way around and grab 'er without getting caught, now can you? He could see that I was right.

Now, I sez, about the paintin of her. What color do you want 'er, Elmer? He said red. Elmer, I sez, I can paint her red, and red makes a beautiful job; or I can paint her bright green, or any one of a half dozen other colors, and they're all mighty pretty; but it ain't practical to use a single solid color, and I'll tell you why. She's too durn hard to see at night. You need contrast—Just like they use on them railroad crossin bars—so you can see 'em in the dark.

If I was you, I'd paint her a bright red, with white trimmin's—just like your barn. Then she'll match up nice in the daytime, and you can spot 'er easy at night, when you ain't got much time to go scoutin around.

Lem continues his discussion of the details of privy building with a warning of the disasters that can occur when an amateur attempts to do a specialist's job. One of the worst tragedies to occur in Sangamon County came when "Old Man Clark's boys thought they knowed something about this kind of work, and they didn't."

Lem's estimate for the work was considered too high by Mr. Clark, so he had his boys—mere amateurs—build one. They made one technical and near fatal error: They didn't anchor it.

You see, I put a 4 by 4 that runs from the top right straight on down five foot into the ground. That's why you never see any of my jobs upset Hallowe'en night. They might pull 'em out, but they'll never upset 'em.

Here's what happened: They didn't anchor theirs, and they painted it solid red—two bad mistakes.

Hallowe'en night come along, dark than pitch. Old Man Clark was out in there. Some of them devilish nabor boys was out for no good, and they upset 'er with the old man in it.

Of course, the old man got to callin and his boys heard the noise. One of 'em sez: "What's the racket? Somebody must be at the chickens." So they took the lantern, started out to the chicken house. They didn't find anything wrong there, and they started back to the house. Then they heerd the dog bark, and one of his boys sez, "Sounds like that barkin is over towards the privy." It being painted red, they couldn't see she was upset, so they started over there.

In the meantime the old man had gotten so confused that he started to crawl out through the hole, yelling for help all the time. The boys reckonized his voice and come runnin, but just as they got there he lost his holt and fell. After that they just called—didn't go near him. So you see what a tragedy that was: And they tell me he has been practically ostracized from society ever since.

An old-fashioned one-holer.

Climbing trees on a hunt.

NOW, DON'T THAT BEAT ALL!

A morning deer hunt is usually over around ten o'clock. Even the most patient of hunters is ready to come off his stand and go back to the camp by that time, particularly if he has not seen a hair. I carry coffee, a pork chop, and a Snickers bar, so I can last a little longer, if I have a mind to. Under the best of circumstances, somebody has stayed at the camp and cooked sausage and eggs with biscuits and gravy for his buddies when they come in from the woods. If not, there might be a cold plate of last night's fried venison backstrap still lying around. The coffee pot is always on, and the hunters report on their morning hunts, usually as they stand backed up to an outdoors log fire.

The hunting report is casual, but it should be accurate because the others listen and learn. "All I saw was a big old black fox squirrel and one armadillo and some fresh hog rubs where that trail comes out of the creek bottom." Or, "When I finally turned around and saw him, he saw me and left the county." You learn two things with those reports: 1) where to put a hog trap and 2) don't turn around when you hear a deer walking up behind you. Reports lead to remembrances and remembrances lead to the kind of hunting tales that have been told after hunts ever since man got the genetic command to kill and eat meat or die.

A great gun story is one Fount Simmons used to tell down in the Thicket. Fount was paralyzed from the waist down, but he was a great market hunter during the time when the railroads were being built in the Thicket and the big saw mills were flourishing. He heard that somebody had an eight-gauge shotgun for sale in Newton, so he took a two-day ride up there and bought it. He tried it out on his way back and said it took him an hour before he could get back on his horse. When Fount got home he charged it pretty heavy and set it in the gun rack and told his brother Rad that that was just the right gun to get the old buck with, the one that always skirted their field just out of range. After a light shower one afternoon Rad took the gun and eased out to the edge of the pasture and took a stand at the forks of a split-rail fence, with the gun barrel resting on the third rail. About three o'clock the folks in the house heard a mighty roar from Rad's direction that shook the trees. About six o'clock Rad came in, considerably bruised up and with his arm hanging kind of limp. He said he had the front end and the back end of the deer hanging down in the woods, and that he had spent most of the afternoon rebuilding the fence.

An old boy came up from Houston to hunt one weekend with Speck Risinger in Tyler County, and of course, since he was pretty new to the game Speck put him on a real meat stand right on this sand road. Speck called them "poison stands!" and it scared you to think what might come out over you.

Speck checked him out on the rules of the hunt, told him not to shoot a doe or any of the hounds, and left him standing there with his brand new Marlin lever-action .30-30. It was a still-frost morning, and the dogs jumped a big buck just as he was coming in to bed down and, dogs a-squawlin', the race was on. Speck fired his gun to let the standers know that a buck was running, and then he took off through the woods trying to keep them in sight. Sure enough, they were headed right toward the sand-road "poison stand."

Speck wasn't far behind when deer and dogs crossed the road, and he was waiting to hear a shot and a yell but there wasn't a sound. When he got there the man was still stuttering in the shakes of buck fever and standing with his gun at his side. He said that it was a big buck and that it just kind of trotted across the road about twenty steps from him—said he had time to fire five shots before the buck hit the brush again. Speck said he hadn't heard a shot, and the old boy swore and be-damned that he had fired five times. That was about the time Speck saw something shining in the sand and looked a little closer and found five .30–30 shells. Not a cap had been busted. The old boy had levered the shells through but had never pulled the trigger.

Chuck Davis said that on another occasion Speck saw this stander and asked him what he had seen. The stander told him that he did see four or five dogs crossing the high line, but that was all. Speck asked him, "Do you think that a deer was chasin' the dogs?"

Jim Hayes, who was teaching in Woodville at the time, was hunkered down on a stand in Sunny Dell Pasture early one cold morning and decided he had to have a cup of coffee. So real slow he got his thermos and poured a cap full and glanced down the road just in time to see a big old rocking-chair buck sneaking out to cross the road. He didn't have time to put down his cup, so he eased his left hand with the coffee out to raise the gun barrel. He got it up just to sight as the buck started into the woods again, and he touched it off. Jim said the gun roared and the whole world turned wet, hot, and coffee brown. And that old buck left the country without even raising his flag.

On another frosty winter morning Jim Snyder climbed up and squatted on a big log for his morning relief. He propped his rifle against the log, and for easy access he spindled a short roll of toilet paper on the rifle barrel. Soon after, but still in the midst of, a young buck stepped out of the woods and gazed in wonder at this large growth on a downed log in his stomping ground. Never removing his eye from the buck target, and pants down and still in a squatting position, Snyder slowly retrieved and shouldered his rifle. He raised it to sight only to be reminded that a roll of toilet paper rested between his back sight and front sight and completely obliterated the deer. The buck, amused and confused at such a picture, strolled back into the brush. Snyder went back to his business with his handily spooled roll of toilet paper.

Noah Platt used to tell of a fellow he was hunting with who took three shots at a deer trotting along just on the other side of a barb-wire fence, and each shot centered a fence post.

On a hunt at Cecil Overstreet's, one of the Moyes got so excited when he heard the dogs bringing game his way that when the deer popped out behind him into the land line he whirled around and threw his gun at him.

Another time, some young man hunting in Cecil Overstreet's pasture in Hardin County was walking down a trail to his stand when a little forked-horn stepped out in front of him. He popped back the bolt, reached in his pocket for a shell, and came out with his cigarette lighter. He claimed that he chambered the cigarette lighter, fired at the buck, and left a burn stripe all the way from his appetite to his asshole. In spite of which, the deer got away.

Closer to the truth, if that's what you're looking for, Bill Clark tells a similar story about a man hunting near Sugar Creek. This fellow had been hunting an old mossy horn for several years without luck. In the early dawn on one frosty morning, he took out his new 20-gauge to test it on some squirrels. Just as he started to cross a fence he spotted his old buck nearby and looking the other way. He chambered a shell and pulled the trigger, and all he heard was the click of the firing pin. Old Mossy heard it too and hit the brush. Disappointed with his new shotgun, he broke it open and saw a roll of Tums in the chamber.

George Doland told about this Fort Worth hunter who was perched in a tree by a thick love-grass pasture waiting for nothing but a trophy buck. The prize buck showed up, the hunter fired, and the deer dropped where he stood, into the tall grass and out of sight. The hunter shinnied down the tree and headed through the tall grass across the pasture. He found the buck and pulled his knife to gut him. He grabbed his buck by his horns—and the buck indignantly rose up with the hunter hanging on and slashing at his throat. After some bloody hand-to-horn combat, the hunter finally subdued his trophy. He was sitting by his buck, trying to get his adrenalin back down and his breath back up, when he saw another buck lying in the deep grass about ten yards away. It was the buck he had shot.

These tales are not over after the hunt. They pop up every time hunters get together, and they're about all sorts of animals, including hogs.

Here's a tale I've told around the campfire, probably more than once. I don't know when I started hunting hogs. I guess it was when I first shot one and brought it home and cooked a ham for Thanksgiving dinner. It beat hell out of a turkey.

I was at Sunny Dell Pasture, hunting out of my leaning post-oak stand on Big Dry Creek when this big old sow came by just at sundown. I popped her. I guess she weighed a hundred pounds or more. Then I got to wondering what I was going to do with all that hog. I sure wasn't going to tote a whole hog back to my pickup a half a mile away, now—in the black dark. I decided to cut it up, deer fashion. I cut off its hams and shoulders and then peeled out the backstrap. I had a mess of meat stacked around in the black dark when I got through, plus a rifle, fanny pack, and climbing hooks.

I was trudging up the hill to the ridge road with a ham in both hands and a backstrap over my shoulder when they opened up. My God but it sounded like all the coyotes in the world, and they were gathering in the edge of the woods about fifty feet away, red-eyed and stirred to a feeding frenzy by the smell of that hog's blood. And I had left my gun for the next trip! I have no doubt that my hair stood on end, like in comic strips. I could feel it. And I could feel my blood which had stopped circulating and had gotten cold. The coyotes got louder and sounded closer, and I finally got back enough in control to start moving again—but not running! I knew I'd never make it in a race.

Looking back, there were probably five or six worn-out coyotes on the other side of the hill. I doubt that they even knew I was in the vicinity. I wasn't looking back that night, however. I made it out to my pickup and would have left the rest of that hog in the bottom with the coyotes, but I had to go back and get my gun and gear.

John Artie McCall and I talk on the phone fairly regularly, usually about hunting and wild animals. John Artie is paranoid about raccoons (and hogs!). Coons steal the corn out of his deer feeders at his camp on the Trinity. They throw chairs out of his deer stands, and tear up his duck blinds. This morning he was telling me how a friend of his was losing lots of corn out of a feeder, so he raised his feeder higher than he figured any coons could reach. He was still losing corn, so he put out a motion camera. What he got was a picture of one coon standing on another's shoulders, raking corn out of the feeder for every other coon in the pasture! "Now, don't that beat all! You think a coon ain't smart!"

The crew of *The Harkness*.

GREATER LOVE . . .

[by George N. Oliver (the Rabbi) 1923–2002 of Tyler, as told to F. E. Abernethy]

We called him "Rabbi" ironically, probably because he could be so outrageously disorderly and unrabbinical. His name was George Oliver, and he was among the veterans who returned from World War II to the Stephen F. Austin State College campus on the G. I. Bill in 1946. He had been in the 169th Infantry, C Company, 43rd Division and had fought up the islands from New Guinea to the Philippines. George and I lived together in old army barracks that had been moved onto the campus to house students. We called it "The Old Folks Home," and it was a den of iniquity.

The Rabbi was one of the wildest, drinkin'est, fightin'est characters I have ever known, and we bonded early when we were thrown in jail together on one of our sprees. But the Rabbi changed. He married a good woman and he became a schoolteacher. He taught at a junior college and in one of the Texas prison units. And he got religion and became a lay preacher. And every one of us who knew him in The Old Folks Home continued to be amazed at his metamorphosis.

The Rabbi never told this war story during the early years that we knew each other. We were all too close to the war to try to impress each other with sea stories. Fifty years later, after we renewed our friendship through frequent visits, he began to tell his war stories. The following story about him and his sergeant became his main story, and I think he defined his life by that story. This episode in his war became the beginning of his redemption. George's family knows this story better than any other of his war stories, so if the story is not legend now it probably will be if the family holds together long enough and closely enough to pass it on.

George's outfit was battling through the jungles of New Guinea when it was pulled out and sent to the rear for R&R. Before they went into town on their first pass, the chaplain called them all together and gave them the regular G. I.'s lecture on how to behave in civilization and how not to get the clap or get hauled in by the shore patrol. As usual, the soldiers were more amused than they were instructed, and the Rabbi, scorner and scoffer that he could be, was among the worst. After the lecture, he took great delight in amusing his comrades with satiric imitations of the Catholic-priest chaplain giving his lecture on sexual activities. Unfortunately, his sergeant, who was a devout Catholic and a close friend of the chaplain, heard George's performance. The result was that the sergeant took a strong dislike to George, and according to George, the sergeant for spite sent him on the most dangerous missions in the following campaigns.

A year later, in 1944, the Rabbi's outfit was in the Philippines. George's company was charged with capturing a hill and the gun emplacements contained thereon. During the advance George was pinned down and a Jap rifleman had him in his sights and was sniping at him, the bullets kicking up dust all around him. George was frantically throwing hand grenades in the Japanese direction, when he slipped and fell, turning as he fell. His hand-grenade pouch swung around and hit him square in the mouth and nose.

Blood poured down his face and front, and the Rabbi was certain that he had been hit and was mortally wounded. He screamed for the medic and then rolled up in a ball of pain waiting for something to happen.

George felt a hand on his shoulder and felt himself being rolled over on his back. He opened his eyes and saw the sergeant leaning over him. The sergeant comforted him, wiped the blood off his face, and told him, "Tex, you're hurt but you aren't shot and you aren't going to die."

Those were Sergeant Buddy Poland's last words. The Jap sniper who had been getting the Rabbi's range sighted in on the sergeant's back as he leaned over helping George. He squeezed the trigger and the sergeant dropped almost on top of George. The sergeant's body made a protective wall for George until the action moved on up the hill and George recovered and moved on with it.

George left his sergeant behind in the advance up the hill, but he never left the memory of that moment and his belief that Sergeant Buddy Poland took the bullet meant for him.

The Rabbi went to that story often as he recounted his own life's evolution from rakehell to a man of God. He got to where that incident became the turning point in his life. It wasn't. At war's end the Rabbi had not even begun to raise all the hell that life had in store from him. But between the love of his wife and some years to mature in, George did achieve a miraculous transformation. He was a naturally loving man, but he became even more so, continually concerned about his old wartime friends. And the moral of his story of a man who saved another man whom he didn't even like was "Greater love hath no man than this: that he will lay down his life for his brother."

As a young sailor.

The Whittler's Bench, Tenaha, Texas.

WHITTLER'S BENCH—TENAHA, TEXAS

[Originally, photographs and text by Francis Edward Abernethy]

Sometimes a man gets the feeling that he's not living life, that it's living him. He cuts the grass, turns around, and there it is whispering to be cut again. He fixes the starter on his car, and the washing machine demands equal time. He spends all his money paying one stack of bills, while another stack stridently insists that it be paid too. He begins to feel that he is running in deep sand, and if he ever slows down all the responsibilities in his life will roll over him and bury him. This is the time, if he has any character, that he will step aside, let it all roll by, and go fishing. Or if that is too much trouble, he can sit down and whittle. Tenaha, Texas, in its infinite wisdom has provided a whittlers' bench for just such an occasion.

Tenaha (of "Tenaha, Timpson, Bobo, and Blair" fame) is in Shelby County, deep in the East Texas pines. It's a small town but it seems satisfied and easy going, and it's what a lot of Houston and Dallas people dream about escaping to. Tenaha is an Indian name and it means "muddy water." One of the whittlers said that the town was called "muddy water" because during the wet years, back when it rained regularly, there was always a pond of red-dirt-muddy water standing between the main street and the railroad tracks. The other whittlers agreed both with the etymology and the fact that it used to rain more.

Tenaha's whittlers' bench is set against the brick east side of Wall Drug Store. It is a weathered-oak two-by-twelve that sits on iron pipe legs. For a long time the bench sat on cedar blocks, but these were slowly whittled away. A part of one of the blocks is still in the wood pile at the end of the bench, still furnishing whittling material for the guests.

The whittlers started off by telling me that the bench had been there since The Beginning. Then some fellow in his mid-eighties said that it had been there all his life, or at least as long as he could remember. They finally decided that since somebody was going to write it down that the bench had been there around fifty years. And it has been the popular gathering place for the Tenaha whittling aristocracy for all that time.

Some days, they tell me, the bench is in such demand that a serious whittler can hardly find space to sit down, and he doesn't dare get up once he gets a place. The number of whittlers varied from six to ten the day I visited. Most of the men are retired, between work, or did what they had to do that morning. One of them said that he used to spend his time fishing but he got saved, and had to give up lying, so he took up whittling instead. They are a strong and hardy crew in spite of the large number of years they stack up among themselves. They are proud of the combination of wit, spirit, strength, and age which characterizes them, and they brag enthusiastically on their oldest member, who is ninety-four, still doesn't wear glasses, and drives Tenaha's only taxicab.

You need the proper tools—and techniques.

They are also proud of their whittling skill. Expert whittling doesn't require a real sharp knife, I learned. In fact, a sharp slicing knife with a long bevel would slice into the wood, which is what a whittler doesn't want to do. A short bevel on a not-too-sharp knife is what is required, one that will plane off long, thin curls of delicate shavings. A real professional can start at one end of his whittling stick and shave a long curl all the way down to the other.

They don't whittle things either, like wooden spoons or fids or candlesticks. Their purpose on that bench is not to create either the useful or the ornamental. They are there asserting their independence and demonstrating their command of their lives by cultivating skill without purpose. They are practicing conspicuous consumption of time, and those of us who speed through Tenaha to make an appointment on time in Shreveport eye them with envy. They know this. They whittle pieces of wood into non-utilitarian forms to show the world that while they are on that bench they don't have to be concerned with clocks or with the frantic struggle to either decorate, maintain, or keep up with life.

Their talk is much like their whittling, an artistic and conspicuous consumption of words. Theirs is one of the few places in our society where conversation is an art form, where telling tales, moralizing, lying, sermonizing, playing with words and figures of speech are practiced and cultivated as an end in themselves. They are masters at the use of colorful and dynamic language, and their speech patterns and dialect will never be diluted or standardized by television, movies, or journalese. And like the whittled stick, their talk is an end in itself and does not require a practical and social application. They can discuss politics, morality, and ethics academically, separated for the time being from the actuality of these things, as a historian might discuss the Napoleonic Wars. Their talk is not an instrument to persuade men to their way of thinking or living or to bring about changes in society. It is talk for the sake of talk, the refinement of man's greatest glory, his gift of speech.

Their daily gathering also satisfies the ancient instinct of males to bond together, to cluster and exalt in their maleness, and to celebrate their masculine command of life and all creatures in it. An interesting female passing by will quicken their conversation considerably and move them out to the edge of the bench, but she is no challenge to their position or territory. The whittlers' bench is a male place, a place of knives and of old hunts and battles and conquests. The uninitiated may sit but he cannot enter.

Ironically, however, the struggle is all. No matter how we might envy the whittlers when we look up from the panic of our own pursuits, most of us would have to be struck down before we could slow down long enough to whittle a decent stick. We are not conditioned for tranquility. Those magic moments are rare when we can truly loaf and invite our souls. They are small glimpses of our fantasies of Paradise, when the lions within us lie down with the lambs. For that reason, because of the rarity of these glimpses, the bench and its occupants stand out as important symbols. Whether they— these men or others like them—are whittling on the city square, at the county courthouse or a filling station, in the park or just in the shade, the whittlers show us that it is possible for a super-charged *homo sapien* in a manicly accelerating machine-of-a-world to step out of the pandemonium for a while, re-assert a little control over his life, and simply savor his humanity.

All in a day's work.

In the faculty lounge.

BACK IN THE OUGHT 'SIXTIES

I (an English teacher whose academic field was Renaissance drama) became a folklorist in the 1960s, and I am going to tell you about a few of those dear souls who stood in loco parentis and showed me the way.

This all started over coffee and moon pie—at five cents apiece, I might add—in the Lamar Tech faculty lounge, in 1959. The subject of the Texas Folklore Society came up, and a colleague told me that I should join up with that group. And fifty years ago I did. The following Easter, in 1960, I took the Greyhound from Beaumont and went to present a paper at my first meeting in San Antonio.

I was much <u>im</u>pressed with the Menger Hotel, but I was much <u>sup</u>pressed by the boisterous jollity of that Thursday evening's TFS gathering at Casa Rio, when I lately arrived. After dinner, people sang. I sat in the last tier, hugging the shadows. Members were in full cry when I crept out and went back to the hotel to go over my paper for the fiftieth time.

I was probably still going over my paper Friday morning at 8:45. Soon after nine, I made my first appearance before the Texas Folklore Society with "East Texas Josey Party Songs." I was pleased that the audience did not go to sleep, walk out, or throw things. I was warmed by their reception. But, the high point of the session—and of many sessions and of many years thereafter—occurred when Hermes Nye, whom I had never heard of, passed me a note that read (I still have that note!), "Delightful! Let's get together this evening."

And we did!

After the banquet that night, Hermes, Américo Paredes, Roger Abrahams, and I and three or four others congregated in a dim corner of the banquet room. Everybody else had gone. Hermes had his guitar, and we circled up our chairs and began to sing, usually singly but sometimes in duet harmony or as a group. We quickly worked it out that each of us would sing two songs and then pass on the guitar. A soldier from Arkansas wandered in and joined us, and a bunch of folks wandered by and sat in the darkness around us. We loved it. Nobody hogged the guitar. Everybody enjoyed everybody else. I remember singing "Precious Jewel" and "Little Green Valley," neither of which anybody knew. It was a close encounter of the very best kind, and I felt a sense of belonging with them and the Texas Folklore Society that I have never gotten over. I have missed only one meeting, last year at Lubbock, since 1960.

Actually, during those morning and afternoon sessions, I enjoyed meeting a whole host of TFS folks, one of whom was Joe Doggett, a long-lost and distant cousin, and Hudson Long whose name was famous on an American lit textbook—and Jim Lee continually confused Hudson Long with Wilson Hudson. Ironically, later generations got confused between Jim Lee (He of Many Households) and Jim Byrd, and they called both of them "Jim Byrd Lee." I met the poet Everett Gillis from Texas Tech and Brownie McNeill, who was famous because he had cut a folk song LP with his picture on the jacket and was to become president of Sul Ross, and John Q. Anderson with the tiny guitar that knew a thousand songs, and many who would become integral parts of my life. That is who I am remembering and celebrating herein, those TFS members of my parents' generation, Back in the Ought 'Sixties, the ones who planted the vines from which I harvested the grapes, the richest part of my academic life—my years with the Texas Folklore Society.

And I also secondarily celebrate those that came into the fold about the same time, because we were on the watershed, and we were the new generation. Jim Lee and Ed Gaston had come a year earlier in 1958, but we all—James Ward and Edwin Jr., Jim Byrd, John O. West, Paul Patterson, Jim Day—came about the same time. And later in the 'Sixties, the much younger Joyce Roach, Sarah Greene, and Sylvia Grider came on board. We were the new TFS generation in the 'Sixties. We were the kids! believe it or not, still wet behind the ears!

Paul Patterson.

And Hermes Nye, he of the generous welcome, was the beginning for me.

Hermes was a fashionably-dressed, would-be hippie lawyer who gave papers on hot rods and armadillos and "hangin' ten." He had come down from the Midwest and married a rich Southern belle. I don't know how much law he practiced, but he was the Society's Counselor until the day he died. During that folk music explosion of the 'Sixties, Hermes sang at all the Dallas cabarets and emceed and performed on his own Big D radio show. During the Society's Thursday night hoot (I had never heard the word "hootenanny" until I came to the TFS.) Hermes was the interlocutor and was the best we ever had, always fully focused on the participant, never stealing the light. Hermes knew how to make first-time performers confident and comfortable. His own annual presentation was a melodramatic and interminable recitation of "Lasca" and/or a musical rendition of the pecadillos of Aimee Semple MacPherson. Hermes wrote the meetings' resolutions in purple Victorian prose and read them in stentorian tones with flourish and gesture. In the 'Seventies, Hermes wrote a semi-fictional autobiography detailing his AC/DC sexual escapades, among other adventures, for which wife Mary Elizabeth forgave him (she said!) but Martha Emmons would not. The title of Hermes' opus was *Sweet Beast, I Have Gone Prowling*, which should give you some idea of the nature of the content. Hermes was a jewel!

Hermes Nye at a hootenanny, c. 1960s.

Martha Emmons read Hermes' *Sweet Beast* and was *not* amused. Miss Martha, from the heart of Baylor Bible-Belt Baptistry in Waco, was the moral arbiter for the Society even then. The meeting papers were liberal in topic and delivery, during those chaotic transitional times, when the world was turning upside down. Martha handled the sexual and social revolution of the 'Sixties with mature sophistication, but she was also not amused by religious flippancy. At the Waco meeting she received Robert Flynn's first presentation of "Growing Up a Sullen Baptist" with pursed lips and tightened eyes. On the other hand, her presentation of "The Adulteration of Old King David," both religious and sexual, was an all-time hootenanny classic: "Sister Uriah, what chu doing with that wash tub on yo' front po'ch?" "Why, Ole King David, it's Satidy, and I'm fixin to take a bath." "Woman, ain't you got no shame? Take that tub inside!" "I would, Ole King David, but I'm just a pore little weak woman, and I cain't tote it inside all by myself." "Well, here, Miz Uriah, let me help you."—And that was the last they seen of Ole King David till come Monday!

Two TFS legends, John O. West and Martha Emmons.

And speaking of young—and old!—liberals, during one Driskell Hotel-Austin meeting we had a passionate and protracted integration discussion supporting Emmett Till or the Freedom Riders or something similar. We were to the point of passing resolutions to send to the Capitol and all Texas newspapers—or maybe we were going to march to the Capitol!—when ultra-liberal Hermes Nye informed us that, satisfying though it might be, such a political outpouring could jeopardize the Society's academic tax-exempt status. Such topics regularly arose thereafter during those parlous times, but they were in softer tones and kept in house.

Another indication of the TFS spirit of the times: Martin Shockley, the impeccably dressed Virginian with the aristocratic Tidewater accent and the strikingly grand white moustache, had the distinction of being fired from the University of Oklahoma in the 1940s for inviting a Negro to speak to an on-campus academic meeting. Martin later resigned as English Department head in Indiana when the president fired a colleague for supporting Henry Wallace of the far-left-wing Progressive Party. Fortunately for Texas and the Folklore Society, Martin spent most of his career at North Texas in Denton. One could not out-liberal Martin Shockley.

Another memorable elder member and episode was Judge Charles Francis II's getting drunk at the 1966 Monahans banquet and Mody Boatright's directing Jim Lee and me to take him back to his motel room. Dutifully we loaded the Judge into his car, poured his honor into his bed, and proceeded to take his long, shiny, black Cadillac on a midnight tour of the Monahans' honky tonks. I watched Lee cut an impressive swath that night, and I have ever since deferred to James Ward's sophistication and worldly ways.

On another evening of alcoholic enlightenment, one of the Society's grande dames took umbrage with one of my folkloric pronouncements and baptized me with a full glass of scotch and soda (It was a Baptist total immersion.) as a group of us discussed "professional matters" in the banquet room of the Shamrock Hotel. Jim Byrd promised to write a sonnet to suit the occasion but he never did.

Mody Boatright was the Secretary-Editor, the Alpha male, and the paterfamilias of the Society. With the forever cigar and a slight stoop, Mody moved with quiet authority among the members, closely trailed by young aspiring writers and presenters ever mindful of their need for upward mobility and the unwritten "publish or perish" clause in their teaching contracts.

Stith Thompson, the editor of PTFS # 1 and the venerated producer of the six-volume *Motif Index*, was a hero of that generation of folklorists, and John Q. Anderson imported him at least twice to TFS meetings, once in the 'Sixties to A&M, John Q.'s academic base. He was much welcomed by his peers, almost fawned upon. I am afraid that my peers were more involved in the night's hoot and where one could get booze in College Station.

Frank Dobie sometimes showed up at the Austin meetings to visit old friends, but he seldom stayed long. Most of us stood around in awe of this Texas icon and dared do little more than try to get a handshake and a howdy. Mr. Dobie and I had corresponded once, and we visited briefly at Mody's house one evening, but I am sorry to say that I never made a solid and personal connection with Texas folklore's Man of the Times. By the 'Sixties Dobie had become a member of the national (or international) folkloric pantheon and was out of the sphere of us ordinary assistant professors of English.

My warmest impression of Frank Dobie came on the night that he was made a Fellow of the Texas Folklore Society in Austin at the Driskill in 1961. (J. Frank Dobie, who was responsible for the early resurrection and the vigor and vitality of the Texas Folklore Society, was made a Fellow twenty years after he retired as Secretary-Editor. That distinction did not come lightly.) Dressed in his white linen suit, Dobie cut an imposing picture at that evening's banquet. He gratefully accepted the Fellowship scroll, briefly thanked the Society and sat down. Martin Shockley, as splendid an orator as Hermes, paid Frank Dobie his tribute, which concluded thusly (What I wouldn't give to orate this in Shockley's mellifluous tones!):

> A Texan not by birth but by choice, I came to
> Texas with about the average ignorance and
> prejudice. I had always considered the coy-
> ote a pesky varmint, a cunning chicken thief,

a sneaky villain best seen over the sights of a .30–30; then I read a book by Frank Dobie and learned that the coyote is a noble creature with a proud and independent spirit and a fierce love of freedom. I had always considered the longhorn to be a stupid cow critter, all bone, gristle, and stringy meat, mean, vicious and hard to handle; then I read a book by Frank Dobie and learned that the longhorn is a noble creature with a proud and independent spirit and a fierce love of freedom. I had always considered the mustang the sorriest specimen of horseflesh, hammer-headed, wall-eyed, ewe-necked, sway-backed, bushy-tailed, ornery and dangerous; then I read a book by Frank Dobie and learned that the mustang is a noble creature with a proud and independent spirit and a fierce love of freedom. Now they tell me Mr. Dobie is writing about rattlesnakes, and I anticipate another agonizing reappraisal.

Frank Dobie laughed out loud, hugged Martin, and spent the rest of the evening going around and visiting with members. That was a grand night, and Dobie was a grand man.

So many others of our, or "my," sainted elders were on stage Back in the Ought 'Sixties. Leland Sonnichsen, famous author-historian of El Paso, was a fine singer and piano player. He was also a charmer, and the ladies flocked around him like birds at a seed feeder. Allen Maxwell, Director of SMU Press, was there, and this was during a time of troubles between the TFS and the SMU publishers, because of late books and unanswered correspondence. Ralph Houston of Southwest Texas and the dearly loved Mabel Major of TCU, who had been a part of the Society since the 'Thirties, were regular presenters.

The most important elder in my professional life was Wilson M. Hudson. Wilson was a UT Phi Beta Kappa with four years in the Air Corps during WWII. He was also a scholar, who did his best to lead the TFS to higher academic levels with use of motif index numbers. He was a serious academic with a Victorian sensitivity and morality that made Miss Martha's standards almost bacchanalian, and he was my guide and mentor during the early years of my membership. Additionally, I shall ever be indebted to Wilson and Gertrude because they rescued Hazel and me from five o'clock Dublin traffic and restored us with brandy. To Wilson M. Hudson I owe the most.

And let us not forget John Lomax, Jr., a son of the Society's founder. John was a regular and bore his Lomax plaid-shirt mantle with due regard to his family's folklore heritage. John loved to sing acapella, and he could carry a tune, but it was in a rusty bucket. However, what he lacked in musical texture he made up for in volume and vitality. He loved to lead a singalong of "The Rivers of Texas," but John is best remembered by some of us for a one-time rendition of "Take This Hammer."

At a Houston folk singing soiree, we noticed at singing time that a six-foot, fifteen-inch-dbh, red-oak log lay half way between the audience's front row and the singers' table. Its presence aroused a flurry of speculation until Big John got up to sing "Take This Hammer." He reached behind the table and pulled out a shiny-sharp, double-bit axe, and stepped up to the log. After a few words explaining that "Hammer" was a work song learned from "Leadbelly" and used to coordinate axe or sledge hammer work, Big John began to sing: "Take this hammer (Whop! The axe bit into the log!) Give it to the Captain (Whop!) Take this hammer (Whop! This time a chip of wood went sailing toward the far end of the front row.) Give it to the Captain (Whop! We could tell, to our dismay, that John flat knew how to chop wood.) Take this hammer (Whop! Chips—Big chips!—were flying by now, and the first two rows were cleared, the previous occupants hugging the wall.) Give it to the Captain (A long pause, then a ferocious Whop! And a chunk of wood the size of a brickbat whizzed into the sheetrock wall and stuck.) Tell him I'm gone, Lawd (Whop!) Tell him I'm gone (Whop! Those of us left were ducking behind chairs.).

The audience was pretty well thinned by then, but Big John had two more verses to go and by golly, he was going to sing his song and chop his wood if it hare lipped the governor. He did. We all crept back to our seats and to a room carpeted with wood chips. Big John, grinning in self-satisfaction, accepted our scattered applause as his due, and took his seat, convinced that Old Daddy John Lomax was somewhere heavenly, applauding his demonstration of reality folklore. John Lomax, Jr., was a hard act to follow.

They were all hard acts to follow—Frank Dobie, Stith Thompson, Mody, Wilson, Sonnichsen, Shockley, Hermes, John Q. These members of the 'Sixties were the TFS builders of their time and their future, and they put the marks of their personalities on this organization. We honor these our ancestors who kept the Society's circle unbroken through their years to ours. We would not be here had they not kept the faith in the Society's future.

A different generation is now building our time and our future, and I can tell you when I look out over this membership of the Texas Folklore Society in its *one hundredth year of existence!!!* (Can you believe it!?) that the Society is larger, stronger, richer, filled with more vitality and imagination and folkloric expertise than it had Back in Ought 'Sixty and much of the time before. I can remember times in this past half-century of the Society's life when its sessions were held in a college classroom and we had empty chairs, times when we had so few acceptable papers on hand that we had trouble publishing an annual, times when we had to wait 'til the year's dues were paid to get money enough to pay for the publication of an annual. *But* I can also call to mind presentations and personalities that thrilled and excited me with their revelations, that were the greatest parts of my education—folkloric, academic, and personal. The richness of the Texas Folklore Society's coming together in this discipline made me rich with understanding of ways of life I would never have learned to see without the Society and its members.

We have come a long way in this last half of the Society's life-time, and I have complete faith in the Society's future and in Ken Untiedt's and Janet Simonds' management and leadership as the Society heads into its next one hundred years.

Now, as then, our future and the Society's future depend on its members' continued interest and involvement in Texas folklore and in the energy that they—you and I!—invest in the collecting, preserving, and presenting of our folklore. I am convinced that beyond the good fortune the Society has had in its membership, the reasons for its success are that it has loved and preserved folklore without embalming it in academic pedantry and *with* presenting it in ways palatable to public tastes and interesting to the eyes and ears of the general.

Folklore classes in colleges and universities have thinned out in the last two decades. Folklore centers at The University and throughout Texas and the U.S. have dwindled or disappeared. The American Folklore Society has diminished in membership and production and is seldom heard from. But the Texas Folklore Society has grown larger and stronger. We have, therefore, an even greater obligation and responsibility to dance with the partner who brung us.

I am convinced also in the good fortune that the Texas Folklore Society has had in its membership. We are a solid bunch of folks, children of many parents and many professions and many cultures, but rich and poor, we have always been kin. No matter what our ways of life and living, we come together as loving kinfolks bound together by our pride in our present and our past, cherishing the same songs and learning new ones, hearing the same stories and learning new ones, joined by the same traditions and beliefs—and learning and understanding and growing into new ones. We folks of the Texas Folklore Society are always learning and always growing, along with people who share with us the love of family and country and the native soil from which we grew.

Long live the Texas Folklore Society! Let us live another hundred years!

The cover photo for *Both Sides of the Border: A Sampling of Texas Folklore,* the 2004 publication.

PREFACE

﹏﹏

Tell me honestly, have you ever cleaned out your files? I don't mean picking through one pittance of a drawer of files while watching *As the World Turns.* I mean thoughtfully and meticulously going through cabinets and closets and garages filled with files that go back to your school days and even before. I thought not. The task out-daunted you, didn't it? You feared the cataclysmic emotional upheaval that would result from delving through the detritus of your past. I urge you to summon your true grit and intestinal fortitude and to do so now. Address yourself to the task so that those who follow you will not have that as one of their onerous duties at your eventual exit.

This "holier than thou" attitude is the result of my having cleaned out my Texas Folklore Society files as I prepare to pass the TFS editorial mantle on to Ken Untiedt. I had to do a massive cleanout and organization some years back when I organized and boxed all of the Society's records from 1971 to 2000 to be deposited with the rest of the TFS records in the archives at the Barker Center at The University. Now I have made the second round of cleaning out files to see if there was anything I missed, and I found some real jewels. These were papers and clippings from years past that had been lying around just looking for a place to make their literary debuts.

The result of all this cleaning out is that this year's PTFS is one of your ultimate bargains—four books in one!—a history monograph, a Tex-Mex book, a miscellany, and a *Family Saga* reprise. Now is that a huge hype or what!

We purposely highlighted the Tex-Mex section and christened this 2004 Publication of the Texas Folklore Society #61 *Both Sides of the Border: A Scattering of Texas Folklore,* because of its emphasis upon recently researched Tex-Mex folklore—and because the opening article is a beautiful autobiographical piece by Lucy West about growing up on both sides of the Rio Grande border. Additionally, we recognize that Texas has other borders besides the Rio Grande. In fact, we considered the ambiguity of the word "Border" as it applied to Texas with its several borders and will use that title with the folklorists' knowledge that all of this state's songs, tales, and traditions have lived and prospered on the other sides of Texas borders at one time or another before they crossed the rivers and became "ours."

The Texas Folklore Society has been publishing Mexican folklore from both sides of the border since its beginning. PTFS #1, now called *'Round the Levee,* included a Mexican border ballad—untranslated! Frank Dobie began his folkloric mission collecting and publishing Mexican folklore that had lived on both sides of the Rio Grande. His *Spur of the Cock* (PTFS #11–1933) and *Puro Mexicano* (PTFS #12–1935) were extensive collections of Texas-Mexican folklore as were Mody Boatright's *Mexican Border Ballads* (PTFS #21–1946) and Wilson Hudson's *Healer of Los Olmos* (PTFS #24–1951). More recently, Joe Graham edited *Hecho en Tejas* (PTFS #50–1991) and the Society published Al Rendon's classic picture study, *Charreada: Mexican Rodeo in Texas* (PTFS #59–2002).

The above list does not include the fact that just about every volume of the Society's sixty-one publications has included Mexican folklore that has lived on both sides of the Texas Rio Grande border. Nor does it include Texas Folklore Society extra books such as Frank Dobie's *Coronado's Children,* Américo Paredes' *With His Pistol in His Hand,* Riley Aiken's *Mexican Folktales from the Borderland,* and John O. West's *Mexican-American Folklore.*

And we must conclude with the observation that Texas has a large population of individuals who have lived on both sides of the border and are now creating a folkloric mix that we will hear much of in the future. Thus, *Both Sides of the Border* is timely.

Both Sides was to have been a traditional miscellany, containing the best of papers presented at TFS meetings over the past few years, as well as casual submissions. We have used that meritorious

miscellany of materials as the center of the book. We concluded
Both Sides of the Border with "*The Family Saga* (Cont'd.)" because
we had several rich family legends and studies of family legends left
over from last year's publication. *The Family Saga* has stimulated a
flow of family legends that will eventually require the publishing of
a companion volume.

I started editing my first PTFS, number thirty-seven, in the fall
of 1971, which was before some of you were even born. I was
determined to start the volume with something by my hero J. Frank
Dobie, so I talked Bertha Dobie into sending me a hunting story
from his unpublished files. You will notice that I start this, my last
volume, with J. Frank Dobie also. I thought such a beginning tribute was fitting.

I bummed and borrowed enough articles to make a passable
TFS miscellany in 1971, and I gave the material to Bill Wittliff at
the newly founded Encino Press. Bill put it artistically all together
in what we clumsily called *Observations & Reflections On Texas
Folklore* (PTFS #37–1972). The title was accurately descriptive but
it lacked euphony, or something. But Lordy! Was I ever proud of
that book! Bill followed the footsteps of Carl Hertzog. He knew
instinctively and aesthetically how to blend paper, print, pictures,
text, etc.—all the elements that make a book—into a unified artistic
whole. It is a rare talent, one much neglected in our fury to get
books on the stands.

I started editing *Both Sides of the Border,* number sixty-one, with
a full hopper of folkloric articles, much richer in material than I
was that first year of this editorship. I realized again—for the twentieth time—how blessed the Society is with its wealth of writers
and researchers. Folklore courses have lost their places in academe
since the beginning of my editorship, but Society members have
continued to collect and preserve and study folklore on their own.
And the Society has been able to continue its publishing program,
always with the support of its members. I take this opportunity to
thank all members who have ever put their literary pens to paper

for the Society's sake. You are the lives of the Society's publishing program, and future generations will bless your names as the carriers of Texas' folkloric torch.

I have not made a survey lately to see what other states have done in the way of preserving and presenting their folklore. But I would venture to say that Texas has done as well as any in maintaining a published record of its folklore studies.

So I am ending much as I began thirty-three years ago with a miscellany of observations and reflections on Texas folklore that I found readable and informative. I used a few old papers that had rattled around in my files for years because I could not find the exact place to use them. I paid tribute to some long departed buddies who still remain dear to my heart. And I hope that ultimately I have organized a PTFS that has some worthwhile academic value.

The editors thank Heather Gotti, our office secretary, for her work in collecting and organizing the articles for this publication, and we thank Karen DeVinney, managing editor at the University of North Texas Press, for her editing.

I shall not sing a swan song until I find one that goes well with a country band composed of fiddle and guitar, banjo and bass— something like the East Texas String Ensemble. And as much as I like the perks more than the works, I will try to keep my hands off the TFS publications so that Ken Untiedt can start putting his stamp on the books of the next thirty-three years.

It's been a blast! It's been my life.

Francis Edward Abernethy
Stephen F. Austin State University
Nacogdoches, Texas
January 31, 2004

Ab in the TFS office, *photo courtesy of Hardy Meredith.*

Janet Simonds with Ab Abernethy.

INDEX

A

Abernethy, Ben, 172, 190–191,
195, 276
Abernethy, Benjamin McCluskey, 195
Abernethy, Deedy, 52, 195
Abernethy, Eileen, 242
Abernethy, Francis Edward "Ab"
"Back in the Ought 'Sixties,"
303–313
Between the Cracks of History,
preface, 8–14
*Both Sides of the Border: A
Scattering of Texas Folklore*,
preface, 315–320
Built in Texas preface, 163–169
"Folk Art in General, Yard Art in
Particular," 39–49
*Observations & Reflections on Texas
Folklore*, preface, 3–7
photos of, 2, 12, 13, 14, 28, 34,
36, 50, 69, 70, 76, 90, 91, 95,
98, 105, 126, 131, 148, 152,
155, 156, 157, 161, 184, 185,
186, 190, 195, 238, 259, 260,
274, 276, 286, 291, 295, 302,
319, 320
"Snakelore," 51–59
*Texas Folklore Society: 1909–1943,
Volume I*, preface, 149–153
*Texas Folklore Society: 1943–1971,
Volume II*, preface, 154–158
*Texas Folklore Society: 1971–2000,
Volume III*, 159–160
"Waggoner's Cowboys," 127–131
"Whittler's Bench—Tenaha,
Texas," 297–301
Abernethy, Hazel, 7, 12, 59, 95, 153,
158, 195, 311
Abernethy, Luanna, 195

Abernethy, Maggie, 195
Abernethy, Robert, 195
Abernethy, Talbot, 125, 242
Abrahams, Roger, 303–304
acoustical communication, 35–37
Adam and Eve stories, 23–24, 51,
93–98
Adams, Marlene, 149
adders, 57
"Adulteration of Old King David"
(Emmons), 85, 140, 307
Aeschylus, 65
African-American folklore
1920s era and, 84–88
African roots and, 87
Afro-American traditions, 45
East Texas, 135–136
Texas history and, 6, 132, 133–146
African Americans
1920s American culture, 84–88
cowboy culture, 138–139
history in Texas, 133–146
Spanish culture and, 133–134
African cultures, 55, 62–63, 87
Agkistrodon piscivorus, 53
Agreda, María de, 110–119
Aguayo, Marques de San Miguel de,
108, 134
Aiken, Jesse, 209
Aiken, Riley, 316
Alamo battle, 136
Alamo Plaza, 236
Alexander, Stan, 193–194
Allen, Barbara, 24
"Amazing Grace" (song), 198
American Folklore Society, 83–84
American Studies Association, 234
amphibians, folk beliefs, 87
"Anchors Aweigh" (song), 249
Anderson, John Q., 193, 304, 309